EMERGING WRITERS

Learn the Tools of Writing

Merlene J. Purkiss

allWrite
publishing

ATLANTA, GEORGIA

Emerging Writers: Learning the Tools of Writing
Third Edition

Copyright © 2018 Allwrite Publishing
All Rights Reserved.

Allwrite Publishing
P.O. Box 1071
Atlanta, GA 30301

info@allwritepublishing.com

Sixth printing December 2018

Printed and bound in the U.S.A.

ISBN: 978-1-9417161-2-0 (Student Edition)

Library of Congress Control Number: 2017947667

Cover design by Melissa Phillips

CONTENTS

UNIT III
Hammer: **SENTENCE BUILDING**

UNIT IV
Building Blocks: _
PARAGRAPH AND ESSAY DEVELOPMENT

UNIT V
Paint: **WRITING CREATIVELY**

Appendix: MECHANICS_

UNIT I Nuts and Bolts:
WORD BASICS

Commonly Confused Words

Words are the foundation of written communication. You will need to become familiar with how to use or manipulate words in order to create effective sentences. Thus, in Unit 1, you will begin with commonly confused words, then spelling rules, and finally, parts of speech. Each lesson is created to help you become a master of words, which will then move you to Unit 2 to begin work on constructing successful sentences.

Some words in the English language are often confused because they may have similar meanings, sounds or spellings. Great writers explore every avenue to make sure they are communicating the right word to their audience. In fact, they use dictionaries and thesauruses to make sure they are conveying the precise meaning of a word. They do this because they know that finding the correct or most appropriate word can clarify the point that they are trying to convey, and using the wrong word or a less effective word can confuse their audience.

Sometimes writers may use the wrong words because the words look or sound alike, but the meaning is different. For example:

She put a classified <u>add</u> in the newspaper. (WRONG)
She put a classified <u>ad</u> in the newspaper. (CORRECT)

The words "add" and "ad" are **homonyms**.

Sometimes writers must find the best word to describe exactly what they mean when two words have similar meanings. For example:

Did you see him <u>smile</u> at me? (GOOD)
Did you see him <u>smirk</u> at me? (BETTER)

The words "smile" and "smirk" are **synonyms**.

Sometimes writers use words that have the opposite meanings to express that a drastic change has occurred. For example:

She was a <u>gracious</u> winner last year. (THEN)
She is an <u>ungracious</u> winner this year. (NOW)

The words "gracious" and "ungracious" are **antonyms**.

TYPES OF CONFUSED WORDS

This chapter is specifically designed to help you learn the precise meaning of commonly confused words. We will discuss *homonyms*, *synonyms*, and *antonyms*.

Homonyms

A homonym is a word that has the same pronunciation as another; however, they both differ in meaning and spelling.

Example: there and their

Synonyms

A synonym is a word that has the same or nearly the same meaning as another word.

Example: love and adore

Antonyms

An antonym is a word that has an opposite meaning to another word.

Example: tall and short

COMMONLY CONFUSED WORDS

Here is a list of *commonly confused words* that will help you determine the correct or most precise word to use in your oral and written communication. If you are unsure about the word you have chosen to fill in the blanks, use the meaning of the selected word to check if you have chosen the right word. The meaning should make sense in the sentence.

Accept, Except

Accept is a verb, which means to receive or to agree with.

Except, on the other hand, is a preposition, which means to omit or to exclude.

Fill in the blanks: The hard-working employee will graciously _____ the award.

All the girls will go on the trip _____ Ann Marie.

Mr. Cardosa does not _____ his employees bizarre comments.

Advice, Advise

Advice is a noun, which means an opinion, a suggestion, or a recommendation.

Advise is a verb, which means to tell, to counsel, to give an advice, or to recommend.

Fill in the blanks: Joan's friends gave her the wrong _____ about her psychology class.

The detective _____ the robber of his rights.

Teachers _____ students to pay attention in class.

Counselors give good _____ to students.

Affect, Effect

Affect is a verb, which means to influence or to produce a change.

Example: That cleaning product affects my sinus.

Effect, on the other hand, can be either a noun or a verb. When *effect* is used as a noun, it means the result of something (the aftermath).

Example: The effect of the medication gave the patient a headache.

When *effect* is used as a verb, it means to cause, or to bring about.

Example: The president effected a change in his policy on same sex marriage.

Fill in the blanks: The current oil crisis will _____ almost every state, but we may not see

the actual _____ until sometime next year.

The president wants oil executives to _____ some changes in their policies.

Already, All ready

Already means earlier, before, or previously.

All ready means completely prepared or ready.

Fill in the blanks: The students have _____ studied for their final exam, so they

are _____ to take it.

Alright, All right

Alright is a nonstandard version of "all right." Avoid using it in written communication.

All right is most times used to affirm a statement. In other words, someone is agreeing with something being said. It's like, "Okay, I agree with you." If possible, avoid using both "alright" and "all right."

Altogether, All together

Altogether means completely or entirely.

All together means in a group.

Fill in the blanks: We were _____ in the courtroom and

_____ pleased with the outcome of the case.

Among, Between

Use *between* to refer to **two** persons or things only.

Use a*mong* to refer to **three or more** persons or things.

Fill in the blanks: _____ you and me, Joan will be the new night supervisor.

Now, she will make sure that the responsibilities will be shared evenly

_____ the five night employees.

Amount, Number

Use *amount* with things that can be measured (an amount of liquid; an amount of money).

Use *number* with things that can be counted (the number of contestants; the number of people).

Fill in the blanks: A _____ of valued employees were missing today.

Therefore, a large _____ of coffee was wasted.

Apart, A part

Apart normally functions as an adverb and means to be separated by distance or time.

A part is a noun, which means a piece of something that forms the whole.

Fill in the blanks: She wants to keep the dancers _____ for now.

Each person has _____ in the upcoming ballet.

Been, Being

Been is the past participle of the verb to be.
(**Tip**: Use *has, have,* or *had* with "been.")

Being is the -*ing* form of the verb to be.
(**Tip**: Use *am, is, are, was,* or *were* with "being.")

Being can also be used as a noun to mean existence of (as in supernatural beings).

Fill in the blanks: Sammy is _____ pardoned for driving without his driver's license.

The mayor has _____ aware of the citizens' needs.

The Transformers have emerged as supernatural _____.

Beside, Besides

Beside means "next to" (by the side of).

Besides means "in addition to" or "except for"

Fill in the blanks: Steven's twin brother always sits_____ him in school.

_____ sitting next to each other, they always wear the same style and

color clothes.

Brake, Break

Brake can be used as a *verb* and a *noun*.
As a *verb*, it means stop or slow.
(**Verb Form:** *brake, braked*)
As a *noun*, it means a device for slowing or stopping a vehicle or other moving objects.

Break means to take apart, to destroy, or to damage.
(**Verb Form:** *Break, broke, broken*)

Fill in the blanks: The child _____ the new toy she received for her birthday.

Tom's mechanic advised him to change the _____ on his car.

"Do not _____ the speed limit," advised the driving instructor.

Buy, By

Buy is a verb, which means to purchase.

By is a preposition, which means near, close to, or no later than.

Fill in the blanks: Whenever Tommy _____ new clothes, he gives away the old ones.

_____ buying a new car, my family saves money on gasoline.

"Please _____ eggs, butter, and milk at the store," said Mother.

I will stop _____ your office in the afternoon.

Coarse, Course

Coarse means a rough surface, unpolished, unrefined (rock salt).

Course means a school subject, part of a meal, or a route.
Course also means the course (path) one will take in life.

Fill in the blanks: To improve his financial status, Bruce took a new _____ of action.

It is evident that his _____ in life will be now be successful.

In the early centuries _____ salt was used to preserve many perishable items.

Compliment, Complement

Compliment is an expression of praise or admiration.

Complement means to complete or perfect something.

Fill in the blanks: Chris' supervisor _____ him for receiving an award for his project.

Richar'd purple tie _____ his shirt, so he gets

several _____.

Continuously, Continually

Continuously means something that occurs nonstop (without pause).

Continually means something that happens frequently or is repeated.

Fill in the blanks: The faucet has dripped _____ for several weeks.

That baby cries_____.

Desert, Dessert

Desert can be used as a noun, which means a hot or dry place.
Desert can also be used as a verb, which means to abandon someone or something.

Dessert is a noun, which refers to something sweet (cake).

Fill in the blanks: The _____ was so dry that every livestock died.

After the honeymoon was over, Nigel _____ his wife and moved away.

My favorite _____ is cheese cake.

Fair, Fare

Fair is an adjective used to describe clear weather; pleasing to the eye or mind; marked by impartiality or to be in a certain condition.

Fair is also a noun, which means a gathering place for the sale of goods.

Fare refers to the cost of a service or good or bad fortune or to turn out.

Fill in the blanks: How did you _____ in last night's game? I _____ well.

The state's yearly _____ has generated millions of dollars.

Willy's 1975 Honda Accord is in _____ condition.

Fewer, Less

Fewer refers to things that can be counted individually.

Less is used with things that cannot be counted individually: (less milk; less coffee; less money)

Fill in the blanks: This year, Manny registered for _____ classes.

His problem is that he received _____ than $1,000 in grants.

Former, Latter

Former means before, earlier, or in the past (the first of two things mentioned).

Latter means after (the second of two things mentioned).

Fill in the blanks: The stylist is available at 8 a.m. and 4 p.m., but Michelle prefers the

_____ because she has morning classes.

Her friend Sue booked the _____ slot.

Hole, Whole

Hole means an empty spot.

Whole means entire.

Fill in the blanks: Susan's _____ family is moving to New York in the summer.

That _____ has been in my backyard since I bought my house.

There is a _____ in the wall.

It's, Its

It's is a contraction of *it is;* or *it has.*

Its means belonging to someone or something (ownership).

Fill in the blanks: _____ obvious that she does not like Sandra.

The company gave all _____ employees an attractive bonus.

Know, Knew, New, No

Know means knowledge of something.

Knew is the past tense of *know.*

New means something that is not old (unused).

No is negative.

Fill in the blanks: Johnnie _____ that he is not ready for his _____ venture.

Everyone _____ this to be true but him.

My answer to your question is _____ because you _____

the _____ rules.

Learn, Teach

Learn means to receive knowledge.

Teach means to give knowledge

Fill in the blanks: Tigers _____ their young ones how to climb, hunt for food, and adapt to

their environments. They _____ these skills quickly. Other animals can

certainly _____ from tigers.

Lose, Loose

Lose is a *verb* meaning to misplace (lose your car keys), or fail to win (game).

Loose an *adjective* meaning not tight (loose shirt; loose wire), or loose change.

Loose can also refer to a loose animal (loose cat).

<u>**Fill in the blanks**</u>:   Did you _____ your cell phone again?

Frankie has a lot of _____ change in his pocket.

If you are not careful with those credit cards, you are likely to _____ them.

The _____ dog injured the cat.

Past, Passed

Past can be used as an *adjective,* a *noun,* or an *adverb.*
<u>Example</u>:   The *past* director was a male (adjective).
<u>Example</u>:   In the *past*, Suzie was a nurse (noun).
<u>Example</u>:   Pamela was so tired that she drove *past* her house (adverb).

Passed as a verb with an object means went ahead, moved past or allowed (passed the test).
Passed as a verb without an object means elapsed or ended (someone passed away; time passed).

<u>**Fill in the blanks**</u>:   The students _____ their final exam with high scores.

George's _____ has been a constant reminder for him.

When you drove _____ me on the highway, I did not recognize your new car.

The incident _____ so quickly that we almost forgot about it.

Peace, Piece

Peace means calmness, tranquility, or agreement.

Piece means a part of something.

<u>**Fill in the blanks**</u>:   Sonya says she finds_____ when she reads.

May I have a _____ of that apple pie?

There is no _____ in Jeremy's household.

A _____ of that land was given to me by my father.

Phase, Faze

Phase refers to an aspect or stage of development:

Faze means to embarrass or to disturb:

<u>**Fill in the blanks**</u>:   Richard's cancer is in its early _____ .

Molly's rude statement about Albert's weight did not _____ him.

Principal, Principle

Principal means the head of a school or main (prime) reason.

Principle is a moral standard or rule by which a person lives.

Fill in the blanks: His _____ reason for working so hard is to purchase a home.

The _____ for Allan's school is Mr. Abott.

My _____ is not to drink or smoke.

Quiet, Quite, Quit

Quiet means silence.

Quite means really, truly, completely, to a considerable extent.

Quit means to stop.

Fill in the blanks: All the girls _____ the basketball team.

The library is a _____ place to study.

The teacher was _____ upset with the students.

Raise, Rise

Raise means an upward movement or advancement: raise a window; raise your hands.
(Verb forms: raise, raised, raised)

Rise means to move upward, usually by its own natural power: the sun rises.
(Verb forms: rise, rose, risen)

Fill in the blanks: My mother _____ 13 children.

The members of the basketball team have_____ to the occasion.

They _____ $600 for their trip.

The congregation will _____ when the bride walks down the aisle.

It is interesting to see how the heat causes the cake to _____.

Should of, Should have

Should of is nonstandard English and should never be used. For one thing, the preposition "of" cannot be used with the helping verb "have."

Should have is the acceptable version for both verbal and written communication.
Example: I *should have* completed my project on time.

Sit, Set

Sit means to be seated.

Set means to put or to place something.
(Tip: A noun usually comes after *set*: to set a table; to set rules)

Fill in the blanks: Carla brags that she can _____ in one position for hours.

                                          Please do not _____ the table until the guests arrive.

Sight, Site, Cite

Sight refers to something that can be seen.

Site refers to a specific location: a construction site, a new facility (stadium).

Cite means to quote; give an example, or to use a reference to support an argument.

Fill in the blanks: The _____ of a tiger terrifies me.

                                          The _____ of the new stadium is a _____ to behold!

                                          In my annual report, I _____ various references.

Stationary, Stationery

Stationary refers to something that is fixed in position (not moving).

Stationery refers to paper, envelopes, pens, pencils, and other writing aids.

Fill in the blanks: The bridge is _____.

                                          The invitation was printed on beautiful _____.

Suppose, Supposed to

Suppose means to assume or guess; to imagine.

Supposed to means ought to.
(**Tip**: It is usually followed by "*to.*")

Fill in the blanks: I _____ we are all going to the same movie.

                                          We are also _____ to return home at the same time.

                                          I _____ you are _____ to do your internship this semester.

Than, Then

Than is used when making a comparison.
<u>Example</u>: Duke is taller *than* Jack, his friend.

Then refers to time; it also means afterward, or next.
<u>Example</u>:   Kiara washed her car and *then* waxed it.

Fill in the blanks: Joan prefers steamed vegetables rather _____ raw vegetables.

                                          Sage is taller _____ Victor, her only cousin.

On Saturday, the soccer team will go to the beach and _____ to a movie.

Everyone prefers this idea _____ having a party.

Their, There, They're

Their is the possessive form of *they* (more than one). It means *belonging to* and is usually followed by an object._
Example: *Their* ideas were not taken seriously.

There is an adverb meaning "at a particular place."

There can also be used as an adverb to introduce a sentence *(there is; there are; there were; there has/have/had been)*.

They're is a contraction of *they are*.

Fill in the blanks: The juveniles were taken to the new facility by _____ counselors.

_____ are 25 of them, and _____ expected to be tried as adults

for _____ crime.

Threw, Through, Though

Threw is the past tense of throw.

Through is a preposition meaning finished (through eating).
Through can also mean going into or coming out of (a building).

Though is a word that is used to show contrast (opposite).
(**Tip**: Though means although, however, despite, but, still.)

Though also means *as if*.

Fill in the blanks: After the 4-year-old child woke up from his nap, he went _____ the

back door and _____ the ball into the pool as _____ he was a pro.

To, Too, Two

To, when used as a *preposition*, means toward (to the bank; to the park).

To may also be used with a *noun* or *pronoun* to form a prepositional phrase (to me, to Joanna).

To can be placed before a verb to form an infinitive (*to have, to sleep*).

Too means also or very (too expensive).

Two refers to the number two (two books).

Fill in the blanks: Saffi's coffee was _____ hot, so it burned his tongue.

He went back to the cafeteria_____ get _____ more cups.

He gave one _____ his supervisor and kept one for himself.

Use, Used

Use means to work with something (use a cookbook).

Used means to become accustomed to (used to someone's attitude).

Used can also be used as an adjective, followed by a noun (used car).

Fill in the blanks: When I was younger, I _____ to dance for a living. At that time, I

could only afford _____ cars. These days I only _____ my

money to buy new cars.

Weather, Whether

Weather refers to the atmosphere (rainy weather; weather report).

Whether means to make a decision or to express doubt (whether or not; if)

Fill in the blanks: Many of the fans did not know _____ they could make the game

because the _____ was unpredictable.

Were, We're, Where

Were is a verb (the past tense of *are*).

We're is a contraction of *we are.*

Where refers to a place or location.

Fill in the blanks: _____ _____ you yesterday? _____

you with the group? We _____ at the place

_____ you told us to go.

Whose, Who's

Whose indicates ownership (something belonging to someone).
(**Tip**: It is usually followed by a noun.)

Who's a contraction of *who is* or *who has.*

Fill in the blanks: _____ keys are these?

_____ is responsible for taking care of the children?

You're, Your

You're is a contraction meaning *you are.*

Your is a possessive pronoun/adjective, which shows ownership.

Fill in the blanks: _____ responsible for purchasing _____ own

ticket when _____ going on the fieldtrip. _____

parents should be aware of this.

OTHER COMMONLY CONFUSED WORDS

Some words that sound alike and look alive can be confused even though they have different spellings. This is particularly tricky with articles, such as **a** and **an**, which precede nouns.

A, An, And

Use *a* before words that begin with a consonant:
   a *book*, a *hat*, a *teacher*, a *nurse*, a car, a *plant*

Also, use *a* before *a* word that begins with a vowel but has a consonant sound:
   a *universe a uniform*, a *unit*, a *university*, a *union*, a *united nation*, a *unicorn*
   (These words take on a "*y*-sound" although they begin with the vowel "u.")

Use *an* before a word that starts with a vowel (*a, e, i, o, u*):
   an *operator*, an *ugly sugar glider*, an *apple*, an *iris flower*, an *egg*

Use *an* before words like *honor* and *hour.*
   (Although they begin with a consonant, the *h* is silent.)

Use *and* to indicate addition.

Fill in the blanks: It is said that "_____ apple _____ day will keep the doctor away."

It takes _____ hour from my house to go to my job. If I wanted to take

a class, _____ university is across the street.

Lay, Lie

Lay means to put or place an object, which is a noun or a pronoun.
   The man will *lay* the **tiles** today; *lay* the **papers** on my desk.
   (**Verb forms**: *lay, laid, has/have/had laid, laying*)

Lay can also mean to lay down rules.
   Sammy will *lay* down specific rules for his guests.

Lie means to recline (lie down on a couch).

(**Verb forms**: *lie, lay, has/have/had lain, lying*)

(**Tip**: *Lie* is usually followed by a preposition (on, down)
and gives no indication that someone does the action.)

The childen *lie* on the carpet for fun.
The toys have *lain on* the floor for hours now.
After work, I will *lie down* for an hour.

Fill in the blanks: As soon as I arrived home last night, I _____ my purse on the table.

The man is _____ the tiles on his kitchen floor.

Richard has _____ in his crib for two hours.

Sage _____ down beside her brother.

_____ your clothes on the bed, Jonathan.

HOMOGRAPHS

Some words have the same spelling but have different meanings. They are called **Homographs**:

Diana's mother bought her a special *present* that she will *present* to her on her birthday.
My mother is *content* with the *content* of her will.

Close (verb, adjective)	**Object** (noun, verb)
Conduct (noun, verb)	**Present** (noun, verb)
Contract (noun, verb)	**Perfect** (adjective, verb)
Digest (noun, verb)	**Record** (noun, verb)
Lead (noun, verb)	**Relay** (noun, verb)
House (noun, verb)	**Wound** (noun, verb)

Can you think of at least two other homographs?

_____   _____

Now, use them to make sentences.

1. _____

_____

2. _____

_____

REVIEW 1

In each of the following sentences, underline the correct word in parentheses.

1. The (effect, affect) of the storm (effected, affected) the entire neighborhood.

2. Fanny has a positive (affect, effect) on Charles' eating habits.

3. The new administration will most likely (affect, effect) several changes in its policies.

4. Did you (loose, lose) money on the bet?

5. Fabian has (a, an) interesting idea about attracting potential club members.

6. (Your, You're) no longer a member of this club.

7. Everyone (except, accept) Molly will (except, accept) our apology.

8. David (past, passed) by my job to congratulate me on my new position.

9. Please inform me (weather, whether) (you're, your) returning to work in July.

10. Although the hospital has financial problems, it gave (it's, its) CEO an attractive raise.

11. I recommend that you put (less, fewer) sugar in your coffee.

12. The county inspectors will visit the work (cite, site) to see if the workers have lost (site, sight) of the building codes.

13. Carlos' (principle, principal) goal in life is to become a firefighter.

14. (Their, There) are numerous people who never read a book. (Their, There) belief is that reading requires too much time.

15. My (advice, advise) to Darius is that he should have (fewer, less) friends.

16. For the final round of the audition, participants are (suppose, supposed) to sing in a group so that they can get (use, used) to each other.

17. It was truly (a, an) honor for me to work for my (latter, former) supervisor.

18. (Except, Accept) for Aaron, all the participants took Virginia's (advice, advise).

19. (Whose, Who's) (your, you're) best friend?

20. I expect Alton to get a higher score on the exam (than, then) his brother.

REVIEW 2

Underline the correct word in parentheses.

1. The tree has (laid, lain) in the street for weeks before the county workers removed it.

2. (Lie, Lay) (you're, your) projects on my desk, please.

3. The children love to go to the beach to (lie, lay) in the sand.

4. (Lying/laying) in the direct sun can be dangerous.

5. Ralph (set, sit) the alarm clock, but he went back to sleep when it sounded.

6. Emily will (sit, set) with her friends at the recital.

7. Please (set, sit) your projects on my desk.

8. It is more polite for students to (rise, raise) their hands whenever they have questions.

9. Did you (rise, raise) when the judge entered the courtroom?

10. As soon as Mr. Roberson (rises, raises) in the mornings, he runs five miles.

11. The book has been (laying, lying) on the desk for several days.

12. Mona has (laid, lain) high morals standards for her siblings.

13. The coach (complimented, complemented) the basketball team for winning the game.

14. At the (fair, fare), I bought several gifts.

15. Carmen's mother complains (continuously, continually) about the loud music in Carmen's car.

16. Tabitha has (laid, lain) on the floor for a long time.

17. In this family, Nadia will (sit, set) the standard for excellence.

18. The rock star's seductive style has (fazed, phased) me.

19. (Peace, Piece) is something that cannot be bought.

20. I have (being, been) blessed by (your, you're) encouraging remarks.

REVIEW 3

Use each of the following words to make short sentences.

Word	Sentence
lie	_____
principal	_____
than	_____
you're	_____
its	_____
affect	_____
effect	_____
too	_____
their	_____
rise	_____
raise	_____
fewer	_____
lay	_____
except	_____
cite	_____

2

Spelling

How many times have you been stuck on the spelling of a word in the middle of writing? Well, many people will admit that this is a common occurrence. However, we live in a technological age where misspelled words are automatically highlighted or underlined, and with the click of a button, you can quickly get the correct spelling. If you are using a computer program to type, do not completely rely on spell check because a computer program will not detect words such as compound words that are spelled incorrectly as two words. For example, the word "mindset" was spelled incorrectly on a professional flyer. It read "mind set," which a computer, even this one, did not detect. In addition, while correct spelling has become secondary in this age of electronic messaging, most of us would still appreciate a personal greeting card or note that isn't filled with spelling errors.

RULES

To improve your spelling, it is essential to learn the rules of spelling. Before you do, however, you need to be familiar with some key terms, which are essential to aid you in becoming a better speller:

<u>Root</u>: The base or main part of a word.

>   **Example:** The word *trust* in *distrust*.

<u>Prefix</u>: A word part (*-pre, -im, -re, -dis*) that is placed in front of a root word. When a prefix is added to the root (base) of a word, it changes the meaning of the word.

>   **Example**: If the prefix *dis-*, which means not, is added to *trust*, it now becomes *distrust*, and the meaning has changed.

<u>Suffix</u>: A word part (*-able, -tion, -ly, -ful*) that is added to the end of a root word. A suffix can change the meaning of a word, and it often changes the part of speech as well.

>   **Example:** By adding the suffix *-ful* to *distrust*, the word now becomes *distrustful*, and the meaning has changed. *Distrust* is a verb; on the other hand, *distrustful* is an adjective.

<u>Vowels</u>: *a, e, i, o, u*

<u>**Consonants**</u>: *b, c, d, f, g, h, j, k, l, m, n, p, q, r, s, t, v, w, x, y, z*

Remember: The letter -*y* can serve *two* functions: It can be either a vowel or a consonant.

> **Example:** In the word *beauty,* for example, -*y* functions as a vowel whereas in the word *yet,* -*y* is used as a consonant.

Here are spelling rules that will help you remember how to spell important words:

RULE 1: Doubling the Final Consonant of Words with One Syllable:

When a suffix is added to a *one-syllable* word that is comprised of a *consonant-vowel-consonant* (*cvc*) arrangement, double the final consonant by adding the same letter and then add the suffix. For words that do not end in *cvc, do not* double the final consonant:

> cvc
> **Example:** plan (plan**n)** + ing = planning
> vcc
> crawl (crawl) + ed = crawled

PRACTICE 1

Before adding the given suffixes to each of the following root words, decide if the final consonants are doubled or not doubled.

	<u>Root Word</u>		<u>Suffix</u>		<u>New Word</u>
	tan	+	ing	=	tanning
	beg	+	ed	=	begged
1.	stop	+	ing	=	_____
2.	ask	+	ed	=	_____
3.	red	+	er	=	_____
4.	lug	+	age	=	_____
5.	hop	+	ed	=	_____
6.	clean	+	est	=	_____
7.	clear	+	ance	=	_____
8.	fret	+	ing	=	_____
9.	brag	+	ed	=	_____
10.	stun	+	ing	=	_____

RULE 2: Doubling the Final Consonant of Words of More Than One Syllable:

When a suffix is added to a word of more than one syllable, add another of the same consonant only if:

The last three letters of the word are *consonant-vowel-consonant* (*cvc*).
The stress (accent) falls on the *last* syllable.

In the word *occur*, for example, the last three letters are *cvc*, and the stress falls on –*cur*; therefore, double the –*r*:

cvc

Example: oc<u>**cur**</u>   (occurr) + ed =   occurred

In the word *offer*, the last three letters are *cvc*, but the stress falls on the first syllable –*of* therefore, do not double the –r:

cvc

Example: <u>**of**</u>fer   (offer) + ed =   offered

Note: Final consonants are *not* doubled before suffixes that begin with a consonant:
commit +   **ment** = commitment
quarrel +   **some** = quarrelsome
rival   +   **ry**   = rivalry

PRACTICE 2

Before adding the given suffixes to each of the following words, decide if the final consonants are doubled or not doubled.

	Root Word		Suffix		New Word
	begin	+	er	=	**beginner**
	hammer	+	ed	=	**hammered**
1.	commit	+	ed	=	_____
2.	happen	+	ed	=	_____
3.	compel	+	ing	=	_____
4.	pardon	+	ed	=	_____
5.	travel	+	er	=	_____
6.	remit	+	ance	=	_____
7	prefer	+	ing	=	_____
8.	transfer	+	ed	=	_____
9.	benefit	+	ing	=	_____
10.	cancel	+	ed	=	_____

RULE 3: Dropping or Keeping the Final -E

If a word ends in a silent *-e* and the suffix begins with a vowel, drop the *-e*:

desire + able = desirable

hope   + ing   = hoping

Keep the *-e* if the suffix begins with a consonant:

hope + ful = hopeful

live   + ly   = lively

EXCEPTIONS		
noticeable	judgment	peaceable
manageable	courageous	knowledgeable
argument	advantageous	acknowledgeable
awful	outrageous	changeable
truly	simple	likeable

PRACTICE 3

In the following exercise, decide whether you keep -e or drop -e:

	Root Word		Suffix		New Word
	use	+	able	=	usable (drop *e*)
	use	+	ful	=	useful (keep *e*)
1.	obese	+	ity	=	_____
2.	dine	+	ing	=	_____
3	nice	+	ly	=	_____
4.	excite	+	ment	=	_____
5.	fame	+	ous	=	_____
6.	rude	+	ness	=	_____
7.	love	+	able	=	_____
8.	sense	+	ible	=	_____
9.	like	+	ness	=	_____
10.	write	+	ing	=	_____

RULE 4: Keeping or Changing the Final -Y

The *y* has *three* rules:

Change -*y* to -*i* if the letter before -*y* is a consonant:

security + es = securities

happy + ness = happiness

Keep -*y* if the letter before -*y* is a vowel (*a, e, i, o, u*):

valley + s = valleys

donkey + s = donkeys

Keep -*y* if the suffix is –*ing*:

play + ing = playing

worry + ing = worrying

EXCEPTIONS				
say	+	d	=	said
pay	+	d	=	paid
day	+	ly	=	daily
lay	+	d	=	laid

PRACTICE 4

In the following exercise, decide whether you keep or drop -y:

	Root Word		Suffix		New Word
	minority	+	es	=	minorities
	attorney	+	s	=	attorneys
	Marry	+	ing	=	marrying
1.	study	+	ed	=	_____
2.	ally	+	es	=	_____
3.	portray	+	ing	=	_____
4.	happy	+	est	=	_____
5.	relay	+	ing	=	_____
6.	alley	+	s	=	_____
7.	study	+	ing	=	_____
8.	silly	+	er	=	_____
9.	angry	+	ly	=	_____
10.	delay	+	ed	=	_____

RULE 5: Adding -S or -ES

For nouns ending in -*s*,-*sh*, -*ch*, -*ss*, -*x*, and -*z*, add -*es* to form their plurals. For all other words, add -*s* only:

book	+	s	=	books	church	+ es	= churches
bush	+	es	=	bushes	boss	+ es	= bosses
buzz	+	es	=	buzzes	tax	+ es	= taxes

For nouns ending in *o*, preceded by a consonant, add *es*:

mosquito	+	es	=	mosquitoes
hero	+	es	=	heroes
tomato	+	es	=	tomatoes

EXCEPTIONS		
pianos	radios	stereos
patios	solos	trios
videos	autos	sopranos
altos	banjos	folios

Tip: For some words ending in -*o*, including all musical words, add -*s* only to form their plurals:

PRACTICE 5

Add -s or -es to the following words to form their plurals:

1. brush _____

2. tomato _____

3. latch _____

4. potato _____

5. box _____

6. buzz _____

7. radio _____

8. rag _____

9. waltz _____

10. index _____

11. flash _____

12. boss _____

13. cargo _____

14. ring _____

15. pillow _____

16. hero _____

RULE 6: -*IE* and -*EI*

Use -*i* before -*e* as in the following words: *believe*, *piece*, *achieve*, *chief*, *belief*.

Exception: Use -*ei* with words that have -*ay* sounds: *weigh*, *neighbor*, *vein*, *eight*, *reign*, *heir*.

After -*c*, use -*ei* as in the following words: *receive*, *deceive*, *ceiling*, *conceive*, *perceive*.

Exception: Use -*cie* with words that have -*shen* sounds: *sufficient*, *efficient*, *ancient*, *proficient*.

OTHER EXCEPTIONS		
their	protein	f o r f e i t
weird	either	caffeine
height	seize	foreign
neither	society	leisure

PRACTICE 6

Add *ie* or *ei* to the following practice:

rev____w	n____ther	rec____ve
fr____nd	sc____nce	____ght
v____n	s____ze	th____r
w____ght	r____gn	for____gn
f____ld	gr____f	th____f
impat____nt	n____ghbor	aud____nce
____ther	soc____ty	w____rd
anx____ty	effic____nt	p____ce

RULE 7: Keeping the First Consonant after a Prefix

The root (base part) of a word does not change even if the *first* letter of the word and the *last* letter of the prefix are the same:

mi**s**	+	**s**pell	=	misspell
di**s**	+	**r**espect	=	disrespect
u**n**	+	**n**ecessary	=	unnecessary
pr**e**	+	**e**minent	=	preeminent
i**r**	+	**r**esponsible	=	irresponsible

PRACTICE 7

Combine the following prefixes and root words:

	Prefix		**Word**		**New Word**
Example:	**bio**	+	**logical**	=	**biological**
	dis	+	appear	=	_____
	im	+	possible	=	_____
	mis	+	trial	=	_____
	il	+	logical	=	_____
	un	+	noticed	=	_____
	over	+	worked	=	_____
	dis	+	satisfied	=	_____
	il	+	legible	=	_____
	mis	+	pronounce	=	_____
	tele	+	phone	=	_____

REVIEW 1 _____

Add the given suffix to each root word.

scar	+	ed	_____	engage	+	ing	_____
clean	+	est	_____	restore	+	ed	_____
occur	+	ing	_____	pursue	+	ing	_____
boast	+	ed	_____	peace	+	able	_____
commit	+	ed	_____	use	+	ing	_____
slam	+	ing	_____	love	+	ing	_____
pardon	+	ed	_____	argue	+	ment	_____
stun	+	ing	_____	use	+	able	_____
travel	+	er	_____	scarce	+	ity	_____
benefit	+	ed	_____	nice	+	ly	_____
happy	+	er	_____	notice	+	able	_____
attorney	+	s	_____	potato	+	es	_____
study	+	ed	_____	usual	+	ly	_____
marry	+	ing	_____	buzz	+	es	_____
ally	+	es	_____	plan	+	ing	_____
pay	+	d	_____	piano	+	s	_____
library	+	es	_____	incidental	+	ly	_____
display	+	ed	_____	mosquito	+	es	_____
worry	+	ing	_____	lonely	+	ness	_____
stop	+	ing	_____	radio	+	s	_____

COMMONLY MISSPELLED WORDS

Even in this age of computer spell check, we must still be able to communicate in professional correspondences without misspellings. Text-based electronic communication mediums, such as e-mail and text messaging, have now forced us to consider the spellings of common words. Moreover, writing students should be aware that many jobs that involve written communication require passing a pre-employment spelling tests. Below is a list of some commonly misspelled words. Study them and take the practice spelling test afterward.

decision	inference	guarantee	noticeable	necessary	referred
discreet	pamphlet	accommodate	liaison	definite	imposter
fluorescent	rhythm	calendar	defensible	cemetery	lightning
publicly	profession	parallel	occurrence	siege	correspondence
seize	knowledge	questionnaire	transcend	subpoena	desperate
sergeant	leisure	solely	grateful	harass	mileage
rehearsal	maintenance	homicide	amendment	circumstance	government
gauge	cannot	responsible	succeed	performance	attendance
license	anoint	achieve	relevant	experience	misspell
a lot (many)	dispensable	advisor	stationery	weight	career
happened	imminent	alleged	newsstand	renowned	minuscule
fertilizer	detach	bookkeeper	omission	recommend	religious
reminisce	Caribbean	category	likable	accidentally	withheld
similar	aggression	separate	weird	commitment	tomorrow
acquit	occasionally	judgment	emigrate	personnel	credible
ceiling	compliment	phase	pastime	proceed	embarrass

REVIEW 2 _____

Circle the correct answer.

1.	necessary	necesary	neccessary
2.	comitment	commitment	committment
3.	seperate	separate	sepirate
4.	tommorrow	tomorow	tomorrow
5.	passtime	pasttime	pastime
6.	minuscule	miniscule	miniscoule
7.	goverment	govorment	government
8.	succed	succeed	suceed
9.	gauge	gage	guage
10.	attendence	attendince	attendance
11.	licinse	lisense	license
12.	rhythym	rhythm	rythymn
13.	acheive	achieve	acheve
14.	religous	relegious	religious
15.	occassion	occasion	ocassion
16.	category	catagory	catigory
17.	acommodate	accomodate	accommodate
18.	notisable	noticeable	noticible
19.	ommission	ommision	omission
20.	judgement	judgment	judgmeant

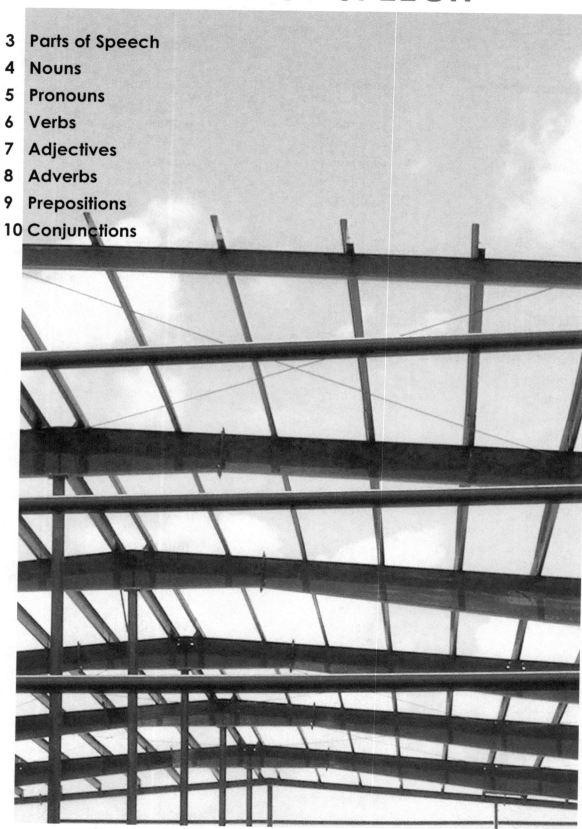

UNIT II Frame:
PARTS OF SPEECH

3 Parts of Speech

Nothing is more essential to understanding the structure of writing than the parts of speech. They are not merely elementary lessons that are learned and reviewed for academic purposes, but rather, they are essential writing tools that should be employed for intentional effect. Choosing the right verb, for instance, can enhance the comprehension, cohesion and color of a composition. Fundamentally, the proper use of grammar is based on this understanding.

OVERVIEW

In order for your writing to make sense, it must be syntactically correct. So, mastering the parts of speech is the key to understanding grammar and expressing your thoughts clearly and comprehensively. Also, if you know your parts of speech, you will not confuse an adverb like well with an adjective like good. Neither will you use the objective pronoun *me* for the subjective pronoun *I*.

Here's a condensed version of the eight parts of speech. Each part of speech, except for the interjection, will be discussed in detail in a section by itself:

NOUNS

A noun names a person, a place, a thing, or an idea. Common nouns are lowercased; proper nouns are capitalized:

Person: *Ms. Brown, boy, doctor*

Place: *church, beauty salon, Cambodia*

Thing (**concrete**): *magazine, Ferris wheel, shoes* (Can be seen or touched.)

Thing (**abstract**): *faith, hatred, truth, freedom*   (Not evident to the senses)

PRONOUNS

A pronoun is a word that can be used as a substitute for a noun. There are several types:

Subjective Pronouns: *I, he, she, it, we, you, they, who, whoever*

Objective Pronouns: *me, us, him, you, it, them, whom, whomever*

Possessive Pronouns: *its, my, her, your, our, their, whose, mine*

Indefinite Pronouns: *anybody, everybody, anyone, everyone, everything, each one, neither, either,* *all, few, many, several, both*

Demonstrative Pronouns: *this, that, these, those*

VERBS

Verbs express an action or state of being. There are *three* types of verbs:

Action: An action verb expresses a physical or mental action.
Examples: *run, walk, sing, dance, think, sleep*

Linking: A linking verb, also known as a "state of being" verb, links a word in the predicate to the subject.
Examples: *am, is, are, was, were, feel, seem, be, taste, look, grow remain, stay, sound, appear, being, been*

Helping: A helping verb, also known as an auxiliary verb, is paired with another verb(s) to form a verb phrase.
Examples: *can, could, shall, should, will, would, must, might, may*

Verbs function alone (main verb) or as groups of words (verb phrase). For example:

- She **completed** her project by noon.
- **Shall** we **go** for a walk?
- Roberto **might be going** to the hockey game tonight.

ADJECTIVES

An adjective modifies or describes a noun or pronoun.

Examples: **a pretty** girl, **this hairy** cat, **that broken** window, **the running** water
(*a, an, the*) are adjectives; they are called articles.

Tip: Wherever you find an article, you will also find a noun either beside or close to it.
Examples: **an** apple, **a humungous** cat, **a white** house, **the hot** chocolate

ADVERBS

An adverb has *three* functions: It modifies a verb, an adjective, or another adverb. It answers the questions: how? when? where?

Examples: *often, very, not, always, soon, most, quite, too,* and most words that end in *-ly*

Modifies a verb: walks **slowly**, speaks **softly**, speaks **well**

Modifies an adjective: **very** hot, **often** misunderstood, **really** friendly

Modifies another adverb: very early, too lonely

PREPOSITIONS

A preposition is a word that is placed before a noun or pronoun to form a phrase
that is related to another word in the sentence.

Examples: *in, on, under, beneath, from, across, beyond, around, before, after, at, for, by, during,*

below, about, through, to
- My father is working ~~in the garden~~.
- The book is ~~on the table~~.
- One ~~of the books~~ is missing.
- Rene will complete the project ~~by midnight~~.
- The games are ~~under the table~~.
- Are you going ~~to the park~~ today?
- The argument is ~~between me and you~~.

CONJUNCTIONS

A **conjunction** is a word that joins two or more words, phrases, or clauses.

> <u>Examples</u>: *for, and, nor, but, or, yet, so, since, because, although, even though, after, if, when, while, as*

INTERJECTIONS

An **interjection** shows strong feelings or sudden emotions.

> <u>Examples</u>: *ouch, wow, ah, hey, oh, hurrah*

- **Hurrah**, I finished my essay!
- **Ouch,** you stepped on my feet!
- **Wow**, Fanny lost twenty-two pounds!

PRACTICE

Identify each underlined word according to its part of speech. Use the following: (n) for noun, (v) for verb, (pron) for pronoun, (adj) for adjective, (adv), for adverb, (conj) for conjunction, (prep) for preposition, and (interj) for interjection.

1. <u>Quietly</u> <u>leave</u> the room.

2. I <u>am</u> <u>honored</u> to be an <u>employee</u> in <u>your</u> company.

3. The <u>aspirin</u> had a <u>negative</u> effect <u>on</u> Sandra.

4. <u>My</u> friends advised <u>me</u> to stop <u>working</u> so <u>many</u> hours.

5. Angela <u>spoke</u> loudly and <u>clearly</u> <u>without</u> a <u>microphone</u>.

6. <u>This</u> is a <u>dangerous</u> intersection; in fact, <u>it</u> is <u>known</u> for <u>causing</u> numerous accidents.

7. As <u>soon</u> as I <u>rise</u> in the mornings, <u>I</u> raise my <u>tinted</u> windows.

8. The <u>broken</u> vase almost <u>caused</u> <u>me</u> to trip and fall.

9. <u>After</u> Hurricane Andrew, <u>several</u> of my windows <u>broke</u>.

10. Olga <u>seems</u> <u>sad</u> by the <u>tragic</u> news <u>of</u> her friend Suzette.

11.   <u>In</u> my car, <u>under</u> the seat <u>are</u> the folders <u>for</u> my meeting.

12.   <u>Hurrah</u>! I am <u>excited</u> that you are <u>going</u> to Egypt <u>with</u> me.

13.   Marcel <u>will be watching</u> the <u>news</u> with <u>me</u> tonight.

14.   <u>After</u> I left the <u>basketball</u> game, <u>I</u> went to dinner with <u>several</u> friends.

15.   Where <u>were</u> you <u>when</u> I knocked <u>on</u> <u>your</u> door <u>this</u> morning?

16.   <u>Andrew</u> and <u>Joana</u> are not <u>working</u> this summer.

17.   I <u>drove</u> my <u>new</u> car home <u>very</u> slowly.

18.   <u>Ah</u>! I was <u>15</u> minutes late <u>for</u> my meeting, <u>so</u> I <u>slowly</u> crept in <u>by</u> the <u>side</u> door.

19.   Diana <u>does</u> not <u>eat</u> meat or <u>drink</u> coffee.

20.   The <u>other</u> day I went shopping, <u>but</u> I only bought <u>some</u> uniforms <u>for</u> my children.

REVIEW

Fill in the correct parts of speech in the blanks.

An _____ modifies a verb, adjective, or other adverbs.

A _____ is the name of a person, place, thing, or an idea.

A _____ is a substitute for a noun.

An _____ modifies a noun or pronoun.

A _____ is a word that is placed before a noun or pronoun to form a phrase.

A _____ joins two or more words, phrases, or clauses.

An _____ shows strong feelings or sudden emotions.

A _____ can be action, linking, or helping.

A _____ implies a state of being or condition for the subject, not an action.

Nouns

BASIC TYPES OF NOUNS

A noun is a word that names a person, place, thing, or idea. A noun can be either singular (one) or plural (more than one.) There are *two* kinds of nouns that name things: **concrete** and **abstract**.

Concrete nouns are objects or persons that can be seen or touched. In other words, they can be perceived by the five senses.

Abstract nouns, on the other hand, cannot be perceived by the five senses.

Proper nouns name a specific person, place, thing, or idea. A proper noun starts with a capital letter. A **common noun** does not start with a capital letter unless it begins a sentence.

COMMON NOUNS				
Persons:	aunt	brother	man	friend
Places:	mountain	bridge	beach	river
Things (concrete):	hat	paper	desk	book
Things (abstract):	faith	love	hatred	courage

Tip: All words that end in *-ion, -ment, -dom, -hood, -age, -ance, -ence, -ness, -ism -or, -er,* and *-ure* are nouns.

PROPER NOUNS				
Persons:	Louise	Thomas	Mr. Fields	Tasha
Places:	Himalayas	Golden Gate	Sun Belt	Harlem
Things (concrete):	Super Bowl	Styrofoam	Dumpster	Bible
Things (abstract):	Godspeed	Prohibition	Pentecost	Easter

RULES FOR FORMING PLURALS

1) Add -*s* to most nouns to form their plurals:

Singular	Plural	Singular	Plural
girl	girls	idea	ideas
chair	chairs	hand	hands
book	books	day	days
rose	roses	clue	clues

2) Add *es* to nouns ending in *s*, *ss*, *sh*, ch, *x*, and *z* to form their plurals.

Singular	Plural	Singular	Plural
glass	glasses	box	boxes
bush	bushes	waltz	waltzes
church	churches	quiz	quizzes
boss	bosses	frizz	frizzes
buzz	buzzes	switch	switches

3) Nouns ending in *y* fall into *two* categories to form their plurals:

(a) If a noun ends in *y*, preceded by a consonant, change the *y* to *i*, and then add *es* to form its plural.

Singular	Plural	Singular	Plural
minority	minorities	worry	worries
battery	batteries	copy	copies
enemy	enemies	study	studies
clergy	clergies	family	families

(b) If a noun ended in *y*, preceded by a vowel (a, e, i, o, u), only add *s* to form its plural.

Singular	Plural	Singular	Plural
alley	alleys	attorney	attorneys
x-ray	x-rays	key	keys
delay	delays	replays	replays

Nouns Ending in o

4) If a noun ends in *o*, preceded by a consonant, add *es* to form its plural.

Singular	Plural	Singular	Plural
potato	potatoes	tomato	tomatoes
cargo	cargoes	hero	heroes
embargo	embargoes	mango	mangoes

Note: Some nouns ending in *o* have *two* plural forms. When in doubt, consult a dictionary, and usually, the first spelling is the preferred one.

Singular	Plural	Singular	Plural
cargo	cargoes/cargos	zero	zeros/zeroes
volcano	volcanoes/volcanos	buffalo	bufaloes/buffalos
mosquito	mosquitoes/mosquitos	motto	mottoes/mottos
tornado	tornadoes/tornados		

EXCEPTIONS

Singular	Plural	Singular	Plural
piano	pianos	stereo	stereos
solo	solos	trio	trios
alto	altos	banjo	banjos
video	videos	cello	cellos
radio	radios	studio	studios
patio	patios	soprano	sopranos
zoo	zoos	photo	photos
auto	autos	tattoo	tattoos

Note: For all musical words, including others that end in *o*, only add *s* to form their plurals.

Nouns Ending in *f* or *fe*

5) For many nouns ending in *f* or *fe*, change the *f* to *v* and then add *es* to form their plurals.

Singular	Plural	Singular	Plural
calf	calves	knife	knives
leaf	leaves	wife	wives
shelf	shelves	half	halves
wharf	wharves	self	selves
wolf	wolves	life	lives

6) For some nouns ending in *f* or *ff*, only add *s*.

Singular	Plural	Singular	Plural
bailiff	bailiffs	belief	beliefs
gulf	gulfs	staff	staffs
roof	roofs	chief	chiefs
cliff	cliffs	reef	reefs
handkerchief	handkerchiefs	chef	chefs

PRACTICE 1

Add *s* or *es* to the following nouns:

1. battery _____

2. trio _____

3. photo _____

4. cliff _____

5. radio _____

6. church_____

7. tomato _____

8. studio _____

9. bush _____

10. shelf _____

11. waltz _____

12. minority _____

13. gulf _____

14. belief _____

15. boss _____

16. attorney _____

SPECIAL CASES OF SINGULAR AND PLURAL NOUNS

Although some nouns end in *s*, they are still singular:

Singular	Singular	Plural	Plural
news	mathematics	scissors	shoes
athletics	wages	pants	socks
economics	phonetics	jeans	goods
civics	species	trousers	tweezers
politics	measles	shears	pajamas
semantics	mumps	pliers	binoculars

Irregular Plurals

Some irregular nouns do not follow standard forms of pluralization. The best way to learn them is to memorize them. Many of them just require a vowel change to go from singular to plural:

Singular	Plural	Singular	Plural
child	children	man	men
woman	women	mouse	mice
foot	feet	tooth	teeth
ox	oxen	goose	geese
louse	lice		

Some English nouns borrow their plural forms from other languages. As a result, some nouns have both foreign and the English plural forms:

Singular	Plural	Singular	Plural
analysis	analyses	crisis	crises
basis	bases	oasis	oases
thesis	theses	parenthesis	parentheses
hypothesis	hypotheses	morphsis	morphses
criterion	criteria	phenomenon	phenomena
bacterium	bacteria	addendum	addenda
medium	media	datum	data
curriculum	curricula/ curriculums	memorandum	memoranda/ memorandums
alumnus (mas.)	alumni	nucleus	nuclei/nucleuses
stimulus	stimuli	syllabus	syllabi/syllabuses
fungus	fungui	cactus	cacti/cactuses
appendix	appendices/ appendixes	index	indices/indexes
alumna (fem.)	alumnae	larva	larvae
formula	formulae/ formulas	antenna	antennae
		vetebra	vetebrae/vetebras

Note: The foreign plurals are formed by just changing their endings.

Nouns That Do Not Change Their Forms

Some nouns do not change their forms. They remain the same in the singular and plural.

Singular	Plural	Singular	Plural
deer	deer	moose	moose
fish*	fish	sheep	sheep
series	series	corps	corps
species	species	equipment	equipment
furniture	furniture	merchandise	merchandise
mail	mail	homework	homework

*Fish may be either *singular* or *plural*. If they are the same types of fish, use *fish*; however, if they are different types, use *fishes*.

Compound Nouns

Compound nouns, which are made up of *three* or more words, form their plurals by adding **s** to the principal word:

Singular	Plural	Singular	Plural
brother-in-law	brothers-in law	father-in-law	fathers-in-law
sister-in-law	sisters-in-law	maid-of-honor	maids-of-honor
court-martial	courts-martial	passer-by	passers-by
mother-in-law	mothers-in-law	on-looker	on-lookers

If the final word in a hyphenated compound word is a preposition, add -*s* to the final word to form its plural:

Singular	Plural	Singular	Plural
follow-up	follow-ups	trade-in	trade-ins
strike-over	strike-overs	write-up	write-ups
check-up	check-ups	pull-up	pull-ups

PRACTICE 2

Write the plural forms of the following nouns:

1. criterion _____

2. crisis _____

3. foot _____

4. child _____

5. trade-in _____

6. hypothesis _____

7. passer-by _____

8. curriculum _____

9. deer_____

10. moose _____

11. furniture _____

12. mouse _____

13. news _____

14. medium_____

Plural Proper Nouns

For most proper nouns ending in *y*, add an *s* regardless if it is preceded by a consonant.

Singular	Plural
Party City	Party Citys
Nancy	Nancys
O'Reilly	O'Reillys

Note: Never form a plural by using an apostrophe.

Family names are most often made plural by simply adding an *s*.

Singular	Plural
Mr. Johnson	The Johnsons
Mr. Brown	The Browns
Mr. Garcia	The Grarcias

For most family names that end in s, es, ch, sh, x, y or z, form the plural by adding *es*.

Singular	Plural
Ms. Jones	The Joneses
Ms. Bush	The Bushes
Ms. Lopez	The Lopezes

Names of companies and other organizations are usually regarded as singular regardless of their ending. For example:

IBM is…
McDonalds is…
Johnson & Johnson is…
Universal Studios is…

Names of sports teams are regarded as plurals regardless of the form of that name. For example:

Miami Dolphins are…
Atlanta Hawks are…
New York Yankees are…
Utah Jazz are…

Note: When a sports team is referred to by the city in which it resides, it is regarded as singular. For example, Miami *is* going to the playoffs this year.

SIGNAL WORDS

Signal words are certain **adjectives** (articles and numbers) and **pronouns** that help identify nouns as being singular or plural.

Singular	Plural	Singular	Plural
a dog	**all** students	**this** watch	**these** watches
an apple	**both** children	**that** idea	**those** ideas
another day	**few** people		
each person	**many** houses		
every cup	**several** opportunities		
one chance	**two** (or more) chances		
the car	**some** nights		
much talk	**most** girls		

PHRASES WITH OF

Look out for *of* phrases. They signal that a noun is coming up. Of utmost importance, the noun that follows an *of* phrase *must* be plural:

- One **of the students** is absent today.
- Another one **of my poems** will be published.
- Several **of my classes** are canceled.

PRACTICE 3

Underline the error in each sentence and then make the correction on the line to the right.

1. Some familys do not believe in taking long vacations.   _____

2. Several reporters lost their life in Iraq.   _____

3. These curriculum are not working well this year.   _____

4. The shelf have fallen and broken in several pieces.   _____

5. The Internet contains information about the radio media.   _____

6. These piano were donated to the church by members.   _____

7. More and more minority student are attending college.   _____

8. All types of fish can be found in the lake close to my house.   _____

9. I left one of my suitcase at the airport last week.   _____

10. The Jones sold their home and moved to Orlando.   _____

COLLECTIVE NOUNS

Collective nouns refer to a group of people or things.

COLLECTIVE NOUNS

group	audience	fleet	number
class	herd	squad	congregation
crowd	tribe	staff	company
team	flock	faculty	congress
choir	panel	army	senate
committee	board	school	government
family	college	jury	crew

Examples: The **class** took a field trip to the zoo.
Do you know if the **jury** reached a verdict?
This year's dance **team** includes two seniors.
The will **army** face a tough battle in the city.
The **herd** of cows ran across the plain.
The **group** announced that the tour begins next summer.
Everyone on the **panel** of experts applauded when he arrived.

PRACTICE 4

Fill in the correct pronouns in the blanks and then underline their antecedents.

1. After the jury deliberates, _____ will announce _____ decision today.

2. The cows ran away from _____ pasture and are going in _____ own direction.

3. The committee will meet in _____ usual room to select a new dean.

4. The college will be honored for _____ commitment to minority students.

5. The Army will be sending 5,000 of_____ best men and women to Iraq.

6. The crowd screamed when _____ favorite team won the football game.

7. The faculty will decide on _____ new textbook for psychology.

8. On Monday, a number of employees were absent from _____ jobs.

9. A herd of goats at the fair went _____ separate ways after the judges left.

10. The crew members are through working and are going to _____ rooms.

11. The government is supposed to reevaluate _____ immigration policies.

12. The group is going to the football game in _____ own cars.

13. The crew is not going to finish _____ shift until midnight.

14. The strike unit disagrees whether to attack _____ enemy tonight.

15. The board will make _____ decision in two days.

16. A number of residents who complained about the loud noise are ready to take _____ complaints to the manager.

Pronouns

The prefix *pro-* means *for*, so a **pronoun** is a word that can be substituted *for* a noun. Pronouns are important in both oral and written communication. For example, if we were to use all nouns in oral or written communication, our speech or writing would certainly be humdrum (boring). Therefore, we sometimes use pronouns in the place of nouns. Look at the following sentences and their revisions:

> **Original**: **Andrew** is a good basketball player although **Andrew** has only been playing basketball for three years.

> **Revised:** **Andrew** is a good basketball player although **he** has only been playing for three years.

> **Original**: **Carmen** is 50 years old, but **Carmen** still lives at home with **Carmen's** mother.

> **Revised**: **Carmen** is 50 years old, but **she** still lives at home with **her** mother.

Pronoun-Antecedent Agreement

An **antecedent** is a word to which a pronoun refers. The prefix *ante-* means before, so the antecedent always comes before the pronoun.

Examples: Julie celebrated **her** birthday when **she** went to Europe.
(**Her** and *she* are referring to Julie, who is the antecedent.)

Raul is not willing to take responsibility for **his** actions.
(**His** is referring to Raul, who is the antecedent.)

A **pronoun** must agree with its antecedent. Thus, if the pronoun is singular, the antecedent to which it refers must also be singular, and if the pronoun is plural, the antecedent to which it refers must also be plural: **(singular/singular) (plural/plural)**.

Examples: The **store** will be closed for **its** annual inventory.
(**Its** is a **singular** pronoun that refers to the **singular** antecedent *store*.)

The **stores** will be closed for **their** annual inventory.
(**Their** is a **plural** pronoun that refers to the **plural** antecedent *stores*.)

PRACTICE 1

In each of the following sentences, underline the pronouns and their antecedents, and then write them on the lines to the right.

	Antecedent	Pronoun
Example: <u>**Manny**</u> was happy with <u>**his**</u> grade.	<u>Manny</u>	<u>his</u>

1. Sage and her parents will take their first vacation in May. _____ _____

2. When Victor was born, he weighed nine pounds. _____ _____

3. The book is not placed in its proper place. _____ _____

4. For the first time, the girls will shop for their own clothes. _____ _____

5. When the students arrived at their dorms, they discovered that there were no towels. _____ _____

6. Has Monica found her stolen purse? _____ _____

7. Some of Maggie's friends want to transfer to her school. _____ _____

8. Frank and William believe they are inseparable. _____ _____

9. When I lost my ring, I was worried until I found it. _____ _____

10. The visitors were not pleased with their first impression of the hotel's lobby. _____ _____

11. Both the sales clerk and the customer believe their accusation of each other were warranted. _____ _____

12. George and Fidel gave their class presentation together. _____ _____

13. America made history when its first African-American president was elected. _____ _____

14. President Obama is known for his eloquent speeches. _____ _____

15. When Angela's brothers arrived home, she had a surprise for them. _____ _____

Pronoun-Antecedent Agreement with Indefinite Pronouns

An **indefinite pronoun** does not refer to any specific person or thing. In other words, its identity is unknown. Some indefinite pronouns refer to unknown people whereas others refer to unknown things. Also, some are always *singular* while others are always *plural*.

SINGULAR AND *PLURAL* INDEFINITE PRONOUNS

Singular	Singular	Singular	Singular	Plural
-body words any anybody everybody nobody somebody	*-one words* one no one anyone any one (of) * someone some everyone every one (of)*	*-thing words* anything nothing something everything	*other words* each (of) either (of) neither (of) another	both few many several

Note: Use the following rules for **singular** and **plural** indefinite pronouns:

- The *-body* and *-one* words are always singular and can only refer to people, so use *he* or *she* or *him* or *her* to refer to them because they are also singular.
- Use *it* or *its,* which is singular, to refer to the *-thing* words which are also singular. Also, they can only refer to singular inanimate objects.
  Write *any one* and *every one* as *two* words when an *"of"* phrase follows.*
- *Each (of), either (of), neither (of)* and *another* are always **singular** and can refer to either people or inanimate objects. Use *he/she*, *him/her*, or *it/its* to refer to them.
- Use *their* or *they* or **them** to refer to plural indefinite pronouns.

Examples: _

- *Anyone* can get a college degree if *he* or *she* works hard.
- *One* should take responsibility for **his** or **her** or (**one's**) actions
- *Anybody* can play monopoly if **he** or **she** tries.
- *Something* is wrong with *its* color.
- *Any one* (of the guards) can escort you to the main office in **his** or **her** car.*
- *Every one* (of the students) passed *his* or *her* final exam.*
- *Either* (of these individuals) is worthy of getting *his* or *her* prize.
- *Each* (of these cars) has *its* flaws.
- *Neither* (of these documents) is ready for *its* publication.
- Only *few* (of the campers) knew *their* way around the park.
- *Several* (of the residents) did not realize *they* had to pay an association fee.

Note: *A **prepositional phrase** between the subject (the antecedent) and verb does not change the antecedent. Pay attention to the **prepositional phrases** in parentheses above.

Singular and/or Plural Indefinite Pronouns

Some **indefinite** pronouns, which are modified by prepositional phrases, may either take singular or plural pronouns. This is determined by the noun in the prepositional phrase that they reference. The noun in the phrase offers a clue as to whether the indefinite pronoun is singular or plural. Look at the following indefinite pronouns and the *underlined nouns* in the prepositional phrases to which they refer:

Singular or Plural

any	some
none	most
all	

- *Some* of the <u>furniture</u> has been shipped in *its* container.
- *Some* of the <u>dogs</u> are wearing *their* collars.
- *All* of the <u>mail</u> is in *its* boxes.
- *All* of the <u>doctors</u> are in *their* offices.
- *None* of the <u>students</u> who cheated on the test thought *they* were wrong.
- *None* of the <u>food</u> tasted good, so the chef threw *it* away.
- *Any* of the <u>furniture</u> you choose will serve *its* purpose.
- *Any* of the <u>administrators</u> can serve as *their* liaison.
- *Most* of the <u>mail</u> is in *its* box.
- *Most* of the <u>people</u> were displeased with *their* bonus checks.

PRACTICE 2

Fill in the correct pronouns in the blanks and then underline their antecedents.

Examples: <u>**Anyone**</u> can dance if **he** or **she** tries.
Did <u>**someone**</u> forget **his** or **her** keys?
<u>**None**</u> of the men in the video thought about **their** audience.

1. Everybody looks as if _____ is exhausted after gymnastics.

2. Everyone ate as if _____ had not eaten for days.

3. One should be aware of _____ surroundings.

4. Each of the doctors will give _____ patients a free consultation in December.

5. None of the women were willing to give up _____ desks to the new employee.

6. Either of the girls will give a review of _____ work.

7. Each of these textbooks has _____ strengths and weaknesses.

8. Several students missed the deadline for _____ projects.

9. Someone left _____ books in the classroom.

10. All the equipment is stored in _____ right place.

11. Some people are good at faking _____ attitude.

12. Few individuals take _____ jobs seriously.

13. All employees are aware of _____ responsibilities.

14. Everything for the party will go well if _____ is planned in advance.

15. Neither of the women passed _____ test.

CLEAR PRONOUN REFERENCE

Every pronoun in a sentence must refer to a specific antecedent. If it does not have a clear antecedent, it is considered unclear. Avoid using **vague**, **repetitious**, and **ambiguous** pronoun references because they can confuse readers. Note the following examples:

Vague Pronouns

A **vague** pronoun means it is unclear. It is usually introduced by the pronouns **they, them** or **it**.

Unclear: **They** told me I can't make up the test. (Who are *they*?)
Revised: The **teacher** told me I can't make up the test. (*Teacher* is substituted for *they*.)
Revised: I was told by the **teacher** that I can't make up the test.

Unclear: At the music store, **they** told me they are out of the video I wanted. (Who are *they*?)
Revised: At the music store, the **cashier** told me the store is out of the video I wanted.
             (*Cashier* is substituted for *they*.)
Revised: When I went to the music store, the **cashier** told me that the video I wanted was not in the store.

Unclear: When will **it** come to an end? (What is *it*?)
Revised: When will **the argument** come to an end? (*Argument* is substituted for *it*.)

Repetitious Pronouns

A **repetitious** pronoun usually repeats the noun that precedes it. It is unnecessary to use a pronoun immediately after its subject. When this occurs, it is considered repetitious. For example:

Incorrect: My **teacher** <u>she</u> says that I am failing my class. (*She* is unnecessary.)
Correct: My **teacher** says that I am failing my class.

Incorrect: The **newspaper** <u>it</u> says toilet paper is on sale. (*It* is unnecessary.)

Correct: The **newspaper** says that toilet paper is on sale.

Ambiguous Pronouns

The prefix *-ambi* means both; therefore, a sentence that is ambiguous is subject to more than one interpretation. Most times this occurs when one pronoun is referring to more than one antecedent. This can certainly confuse readers because it is unclear as to which of the antecedents the one pronoun is referring. Look at the following ways in which *ambiguous* pronouns can be corrected:

Example: <u>**Ciara**</u> told <u>**Mindy**</u> that <u>**she**</u> has a doctor's appointment.

It is unclear who has the appointment. Is it Ciara or Mindy? It is not clear because "she" could be referring to Ciara or Mindy.

To fix the ambiguity, *two* solutions can be used:

Substitute the pronoun *she* for Ciara or Mindy, or use direct quote, which is always the best choice.

Solution 1: <u>Ciara</u> told <u>Mindy</u> that <u>Ciara</u>^(she) has a doctor's appointment.
                 <u>Ciara</u> told <u>Mindy</u> that <u>Mindy</u> has a doctor's appointment.

Solution 2: Ciara told Mindy, "I have a doctor's appointment."

In solution 1, it is now clear that "she" is referring to either Ciara or Mindy.
In solution 2, the direct quote makes it is clear that Ciara is the one who has the doctor's appointment.

PRACTICE 4

Revise the following **vague**, **repetitious**, *and* **ambiguous** *pronoun references to make them clearer.* **Answers will vary**.

1.   When I went to the testing department to take my final exam, they told me I was not mentally prepared to take the test.

      _____

      _____

2.   When Andrea first met Louise, she was overweight.

      _____

      _____

3.   The jar it fell on the tile and broke in several pieces.

      _____

      _____

4.   Madge invited Erica and her sister to go to Europe with her this summer.

_____

_____

5.   At the dentist office, they said that I have several cavities.

_____

_____

6.   Eileen told Patricia that she is going to have surgery on her left knee.

_____

_____

7.   When will it come to an end?

_____

_____

8.   The teacher told the student that it was time for her to leave.

_____

_____

9.   While I was working on my research paper, my computer it crashed.

_____

_____

10.   The girls took the gifts from their friends even though they did not like them.

_____

_____

11.   The van hit the parked car, but it was not damaged.

_____

_____

12.   Are you aware that they won't let you on the flight with such a huge hand luggage?

_____

_____

PERSONAL PRONOUN CASES

There are *three* pronoun cases or forms: *subjective, objective,* and *possessive.*

Subjective Case

Use the **subjective case** when it is used as the subject of a verb:

- **We** <u>washed</u> our car today.
  (The subject pronoun *we* answers who *washed our car.*)

- **She** <u>will take</u> the test after her class.
  (The subject pronoun *she* answers who *will take the test.*)

Use the **subjective case** after a *linking* verb: *am, is, are, be, was, and were.*

Incorrect: It <u>was</u> **her** who stole John's wallet.
Correct: It <u>was</u> **she** who stole John's wallet.

Incorrect: If anyone could do the job, it <u>would be</u> **him**.
Correct: If anyone could do the job, it <u>would be</u> **he**.

Incorrect: It <u>was</u> **them** who made the decision for me.
Correct: It <u>was</u> **they** who made the decision for me.

Objective Case

Use an **objective pronoun** after an *action* verb:

- She <u>told</u> **me** about her exciting trip.
  (Notice that the objective pronoun *me* follows the action verb *told*.)

- My daughter bought **him** perfume for his birthday.
  (Notice that the objective pronoun *him* follows the action verb *bought*.)

Use an **objective pronoun** after a *preposition*:

- Ada loaned her dress **to me** to wear to the wedding.
  (Notice that the object pronoun *me* follows the preposition *to*.)

- That book was bought **for them**.
  (Notice that the object pronoun *them* follows the preposition *for*.)

Possessive Case

Use the **possessive case** to show ownership. It can also be used as an adjective when it modifies or gives information about a noun:

Incorrect: The company gave **it's** (it is) employees a raise.
Correct: The company gave **its** employees a raise.

Incorrect: The problem is **their's** (their is)
Correct: The problem is **theirs**.

Note: Do <u>not</u> use apostrophe with pronouns that are already possessive: *mine, his, her,* **hers**, *their,* **theirs,** *your,* **yours, its, our, ours.**

Below is a chart that will allow you to easily recognize and utilize the proper pronoun case.

PRONOUN CASE CHART

SINGULAR	Subjective	Objective	Possessive
1st person	I	me	my/mine
2nd person	you	you	your(s)
3rd person	he	him	his
	she	her	her(s)
	it	it	its
	who(ever)	whom(ever)	whose

PLURAL	Subjective	Objective	Possessive
1st person	we	us	our(s)
2nd person	you	you	your(s)
3rd person	they	them	their(s)
	she	her	her(s)

PRACTICE 5

On the first blank, select the correct pronoun; on the second blank, select the correct pronoun case.

Example: (<u>She</u>, Him) will go to the bank.   <u>she</u>   <u>subjective</u>

1.   This situation is between (we, us).   _____   _____

2.   She told (me, I) about her new child.   _____   _____

3.   (They, Them) will cook tonight.   _____   _____

4.   It was (he, him) who gave us instructions.   _____   _____

5.   The decision is certainly (their's, theirs).   _____   _____

6.   (Us, We) students like easy assignments.   _____   _____

7.   Is this new car (her's, hers)?   _____   _____

8.   Every child except (he, him) will go to the   _____   _____

new play.

9. It is (she, her) who will represent us.   _____   _____

10. Sears will give (it's, its) workers a bonus.   _____   _____ -
11. These are (them, they) who won the prizes.   _____   _____

12. The idea was (ours, our's) originally.   _____   _____

13. Tracy talked to (I, me) about her decision.   _____   _____

14. To Josh and (I, me), Tom is a winner.   _____   _____

15. Is this plate meant for (he, him)?   _____   _____

Compound Constructions

Errors in pronouns mainly occur when they are used in pairs or when a noun and a pronoun are used together:

Incorrect: **Her** and **I** are taking the same courses.
(*Her* can't take courses.)

Correct: **She** and **I** are taking the same courses.
(***She*** can take courses, and *I* can take courses.)

Incorrect: **Fabian** and **me** will go to Europe this year.
(*Fabian* can go, but *me* can't go anywhere.)
Correct: **Fabian** and **I** will go to Europe.
(***Fabian*** will go, and *I* will go.)

Tip: If you can't decide which construction to use, take time to use each pronoun individually:

<u>**Original:**</u>   **Her** and **I** live on the same street for years.

Incorrect: **Her** live on the same street for years.
Correct: **I** live on the same street for years.

The same technique can be used for the following pairs:

<u>**Original:**</u>   (**Her** and **me**)/(**She** and **I**) speak Spanish.

Incorrect: **Her** speak Spanish.
Incorrect: **Me** speak Spanish.

Correct: **She** speaks Spanish.
Correct: **I** speak Spanish.

<u>**Original:**</u>   Joan will visit (**him, I**) this summer.

Incorrect: Joan will visit **I**.
Correct: Joan will visit **him**.

<u>**Original**</u>:   This argument is between Andrew and (**I**, **me**).

Incorrect: This argument is between **Andrew** and **I**.
Correct: This argument is between **Andrew** and **me**.

Remember: Use an *object* pronoun after an **action verb** and a **preposition**.

PRACTICE 6

In the following sentences, underline the correct pronoun or pronouns.

1. Maria, Alfredo and (me, I) are sorry about your accident.

2. Fanny and (her, she) were once best friends.

3. (She, Him) and (me, I) were nominated for the prize.

4. The argument between (he, him) and (me, I) lasted five years.

5. It was (they, them) and (I, me) who decided to take geography.

6. Last summer, (she, me) went to Disney World.

7. Leona talked to (he, him) about his testing anxiety.

8. The property will be shared among the Johnson family and (us, we).

9. (They, Them) and (I, me) will attend the annual conference.

10. If anyone should get a raise, it should be Mina and (him, he).

11. (We, Us) coaches care about our baseball players.

12. Everyone except (him, he) showed up for English class on time.

Pronouns in Comparison

When a pronoun is followed by *than* or *as*, it means that a comparison is being made. Two people or things can be compared in the ***subjective, objective***, or ***possessive*** case. Figuring out the correct pronoun case in comparisons can be somewhat challenging. The possessive case is quite simple; however, the subjective and objective case can be confusing.

When you use a pronoun after *than* and *as* to make a comparison, finish the sentence with the appropriate verb or pronoun case, according to the meaning of the sentence. Look at the following examples in the *three* cases:

<u>**Subjective Case:**</u>   Charles is older *than* (I , me) [**am**].
                                        She likes sodas more *than* (we, us) [**do**].

Objective Case: Jeremy loves him more *than* [**he loves**] (I, me).
Brenda pays her more *than* [**she pays**] (we, us).

Possessive Case: Her hair is longer *than* mine [**is**].
Your ideas are better *than* hers [**are**].

PRACTICE 7

In the following sentences, choose the correct pronoun case.

1. Nadia helps her as much as (I, me).

2. The professor gave Marlon just as much praise as (her, she).

3. Suzette is more jealous of her than (me, I).

4. Is Calvin funnier than (him, he)?

5. Gayle is not as beautiful as (them, they).

6. My neighbors have a nicer lawn than (I, me).

7. According to my doctor, I am in better health than (her, she).

8. My friends say I can dance better than (them, they).

9. Jonathan gives her more attention than (I, me).

10. Her morals are better than (her's, hers).

11. Do you think Iman's supervisor pays her more than (me, I).

12. Eric gets better grades than (I, me).

Relative Pronouns: Who/Whoever and Whom/Whomever

Most people have difficulty figuring out when to use *who* and *whom*. The difference is that *who* and *whoever* are in the **subjective case** whereas *whom* and *whomever* are in the **objective case**. In other words, who/whoever does the action, and whom/whomever receives the action.

The Subjective Case: When there is no other subject *before* the verb, use *who* or *whoever*.

Examples: *Who* <u>walked</u> on the carpet?
(*Who* is doing the walking.)

Give the prize to *whoever* <u>produced</u> the best project.
(*Whoever* is doing the producing.)

The Objective Case: If the verb already has a subject, use *whom* or *whomever*.

Examples: Judge Robinson <u>is</u> the person *whom* you <u>should see</u>.
(Because *is* and *should see* are verbs and have subjects, use *whom*.)

We <u>stopped</u> *whomever* the investigators <u>identified</u> as a suspect.
(Because *stopped* and *identified* have subjects, use *whomever*.)

In the case of **questions beginning with relative pronouns**, you may answer the question with a personal pronoun to determine the correct case. Subjective case in the answer means the same for the question; objective case in the answer means the same for the question. Look at the following examples:

- **Who** <u>will open</u> the mail?
  (*He* or *she* will open the mail.)
- **Whom** <u>are</u> you <u>giving</u> instructions?
  (You are giving *him* or *me* instructions.)

Tip: If a **preposition** is at the very ***beginning*** of a sentence, automatically use ***whom***:

- **To whom** are you speaking? (***To*** is a preposition.)
- **By whom** are you sitting?   (***By*** is a preposition.)
- **For whom** are these files?   (***For*** is a preposition.)

Note: To test if *whom* is the correct choice, remember, it must be followed by a subject and a verb.
In sentence one, the subject is "you" and "are speaking" are the verbs.
In sentence two, the subject is "you" and "are sitting" are the verbs.
In sentence three, the subject is "files" and the verb is "are."

PRACTICE 8

In the following sentences, underline who/whoever or whom/whomever.

1.   Give the promotion to (whoever, whomever) deserves it.

2.   By (who, whom) did you sit at the game?

3.   My supervisor rewarded the person (whom, who) produced the most sales.

4.   Will you select the individual (who, whom) I recommend?

5.   The flowers were given to the senior citizen (whom, who) did the best project.

6.   It would be wise to give a gift to (whoever, whomever) supports your ideas.

7.   For (who, whom) are these lovely red roses?

8.   The chocolate is intended for the athlete (whom, who) you choose.

9.   (Whom, Who) will be the most advanced employee this month?

10.   Are you prepared to confront (whomever, whoever) does the least work?

11.   (Who, Whom) encouraged you to apply for the job?

12.   To (who, whom) do these books belong?

13.   (Whom, Who) did Mr. Jones select for the new position?

14.   With (who, whom) will you be traveling to the workshop.

15.   The new president of the league would like to meet with (whomever, whoever) is in charge of the team.

16.   Gary is the individual to (who, whom) Jasmine is engaged.

17.   Beside (who, whom) were you sitting at the basketball game.?

18.   Except for Rex, (who, whom) is deserving of the award?

19.   (Whom, Who) will be responsible for tonight's big event?

20.   I told (whoever, whomever) called that you were out of town.

Intensive and Reflexive Pronouns

Intensive and reflexive pronouns are often confused because they both share the -*self* pronouns.

Intensive pronouns
An **intensive** pronoun is used to give emphasis to its antecedent (the subject). In other words, the pronoun points back to the subject:

- They **themselves** did the landscaping.
- I **myself** would like to take a French class.
- We **ourselves** are capable of doing the plans for the house.

Reflexive Pronoun
A **reflexive** pronoun, on the other hand, is used to demonstrate that a person performs an action on himself or herself or a thing does something to itself:

- I taught **myself** to speak Spanish.
- The students praised **themselves** for completing the project on time.
- The cat hurt **itself** while jumping the fence.

REFLEXIVE OR INTENSIVE PRONOUNS

SINGULAR		PLURAL	
I	myself	we	ourselves
you	yourself	you	yourselves
he	himself	they	themselves
she	herself		
it	itself		

Note: Neither **intensive** nor **reflexive** pronouns can be used as subjects.

PRACTICE 9

*For each boldface pronoun, write **I** for intensive pronoun and **R** for reflexive pronoun.*

Example: Marlon shaved **himself** today. ____R____

1. This summer I will buy **myself** a new car. _____

2. The president **himself** said he will send more troops to Iraq. _____

3. Marla says she **herself** will take her child to school. _____

4. Carla and Ciara say they will give **themselves** a haircut. _____

5. You **yourself** should take the money to the bank. _____

6. The dog bit **itself** while it was chasing a lizard. _____

7. My sister gives **herself** insulin twice per day. _____

8. My son bought **himself** a Dodge van. _____

9. They **themselves** will make the presentation. _____

10. The frog hid **itself** in my plant because it has lots of water. _____

Verbs

TYPES OF VERBS

If you asked most people "what is a verb," most of them will quickly say, "A verb is an action word." This is only partially true. A **verb** does not always show action. A verb can be *action*, *linking*, or *helping*. A **verb** can also express a condition.

Action Verbs

An **action verb** is usually easy to spot because the subject is usually doing something physical or mental.

Look at the following sentences:

> Jeffrey <u>swims</u> every day to stay in shape.
> (*Swims* is an action verb.)
>
> Diana <u>remembers</u>.
> (*R*emembers expresses mental action.)

An **Action verb** can also be *transitive* or *intransitive.*

Transitive Verbs

Transitive verbs take **direct objects**, which answers *what* or *whom* after the action verb:

> _{subj.   action verb}
> Natalie <u>sings.</u>
> ("Natalie sings" is a **sentence fragment** because it does not answer what or whom after the action verb "sings.")
>
> _{subj. action verb   d.o.}
> Natalie sings a beautiful song.
> (This is now a complete sentence because it answers what Natalie sings.)

Intransitive Verbs

An intransitive verb, on the contrary, does not take a **direct object** because the action is complete without adding a direct object after the action verb.

> subj.   action verb
> Martin <u>jogs.</u>
> ("Martin jogs" **is a complete sentence**, which does not require a direct object.)

Linking Verbs

Linking verbs express a state of being or condition. Unlike action verbs, they *never* take direct objects.

Nevertheless, **linking verbs** are usually followed by a *noun* or a *subjective pronoun (he, she, it, we, you, or they)* to tell *who* are *what* the subject is:

> Lisa is a college professor.
> (*College professor* is a **noun** that tells who Lisa is.)

> This is (he, she it, we, you, they).
> (*He, she, it, we, you, they* are **subject pronouns**.)

A **linking verb** may also be followed by an **adjective**, which describes the subject in some way:

> Sofia is **worried**.
> She is also **sad**.
> (*Worried* and *sad* are **adjectives** that describe Sofia.)

Here are some common **linking verbs:**

is	being	look	turn
are	been	remain	prove
am	become	seem	stay
was	taste	sound	keep
were	act	appear	smell
be	grow	act	feel

Examples:

I <u>am</u> **she**.	(*She* renames the subject, *I.*)
Will <u>is</u> **worried**.	(*Worried* describes the subject, *Will.*)
Ms. Francis <u>is</u> my English **teacher**.	(*Teacher* is telling who Ms. Francis is.)
It <u>was</u> **he** who stole my car.	(*He* is identifying who stole my car.)
This banana <u>tastes</u> **terrible**.	(*Terrible* is describing banana.)

Verbs like *taste, act, feel, remain sound, appear, smell,* and *look,* which deal with the senses, can be either **action** or **linking**. They are **action** verbs when the subject is performing the action. When they connect the subject to a word (**subject complement**) that renames (noun) or describes (adjective), they are **linking** verbs:

Sage looks at the frog.
(*Looks* is an **action verb** because *Sage* is doing something. She "looks.")

Tory looks charming in his bathing suit.
(*Looks* is a **linking** verb because it is describing Tory.)

Even verbs like *keep, get, act,* and *grow* can be linking verbs depending on their use.

Tip: To determine if a verb is **action** or **linking**, substitute the verb with the word "seem(s)." If the sentence makes sense, then the verb is a linking verb and not an action verb:

He feels worried.
He seems preoccupied.

Seems makes sense, so *feels* is a **linking** verb.

I smelled the perfume.
I seemed the perfume.

Seemed makes no sense, so *smelled* is an **action** verb.

PRACTICE 1

Underline the verbs in the following sentences and then determine if they are action or linking verbs.

1.   The babies appeared frustrated.   _____

2.   Wilfred stayed in the army for four years.   _____

3.   Sylvia's child looked cold.   _____

4.   Maureen smelled the curried chicken throughout the neighborhood.   _____

5.   Officer Durant kept quiet about the rape investigation.   _____

6.   Stay calm until help arrives.   _____

7.   Does Alex act this hyper before his bedtime?   _____

8.   Manny sounds the bell at dinnertime.   _____

9.   Larry and Jesus remained friends.   _____

10.   Don't become too frustrated with your family.   _____

11.   The spaghetti smells good.   _____

12.   Robert tasted the food several times before serving it.   _____

Helping or Auxiliary Verbs

Helping verbs, which are sometimes called **auxiliary verbs,** are combined with main verbs to form verb phrases. There are *nine* of them, and they are the **only** verbs in the English language that cannot be used by themselves. They act as helpers; thus, they need *other verbs at all times* (will *go,* must *give,* should *walk,* may *teach,* etc.) Here are the nine main helping or auxiliary verbs:

can	might	should
could	may	will
must	shall	would

Other Helping Verbs

<u>Verb</u>	<u>Forms of the Verb</u>
be:	*am, is, are, was, were, been, being*
have:	*has, have, had*
do:	*do, does, did*

These verbs and their forms may function as main verbs or helping verbs. In other words, they can stand alone or they can be linked with other main verbs:

Examples: Suzie <u>was</u> once a dancer.
Shelly <u>is doing</u> her math assignments.
Jim <u>has</u> a way of going to work late.
Manny <u>has missed</u> two classes.
Liz <u>did</u> her portion of the assignment.
Loraine <u>has</u> <u>had</u> a successful career.

Verbs That Cannot Stand Alone

Been is a verb that cannot be a verb by itself. It must be combined with **has, have,** or **had:**

Rita <u>has</u> <u>been</u> a treasured colleague.

Being should be linked with a form of the verb *to be:* **am, is, are, was, were:**

I am <u>being</u> accused of giving too many writing assignments.

PRACTICE 2

Underline the verbs in the following sentences.

1. Laurence is a law enforcement officer.

2. Harold was in the army for four years.

3. Richard's baby has a bad cough.

4. Lisette has been in a coma for four months.

5. Mr. Jones will send you an airline ticket.

6. Sandy must pay for the ticket today.

7. Sonia, you may have eggs and grits for breakfast.

8. For sure, Sally will start college this semester.

9. The Andersons have been good neighbors.

10. The Joneses are being taken to their seats by the server.

11. Those girls seem depressed about their grades.

12. Suzanne will go to the party by herself.

13. Al shall remain in California until he graduates.

14. Molly should have been a lawyer rather than a teacher.

15. Marlon returned to the Virgin Islands after graduating from college .

VERBALS

Verbals are words that are formed from verbs, but they *do not* function as verbs. They look like verbs, but they are not. There are *three* types of verbals:

Gerunds: *-ing* word acting as the subject of a sentence
Infinitives: the preposition *to* + a verb
Participles: end in *-ing*, *-ed*, *-t*, or *-k*.

Gerunds

Words ending in *–ing,* that function as nouns are called **gerunds**.

An *-ing* word as a **gerund** in a statement:

> **Walking** is a good exercise.
> (*Walking* is a noun; *is* is the verb.)

> **Understanding** the math problem is quite difficult.
> (*Understanding* is a noun; *is* is the verb.)

An *-ing* word as a **gerund** in a question:

> Do you enjoy **drawing** on paper instead?
> (*Drawing* is a noun; *enjoy* is the verb)

An -*ing* word as a **verb** in a statement:

> Justin <u>is</u> <u>doing</u> well today.
> (*is* and *doing* are the verbs)

An **-***ing* word as a **verb** in a question:

> <u>Are</u> you <u>working</u>?
> (*Are* and *working* are the verbs)

Note: When an -*ing* word is used as a verb, it *must* be accompanied by a form of the verb to be: ***am, is, are, was,*** or ***were.***

Infinitives

Infinitives begin with the preposition *to*, followed by the base form of a verb. A verb will never have *to* before it. Infinitives and infinitive phrases function as *nouns, adjectives,* and *adverbs.*

Example: I <u>want</u> you **to look** at your new car.
("To look" is an infinitive; *want* is the verb.)

Infinitive: *to* + verb
Prepositional Phrase: *to* + noun

Infinitive: *to see*
Prepositional Phrase: *to school*

Participles

Participles are words that function either as verbs or adjectives; usually, they appear next to the noun or pronoun they modify. There are *two* types of participles:

- **Present participles** end in –*ing* (working, singing).
- **Past participles** usually end in –*ed* (tired), –*t* (burst), –*k* (drunk), or –*n* (broken).

Examples: My roommate's **barking** dog <u>kept</u> me up until 1 a.m.
(*Barking* is an adjective, which modifies *dog*; the verb is *kept*.)
Angelina <u>acts</u> as if she is the **chosen** athlete.
(*Chosen* describes the noun *athlete*; the verb is *acts*.)

The **determined** child <u>touched</u> the hot stove.
(*Determined* describes the noun *child*; the verb is *touched*.)

The **broken** vase <u>fell</u> on my right foot.
(*Broken* describes the noun *vase*; the verb is *fell*.)

VERBAL PHRASES

A **verbal** is a verb form that cannot function as a verb. There are *three* kinds of verbal phrases: *participles*, *gerunds*, and *infinitives*:

Participial Phrase

A **participial phrase** is a group of words that begin with a participle. Participles tell *which one*, *what kind*, or *how many* about a noun or pronoun.

Examples:
The man **wearing the black coat** <u>scared</u> me.
(*Wearing the black coat* is a **present participial phrase** telling **which man;**
scared is the verb; *wearing* is the participle.)

Running toward her mother, the child <u>fell</u> and <u>bumped</u> her head.
(*Running toward her mother* is a **present participial phrase** telling **what kind** of child,
a running child; *fell and bumped* are the verbs; *running* is the participle.)

Stopped by the huge guard, the celebrity <u>panicked</u>.
(*Stopped by the huge guard* is a **past participial phrase** telling **what kind** of guard,
a huge guard; *panicked* is the verb; *stopped* is a past participle.)

Note: Both the **present** and **past participle** can come at the **beginning** or at the **end** of a sentence. Pay attention to the punctuation of both.

Gerund Phrase

Gerunds are *–ing* verb forms that can function as *nouns, direct objects, indirect objects, subject complements,* or *objects* of a preposition:

Examples:
Working with the elderly <u>takes</u> patience.
(*Working with the elderly* is a **subject** gerund phrase; *working* is the gerund.)

Julie <u>enjoys</u> **baking cakes** during the Christmas season.
(*Baking cakes* is a **direct object** gerund phrase; *baking* is the gerund.)

Trina <u>makes</u> **doing her homework** her number one priority.
(*Doing her homework* is a **direct object** gerund phrase; *doing* is the gerund.)

Maria <u>is</u> **planning to go to Europe** this summer.
(*Planning to go to Europe* is a **subject complement** gerund phrase; *planning* is the gerund.)

After **washing my car**, it rained.
(*Washing my car* is an **object of the preposition** gerund phrase; *after* is the preposition.)

Infinitive Phrase

An **infinitive** is a form of the verb, which is usually preceded by the preposition *to*. Infinitives can act as *nouns, adjectives* or *adverbs*.

Infinitives as Nouns
Act as subjects, direct objects, subject complements, or objects of prepositions:

> **To win** this tournament <u>took</u> skill. (subject)
> Dennis <u>wants</u> **to do** all the projects. (direct object)
> Melissa's ambition <u>is</u> **to record** an album. (subject complement)
> While in the line **to see** the lion, the child <u>screamed</u>. (object of a preposition)

Infinitives as Adjectives
Modify nouns and pronouns, and they tell *which one, what kind,* or *how many*:

> The person **to eat** the most hot dogs <u>will win</u> the contest. (modifying a noun)
> The individual who desires **to enter** this contest <u>should</u> <u>wait</u> in line. (modifying a pronoun)

Infinitives as Adverbs
Modify **verbs**, ***a*djectives**, or **other adverbs**, and they tell *where, when, why, how,* or to *what extent*.

> **To see** the letters, sit up straight. (modifying a verb)
> Moriah <u>is</u> ready **to go** with the group. (modifying an adjective)
> <u>Go</u> early **to work** with the group. (modifying an adverb)

Remember: A verb preceded by *to* cannot be the verb of a sentence.

Finding the Complete Verb

Verbs can have *one* main verb or a series of other verbs to form a verb phrase. Thus, a complete verb phrase can have from *two* to *four* verbs. Like a single main verb, verb phrases have tenses, or show changes in time.

One verb: Jordan <u>is</u> smart.
Two verbs: Jordan <u>is</u> <u>getting</u> smart.
Three verbs: Jordan's parents <u>must have been</u> smart.
Four verbs: Jordan <u>should have been</u> <u>studying</u> for his weekly quizzes.

Watch Out for Adverbs

Adverbs often come in the middle of a verb phrase; however, they are *not* part of the complete verb. Most times adverbs end in *–ly*. They can, no doubt, be very tricky since they usually come between a helping verb and the main verb.

All adverbs *do not* end in *–ly*. These include: *not, always, never, very, rather, somewhat, often.* (For more on adverbs, go to the chapter titled *Adjectives* and *Adverbs*.)

Billy <u>has</u> **finally** <u>completed</u> his dissertation.
(*Finally* is an adverb and is not a part of the verb.)

Victor **often** <u>screams</u> for his bottle.
(*Often* is an adverb and not part of the verb.)

Watch Out for Contractions

Not is an adverb; when it is attached to a verb, it is *not* part of the verb:

Sally <u>would</u>n't <u>go</u> to sleep early.
(The verbs are *would go* and not *would not go*.)

Compound Verbs

Compound verbs are joined by conjunctions (*and, or*):

The child <u>tossed</u> **and** <u>turned</u> all night.
She either <u>jumped</u> **or** <u>slid</u> off her bed.

PRACTICE 3

In the following sentences, underline the helping verb(s) once and the main verb twice.

Examples: Aaron <u>has been</u> <u>studying</u> for hours.
<u>Are</u> you <u>planning</u> to go the beach this weekend?

1. Josh has been mowing the lawn for the past hour.

2. The students may have been studying for their final exam.

3. Shouldn't Maria and Andrea be in class?

4. Eating rapidly is unhealthy.

5. Stop working on the project, right now.

6. My mother often calls me on the weekend.

7. Aren't you going to Diana's party?

8. You should not have been drinking so much water.

9. Staying on top of your assignment was a wise decision.

10. Sandy's supervisor would like to give her the good news about her promotion.

11. Is Joan thinking about quitting school?

12. You should not have invited Percy to go to the picnic with you.

13. Are those students taking international business in the spring term?

14. Sonia danced and sang at Mercy's retirement party.

15. Shouldn't you leave work early to go to the meeting?

16. After taking the CPA exam twice, Veronica has finally passed.

17. Serena's mother would like to give her a gift for keeping her room clean.

18. Carmen is being singled out by her teacher for not turning in her biology assignment on time.

19. Dora has been thinking about taking a vacation for the past five years.

20. Please make an appointment to see the doctor next week.

VERBS CHANGING FORMS

Depending on the *time*, *mood*, *voice*, *person*, or *number*, the form of a verb changes.

Time

When a verb indicates a change in time, it means that the *tense* has changed.

Regular verbs have *four* principal parts that form their tenses:

Present Form
(Regular form has an *–s* ending to express a current time *only* if the subject is singular)

>   Manny <u>works</u> for himself.

Past Tense Form
(Regular form has an *–ed or –d* ending to express a time in the past)

>   Manny <u>worked</u> for himself.

Present Participial Form
(Helping verb + Simple verb ending in *–ing*)

>   Manny <u>is working</u> for himself.

Past Participial Form
(Helping verb + Simple verb ending in *–ed* or *–d*)

>   Manny <u>has worked</u> for himself.

Common Regular Verbs

Simple	Past	Present Participle	Past Participle
talk	talked	(is/am/are/was/were) talking	(has/have/had) talked
play	played	(is/am/are/was/were) playing	(has/have/had) played
jump	jumped	(is/am/are/was/were) jumping	(has/have/had) jumped

PRACTICE 4

*Write the **regular past tense** of the verbs in parentheses.*

1. After dinner, we_____ (watch) a video.

2. Candy_____(purchase) a new Mercedes Benz for her birthday.

3. Grissel's father_____(escort) her down the aisle at her wedding.

4. Because Ania_____ (protest) about police brutality, she was arrested.

5. The media _____(report) the wrong story.

6. I _____ (invite) 150 people to my birthday bash.

7. I did not believe Denia's story, but it_____ (turn) out to be credible.

8. Wilfred _____ (study) all night for his English test.

9. Josh_____(accompany) his brother to the basketball game.

10. Jeffrey _____ (attack) the robber when the robber _____ (point) the gun at him.

11. Stephanie _____(want) to go to New York to her friend's wedding.

12. The child _____(scream) when her mom left her at school the first day.

Irregular Past Tense Verbs

Irregular verbs *do not* form their past tense and past participle by the addition of *–ed* or *–d* like the regular verbs. They create *their past and past participle by changing some (break/broke/broken), no change (cost/cost/cost), or all (be/was/been) (go/went/gone).* Also, they often end in *-t, -k,* or *-n*.

Mastering these verbs can sometimes be very difficult, especially for non-native speakers because the endings differ from word to word. Therefore, irregular verb forms *must be* memorized:

> Professor Frank <u>began</u> to grade all the papers.
> Abel <u>taught</u> English in high school.
> Last summer, my friends and I <u>took</u> a trip to Paris.

Participle Forms
(**Present**: Helping verb + Simple verb ending in *-ing*)
(**Past**:   Helping verb + Simple verb that changes some, none or all of its form. Often ends in *-t* or *-n* ending)

Present: Johnnie <u>is trying</u> to prepare for the test.
Past: He <u>has begun</u> to outline the chapters.
                 Freddie <u>has taught</u> economics for several years now.

Common Irregular Verbs:

<u>Simple</u>	<u>Past</u>	<u>Present Participle</u>	<u>Past Participle</u>
arise	arose	(am) arising	(has/have) arisen
awake	awoke	(am) awaking	(has/have) awaken
be	was/were	(am) being	(has/have) been
bear	bore	(am) bearing	(has/have) born
beat	beat	(am) beating	(has/have) beaten
become	became	(am) becoming	(has/have) become
begin	began	(am) beginning	(has/have) begun
bet	bet	(am) betting	(has/have) bet
bite	bit	(am) biting	(has/have) bitten, bit
bleed	bled	(am) bleeding	(has/have) bled
blow	blew	(am) blowing	(has/have) blown
break	broke	(am) breaking	(has/have) broken
bring	brought	(am) bringing	has/have) brought
build	built	(am) building	(has/have) built
burst	burst	(am) bursting	(has/have) burst
buy	bought	(am) buying	(has/have) bought
cast	cast	(am) casting	(has/have) cast
catch	caught	(am) catching	(has/have) caught
choose	chose	(am) choosing	(has/have) chosen
come	came	(am) coming	(has/have) come
cost	cost	(am) costing	(has/have) cost
creep	crept	(am) creeping	(has/have) crept
cut	cut	(am) cutting	(has/have) cut
deal	dealt	(am) dealing	(has/have) dealt
do	did	(am) doing	(has/have) done
draw	drew	(am) drawing	(has/have) drawn
dream	dreamed/dreamt	(am) dreaming	(has/have) dreamed/dreamt
drink	drank	(am) drinking	(has/have) drunk
drive	drove	(am) driving	(has/have) driven
eat	ate	(am) eating	(has/have) eaten
fall	fell	(am) falling	(has/have) fallen
feed	fed	(am) feeding	(has/have) fed
feel	felt	(am) feeling	(has/have) feeling

fight	fought	(am) fighting	(has/have) fought
find	found	(am) finding	(has/have) found
fly	flew	(am) flying	(has/have) flown
forbid	forbade/forbad	(am) forbidding	(has/have) forbid/forbidden
forecast	forecast/(ed)	(am) forecasting	(has/have) forecast/forecasted
foresee	foresaw	(am) foreseeing	(has/have) foreseen
forget	forgot	(am) forgetting	(has/have) forgotten
forgive	forgave	(am) forgiving	(has/have) forgiven
freeze	froze	(am) freezing	(has/have) frozen
get	got	(am) getting	(has/have) forgotten/forgot
give	gave	(am) giving	(has/have) given
go	went	(am) going	(has/have) gone
grow	grew	(am) growing	(has/have) grown
hang	hanged (**person**)	(am) hanging	(has/have) hanged (**execution of a person**)
hang	hung (**thing**)	(am) hanging	(has/have) hung (**a thing**)
have	had	(am) having	(has/have) having
hear	heard	(am) hearing	(has/have) heard
hide	hid	(am) hiding	(has/have) hidden
hit	hit	(am) hitting	(has/have) hit
hold	held	(am) holding	(has/have) held
hurt	hurt	(am) hurting	(has/have) hurt
keep	kept	(am) keeping	(has/have) kept
know	knew	(am) knowing	(has/have) known
lay (to put)	laid	(am) laying	(has/have) laid
lead	led	(am) leading	(has/have) led
leave	left	(am) leaving	(has/have) left
let	let	(am) letting	(has/have) let
lie (down)	lay	(am) lying	(has/have) lain
light	lit	(am) lighting	(has/have) lit
lose	lost	(am) losing	(has/have) lost
make	made	(am) making	(has/have) made
mean	meant	(am) meaning	(has/have)meant
meet	met	(am) meeting	(has/have) met
mistake	mistook	(am) mistaking	(has/have) mistaken
overcome	overcame	(am) overcoming	(has/have) overcome
put	put	(am) putting	(has/have) put
quit	quit	(am) quitting	(has/have) quitting
read	read	(am) reading	(has/have) read
ride	rode	(am) riding	(has/have) ridden
ring	rang	(am) ringing	(has/have) rung
run	ran	(am) running	(has/have) run
say	said	(am) saying	(has/have) said
see	saw	(am) seeing	(has/have) seen
seek	sought	(am) seeking	(has/have) sought

sell	sold	(am) selling	(has/have) sold
send	sent	(am) sending	(has/have) sent
set	set	(am) setting	(has/have) set
shake	shook	(am) shaking	(has/have) shaken
shine	shone (light)	(am) shining	(has/have) shone
shine	shined (polished)	(am) shining	(has/have) shined
shoot	shot	(am) shooting	(has/have) shot
show	showed	(am) showing	(has/have) shown/showed
shrink	shrank/shrunk	(am) shrinking	(has/have) shrunken/shrunk
shut	shut	(am) shutting	(has/have) shut
sing	sang	(am) singing	(has/have) sung
sink	sank/sunk	(am) singing	(has/have) sunk
sit	sat	(am) sitting	(has/have) sat
sleep	slept	(am) sleeping	(has/have) slept
speak	spoke	(am) speaking	(has/have) spoken
speed	sped/speeded	(am) speeding	(has/have) sped/speeded
spend	spent	(am) spending	(has/have) spent
spin	spun	(am) spinning	(has/have) spun
spit	spit/spat	(am) spitting	(has/have) spit/spat
split	split	(am) splitting	(has/have) split
spread	spread	(am) spreading	(has/have) spread
spring	sprang/sprung	(am) springing	(has/have) sprung
stand	stood	(am) standing	(has/have) stood
steal	stole	(am) stealing	(has/have) stolen
stick	stuck	(am) sticking	(has/have) stuck
sting	stung	(am) stinging	(has/have) stung
stink	stank	(am) stinking	(has/have) stunk
strike	struck	(am) striking	(has/have) struck
strive	strove	(am) striving	(has/have) striven
swear	swore	(am) swearing	(has/have) sworn
sweat	sweated/sweat	(am) sweating	(has/have) sweated/sweat
sweep	swept	(am) sweeping	(has/have) swept
swim	swam	(am) swimming	(has/have) swum
swing	swung	(am) swinging	(has/have) swung
take	took	(am) taking	(has/have) taken
teach	taught	(am) teaching	(has/have) taught
tear	tore	(am) tearing	(has/have) torn
tell	told	(am) telling	(has/have) told
think	thought	(am) thinking	(has/have) thought
throw	threw	(am) throwing	(has/have) thrown
undergo	underwent	(am) undergoing	(has/have) undergone
understand	understood	(am) understood	(has/have) understood
wake	woke/waked	(am) waking	(has/have) woken/waked
wear	wore	(am) wearing	(has/have) worn

weave	wove	(am) weaving	(has/have) woven
weep	wept	(am) weeping	(has/have) wept
win	won	(am) winning	(has/have) won
wind	wound	(am) winding	(has/have) wound
withdraw	withdrew	(am) withdrawing	(has/have) withdrawn
withhold	withheld	(am) withholding	(has/have) withheld
wring	wrung	(am) wringing	(has/have) wrung
write	wrote	(am) writing	(has/have) written

Here are examples of the verb tenses:

Present Tenses	**Regular Verb** (talk)	**Irregular Verb** (fall)
<u>simple present</u>	I talk	I fall
<u>present progressive</u>	I am talking	I am falling
<u>present perfect</u>	I have talked	I have fallen
<u>present perfect progressive</u>	I have been talking	I have been falling

Past Tenses		
<u>simple past</u>	I talked	I fell
<u>past progressive</u>	I was talking	I was falling
<u>past perfect</u>	I had talked	I had fallen
<u>past perfect progressive</u>	I had been talking	I had been falling

Future Tenses		
<u>simple future</u>	I will break	I will fall
<u>future progressive</u>	I will be talking	I will be falling
<u>future perfect</u>	I will have talked	I will have fallen
<u>future perfect progressive</u>	I will have been talking	I will have been falling

Perfect Progressive Tenses

The *present perfect progressive tense* indicates that an ongoing action that began in the past is continuing in the present or recently ended.

They **have been dating** for many years.
They **have** not **been dating** for many years.
Have they **been dating** many years?

The *past perfect progressive tense* indicates that an ongoing action in the past ended.

She **had been painting** the door before the dog scratched it.
She **had** not **been painting** the door.
Had she **been painting** the door?

The *future perfect progressive tense* indicates than an ongoing action will be completed at some specified time in the future.

I **will have been playing** tennis for 20 years by December.
I **will** not **have been playing** tennis for 20 years by December.
Will I **have been playing** tennis for 20 years by December?

PRACTICE 5

*Write the **irregular past tense** of the verbs in parentheses.*

1.   Harry _____(have) a difficult time adjusting to his new environment.

2.   Miss Jordan _____(break) the vase her daughter _____(give) her for her birthday.

3.   Sofia _____(fall) twice in one month.

4.   Who _____(drink) all that water?

5.   After jogging for two hours, Fred _____(drink) two bottles of water.

6.   To finish her degree rapidly, Janice _____(take) 18 credits per semester.

7.   Who _____(teach) you to dance so well?

8.   My automobile insurance _____(cost) more than my homeowner's insurance.

9.   Yesterday, the children _____(swim) for two hours.

10.   Elsa _____(forget) the lyrics to the song.

11.   After the woman _____(fall) down the stairs, she _____(bleed) until the paramedics arrived.

12.   Monique _____(take) five years to finish her two-year nursing degree

PRACTICE 6

*Write the correct **past** or **past participle** form of the verbs in parentheses.*

1.   For months, Maria has (seek) _____ after a dedicated computer analyst.

2.   After she gave blood, she (bleed) _____ for several minutes.

3.   Two contestants have been voted off *Britain Has Talent* because they (forget) _____ some of the lyrics to their songs.

4.   Joel has (drive)_____ 200 miles to attend his friend's graduation ceremony.

5.   While Anthony was on vacation last summer, he (read) _____ the entire Bible.

6.   Several tornadoes have been (forecast) _____ between June and September.

7.   Alexis has (bear) _____ her grudge against her best friend very well.

8.   To satisfy his thirst, Frank has (drink) _____ six cans of Sprite.

9.   I (be) _____ in Hawaii for two weeks.

10.   My nephew (draw)_____ a picture of his mom for show and tell.

PRACTICE 7

*Write the **past** and **past participle** of the following **irregular** verbs.*

	Present	Past	Past Participle
1.	cut	_____	_____
2.	bleed	_____	_____
3.	put	_____	_____
4.	wear	_____	_____
5.	write	_____	_____
6.	speak	_____	_____
7.	shake	_____	_____
8.	see	_____	_____
9.	swear	_____	_____
10.	become	_____	_____
11.	hang (thing)	_____	_____
12.	come	_____	_____
13.	go	_____	_____
14.	run	_____	_____
15.	cost	_____	_____
16.	beat	_____	_____

VERB TENSES

Tense means time. In English, *six* tenses demonstrate the divisions of time. Of the six, *three* are **primary** and *three* are **secondary**.

Primary Tenses_

The *three* primary basic (simple) tenses that indicate the time of an action or condition are **present tense**, **past tense** and **future tense**:

Present Tense

The **present tense** indicates that an action or condition is in progress (going on) or exists now.

Example: He dances at the club on Saturdays.

Past Tense

The **past tense** indicates that an action or condition is completed or once existed at some definite time in the past.

Examples: She attended the University of Miami. (*Regular past tense*)
Marlon became a United States citizen last year. (*Irregular past tense*)

Future Tense

The **future tense** indicates that an action or condition will take place in the future. It uses **will** or **would** with the base form of the verb.

Examples: Jason **says** he will graduate in two years.
(The main verb "*says*" is in the present tense, so *will* is used.)

His friend **said** he would graduate in four years.
(The main verb "*said*" is past, so *would* is used.)

Secondary Tenses_
The *three* secondary tenses or compound tenses are **present perfect tense**, **past perfect tense**, and **future perfect tense**:

Present Perfect Tense

The **present perfect tense** indicates that an action or condition has just been completed or
has started in the past and is still continuing in the present. It uses the helping verb *has* or *have* plus the *past participle* form of the verb.

Examples: Ms. Smith has spoken for an hour.
(*She is still speaking.*)
Anita and Candy have lived at the same address for several years.
(*They are still living at the same place.*)

Past Perfect Tense

The **past perfect tense** indicates that *two* past actions took place (the *past perfect* and the *simple past*), but the past perfect occurred before the simple past. It is combined with the auxiliary verb *had* plus the past participle of the main verb.

Examples: Before Fanny came home, her mother <u>had</u> already <u>cleaned</u> the house.
(First, Fanny's mother *had cleaned*; then, Fanny *came* home.)

Last week, Justin <u>wore</u> tennis shoes to work because he <u>had sprained</u> his ankle.
(First, Justin *had sprained* his ankle; then, he *wore* tennis shoes to work.)

Future Perfect Tense

The **future perfect tense** indicates that an action or condition will be completed at a future (specific) time. It uses *will have* or *shall have* plus the past participle form of the verb.

Example: The professor <u>will have</u> <u>changed</u> Lauretta's grade before the class ends.
Ramon <u>shall have</u> <u>finished</u> college by the time his sister finishes high school.

Progressive Tenses

Verbs also have **progressive tenses** to indicate that an action or condition was continual in the *past* or continues in the *present* or *future*.

The **present progressive tense** uses the present form of the verb to be (*am, is, are*) as a helping verb plus an *–ing* verb:

Example: Josie <u>is</u> <u>reading</u> his favorite novel.

The **past progressive tense** uses the past form of the verb to be (*was, were*) as a helping verb plus an *–ing* verb:

Example: Josie <u>was</u> <u>reading</u> his favorite novel.

The **future progressive tense** uses *will be* as helping verbs plus an *–ing* verb:

Example: Josie <u>will be</u> <u>reading</u> his favorite novel.

PRACTICE 8

In the space to the right, indicate the tense of the verbs in italics.

Example: Andrea *is studying* for her final exam.   <u>**Present Progressive**</u>

1. Andrew ***has completed*** his homework.   _____

2. By the fall semester, Joe ***will have satisfied*** the requirements
   for his bachelor's degree.   _____

3. The police captured the robber who ***had stolen*** his neighbor's car.   _____

4. Sonia *works* at a huge law firm in New York City. _____

5. Despite Warren's accident, he *went* to work. _____

6. Anita's grandson *broke* her new phone. _____

7. This summer, Anthony *will go* to Colombia for a month. _____

8. The softball team *will be going* to Islands of Adventure. _____

9. Susan *had finished* cooking by the time her relatives arrived. _____

10. Pedro *has been* a U.S. citizen for more than ten years. _____

11. Ericka *will have announced* her wedding plans by the time her mother arrived at the engagement party. _____

12. Alina said she *would like* to become a lawyer. _____

13. The employees *were thinking* about quitting their jobs. _____

14. Olga *has become* a hostile person to her parents. _____

15. George *had* not *heard* about his surprise birthday party before he arrived. _____

16. Suzette *is considering* whether to take a math course. _____

17. Mike *shall have done* the project by Friday. _____

18. Muriel *has made* the same dinner every other night. _____

19. Johnny *was hoping* to find a more experienced assistant. _____

20. The student *will have completed* the project by the due date. _____

Mood

The mood or (mode) of a verb indicates how an action should be regarded: as a *fact*, *command*, *wish*, an *uncertainty*. Based on this, there are **three** moods:

The **indicative mood** is used to make a statement of fact or ask a question:

- The house is clean.
- What are your plans for the future?

The **imperative mood** is used to give a command, or an order:

- Clean the house.
- Study for your final exam.

Note: In the imperative mood, the subject *you* is understood by the person to whom you are speaking or by a reader. Therefore, it is not written:

- [*You*] Clean the house. (The subject *you* is understood)
- [*You*] Study for your final exam. (The subject *you* is understood)

The **subjunctive mood** is used in the following ways:
- to express a desire, to make a wish, recommendation, a request or hope
- to express a condition that is contrary to fact
- to express doubt or uncertainty

Regardless if the subject is singular or plural, the subjunctive mood of the verb **to be** is "**be**" in the present tense and "**were**" in the past. The subjunctive for the present tense third person singular drops the *-s* or *-es*.

Incorrect: He *insists* is that everyone **is** present.
Correct: He *insists* is that everyone **be** present. (use: *request*)

Incorrect: If I **was** you, I would quit.
Correct: If I **were** you, I would quit. (use: *nonfactual condition*)

Incorrect: She *suggested* that each woman **reports** her tips.
Correct: She *suggested* that each woman **report** her tips. (use: *desire*)

PRACTICE 9

In the following sentences, identify whether the sentence is written in the indicative, imperative, or the subjunctive mood.

1. If you were here, we would have completed the project.   _____

2. Where were you when I stopped by your house?   _____

3. Give me your recommendation for the nominees.   _____

4. Sam's mother requests that he take his final exam.   _____

5. If I were like you, I would not go on that dangerous ride.   _____

6. Please do not speak so loudly.   _____

7. David has been a student for 15 years.   _____

8. The girls act as if they were under stress.   _____

9.   That spinach is certainly tasty.   _____

10. It is imperative that the child sees a doctor soon.   _____

11. Tell your friends to be prepared for the interview.   _____

12. My dad suggests that Tim only work part time this summer.   _____

Voice

Verbs occur in *active* or *passive* voice. When the subject of a sentence performs the action of a verb, the verb is in the *active voice*.

The **active voice** takes **transitive verbs** with **direct objects** and shows that the subject of the sentence is doing the action:

    subj   verb   do
- Ida <u>found</u> the check. (action with direct object)

    subj verb   do
- I <u>hope</u> that he wins. (action with direct object)

Note: Only transitive verbs (those that take a direct object) can be made passive. For example:

- John <u>cried</u>. (*cried* is an intransitive verb, so this sentence can't be made passive)

The **passive voice**, on the contrary, shows that the subject of the sentence is receiving the action or condition of the verb. In other words, the action is being done to the subject.

The **passive** form of a verb is formed by combining the verb *to be* (*am, is, are, was, were, is being, has been*) with the past participle:

- The check <u>was</u> <u>found</u> by Ida. (helping verb *was* + the past participle)

- It <u>is hoped</u> that he wins. (helping verb *is* + the past participle)

In the **passive voice**, the direct object becomes the subject.

             subj   verb   d.o.
Active voice: The football <u>hit</u> Doreen in the head.

             subj   verbs
Passive voice: Doreen <u>was hit</u> in the head by the football.

The preposition *by* commonly indicates a passive sentence construction. In the following sentences, compare the **active voice** with the **passive voice**:

Active voice:	The truck <u>hit</u> the car.
Passive voice:	The car <u>was</u> <u>hit</u> *by* the truck.

Active voice:	Tory <u>received</u> a gift at the party.
Passive voice:	A gift <u>was</u> <u>received</u> *by* Tory at the party.

Active voice:	My daughter <u>taught</u> me to drive.
Passive voice:	I <u>was</u> <u>taught</u> to drive **by** my daughter.

PRACTICE 10

*In the following sentences, change the active voice to the passive voice. If a sentence is written in the past tense, use **was/were** with the past participle. If it is written in the present tense, use **am/is/are** with the past participle.*

1. The supervisor warned the employee about her constant tardiness.

    _____

2. Professor Williams' students aced their final exam.

    _____

3. Suzie returned the Mother's Day gift because she did not like it.

    _____

4. Nancy eats a sandwich for dinner.

    _____

5. The elderly woman received free medication from the doctor.

    _____

When the verb is in the **passive voice,** the sentence is considered weak and wordy. Therefore, using the active voice is preferred to the passive voice. For one thing, the active mode is more concise, clear, and direct. Also, writers can create more interesting, sensory stimulating sentences in the active voice.

However, the **passive voice** is typically reserved for deliberate uses. The **passive voice** is particularly useful – even recommended – in *two* situations:

When emphasizing the person or thing acted upon is more important:

> The child <u>was</u> <u>hit</u> by the speeding van.
> (The *passive voice* rightly emphasizes who was hit.)

The federal building <u>has been</u> on high security alert all weekend.
(Emphasis is on what is on alert, not who issued the alert.)

When the actor in a situation is unimportant or unknown:

Bacteria <u>was discovered</u> in the wound.
(The *passive voice* emphasizes the discovery of bacteria, not who found it.)

Employees <u>are required</u> to wear uniform to work.
(The *passive voice* emphasizes what they had to do, not who made them do it.)

The **passive voice** can be used in any tense.

Tense	Subject	Helping Verbs		Past Participle
		Singular	Plural	
Present	The truck/trucks	is	are	parked.
Present Perfect	The truck/trucks	has been	have been	parked.
Past	The truck/trucks	was	were	parked.
Past Perfect	The truck/trucks	had been	had been	parked.
Future	The truck/trucks	will be	will be	parked.
Future Perfect	The truck/trucks	will have been	will have been	parked.
Present Progressive	The truck/trucks	is being	are being	parked.
Past Progressive	The truck/trucks	was being	were being	parked.

The **passive voice** in each construction above emphasizes when the truck was parked, not who is doing it.

PRACTICE 11

*In the following sentences, change the **passive voice** into the **active voice only** if it is more effective. Some sentences will remain unchanged while others will require you to create a subject.*

1. A cure for cancer has been written about in many medical publications.

    _____

    _____

2. Johnnie was given an award for saving the child's life.

    _____

    _____

3. Andrea's house was damaged by the huge palm tree on the side of her house.

    _____

    _____

4. The children are lined up along the fence.

_____

_____

5. The soccer players are known for their winning history.

_____

_____

Person

Person refers to the change in the form of a verb or pronoun based whether a person is speaking in the first, second, or third person.

Person	Singular	Plural
First (the person speaking)	I	We
Second (the person spoken to)	You	You
Third (the person or object spoken about)	He, She, It	They

In the third person singular (he, she, it), the verb gets an _–s_ or _–es_ ending.

Person	Singular	Person	Plural
First	I _walk_	**First**	We _walk_
Second	You _walk_	**Second**	You _walk_
Third	He, She, It _walks_	**Third**	They _walk_

Number

Number refers to the change in the form of a noun, pronoun, or verb to indicate whether more than one subject is indicated. Unlike most nouns and pronouns, adding an _–s_ or _–es_ ending to a verb creates a singular form.

Examples: The baby <u>runs</u>. (Singular)
The babies <u>run</u>. (Plural)

The athlete <u>runs</u> three miles twice a day. (Singular)
The athletes <u>run</u> three miles twice a day. (Plural)

Note: When the subject of a sentence is a plural noun that doesn't end in –s (men, women, children), the verb also gets no –s or –es ending.

Examples: The woman <u>moves</u> too slowly. (Singular)
The women <u>move</u> too slowly. (Plural)

His mouse <u>dashes </u>toward the cheese . (Singular)
His mice <u>dash </u>toward the cheese . (Plural)

Linking verbs also indicate whether more than one subject is indicated.

<u>Singular</u>	<u>Plural </u>
(*he, she, it*) **is**	(*they*) **are**
(*I*) **am**	(*we*) **are**
(*I, he, she, it*) **was**	(*we, they*) **were**
(*he, she, it*) **has been**	(*we, they*) **have been**
(*he, she, it*) **feels**	(*we, they*) **feel**
(*he, she, it*) **seems**	(*we, they*) **seem**
(*he, she, it*) **looks**	(*we, they*) **look**
(*he, she, it*) **appears**	(*we, they*) **appear**

Adjectives

Like the invention of color television, adjectives add color to both oral and written communication. In other words, they create vivid pictures in the minds of readers and listeners. **Adjectives** modify nouns or pronouns and answer the questions **which one**, **what kind**, and **how many**. Most of the time, they are placed immediately in front of the words they modify.

Adjectives

    adj noun
The **new car** belongs to Manny.
(*New* answers **which one**.)

   adj   noun
Gigantic mountains can be found in Chile.
(*Gigantic* answers **what kind** of mountains.)

   adj   noun
Several workers left work early.
(*Several* answers **how many** workers.)

ADJECTIVES AFTER LINKING VERBS

An **adjective** can also be used as a modifier after a linking verb (*am, is, are, was, were, become, look, appear, smell, taste, feel, sound*) to describe its subject:

        LV   adj
The children **looked sad**.

       LV adj
Michael **was happy** about the news.

EASILY IDENTIFIED ADJECTIVES

Some adjectives can easily be identified because of their endings: *-ible/able, -ful, -ous, -some,* and *-ary*. Here are a few:

respons**ible**	favor**able**	cred**ible**	desir**able**
faith**ful**	duti**ful**	use**ful**	harm**ful**
marvel**ous**	gener**ous**	numer**ous**	ridicul**ous**
tire**some**	hand**some**	trouble**some**	whole**some**
vision**ary**	contr**ary**	prim**ary**	second**ary**

PRACTICE 1

Fill in the blank with an appropriate adjective.

1.   Ricky is popular, but Tom is _____ .

2.   Does Raymond live in a _____ house?

3.   Johnny is a _____ student.

4.   Do you go to a _____ church?

5.   Sue acted _____ in front of everyone.

6.   Is this a _____ mountain?

7.   Francisco is an_____ person?

8.   Paulina has_____ hair.

9.   Was it a _____ movie?

10.   Maria was _____ about going on the trip.

FORMING THE COMPARATIVE AND THE SUPERLATIVE

- Use the **comparative** to compare *two* persons, places, or things.
- Use the **superlative** to compare *three or more* persons, places, or things.

For all **one-syllable** words, use *-er* for the comparative and *-est* for the superlative:

Adjective	Comparative	Superlative
	(2 = "**er**")	(3 or more = "**est**")
red	redder	reddest
fat	fatter	fattest
tall	taller	tallest
large	larger	largest

Adjectives with More Than One Syllable

For two-syllable adjectives ending in –y, drop the –y and add –ier to form the comparative and –iest to form the superlative.

Adjective	**Comparative** (2 = "er")	**Superlative** (3 or more = "est")
happy	happier	happiest
silly	sillier	silliest
funny	funnier	funniest
rocky	rockier	rockiest
pretty	prettier	prettiest

For words of more than one syllable that *do not* end in *y*, use "more "for the comparative and "most" for the superlative:

Adjective	**Comparative** (2 = "**more**")	**Superlative** (3 or more = "**most**")
yellow	more yellow	most yellow
common	more common	most common
intelligent	more intelligent	most intelligent
difficult	more difficult	most difficult
careful	more careful	most careful
knowledgeable	more knowledgeable	most knowledgeable
important	more important	most important
beautiful	more beautiful	most beautiful
handsome	more handsome	most handsome

A number of adjectives have **irregular** forms. Here are a few.

Adjective	**Comparative**	**Superlative**
good	better	best
bad	worse	worst
little	less	least
much, many	more	most
some	more	most

Note: Some adjectives such as *unique, universal, rare,* and *perfect* **do not** have comparisons.

PRACTICE 2

In the following sentences, use the comparative or the superlative.

1. Allan would make a _____ (good) baseball player than his brother.

2. Your first essay is _____ (bad) than the second.

3. Marcia is the_____ (intelligent) of her sisters.

4. Which of these stories is the_____(funny) one?

5. Jason is the_____ (contrary) person I have ever met.

COMPOUND ADJECTIVES

A **compound adjective** combines two or more words to express a single idea about a noun. Compound adjectives are formed to avoid possible confusion or ambiguity. When a compound adjective is used **before a noun**, use a hyphen(s):

- Carmen enrolled as a **full-time** student.
- I mailed my **up-to-date** bills yesterday.
- He made two **first-quarter** touchdowns.
- My **three-year-old** son likes to skate.

By combing the words with a hyphen, they express one complete description. However, some combinations of modifiers that appear **after a noun** are not hyphenated:

- Carmen attends school **full time**.
- He paid his bills **up to date**.
- He scored six points in the **first quarter**.
- My son, who just turned **three years old**, likes to skate.

When a hyphenated compound adjective comes **after the verb** *be* (*is*, *are*) and the noun can be implied, retain the hyphen(s):

- Carmen is **full-time** here.
- She is **well-known**.
- He is a **three-year-old**.

For better mastery, include the implied words. The sentences could have read:

- Carmen is [a] **full-time** [student] here.
- She is [a] **well-known** [person].
- He is a **three-year-old** [boy].

The same rule applies when a compound adjective comes before an implied noun:

- My 10-year-old is crying.
- My 10-year-old [boy] is crying.

Remember: The adverb *very* and others that end in *–ly* can never be part of a compound adjective. Also, proper nouns should not be hyphenated.

PRACTICE 3

In the following sentences, choose the correct compound adjective.

1. The girl who lives in the (two-story, two story) apartment is moving.

2. Frances takes great pride in making sure her payroll records are (well-done, well done).

3. We saw Andrea's (much-anticipated, much anticipated) play at the Fox Theater.

4. Those (very-hardworking, very hardworking) students are in each of my six classes.

5. Mrs. Brown is a (six-time, six time) boxing champion.

8

Adverbs

Adverbs modify *verbs*, *adjectives*, or *other adverbs*. They usually tell **how, when, where, why, how often,** or **how much**. Like adjectives, adverbs can come before or after the word they modify. They are easy to identify because they most often end in *-ly*.

Examples:　Jesse drives **slowly**.
(*Slowly* is an adverb that answers **how** Jesse drives.)

Keith finished his essay **today**.
(*Today* is an adverb that answers **when** (the time) Keith finished his essay.)

Emory is **very** tall for his age.
(*Very* is an adverb that modifies the adjective *tall*. It answers **how** tall Emory is.)

Jon delivered his speech **too slowly**.
(*Too* and *slowly* are adverbs; they describe **how** slowly Jon delivered his speech.)

Many adjectives can be transformed into adverbs by just adding *-ly*. Here are some:

Adjective	**Adverbs**
quick	quickly
slow	slowly
quiet	quietly
prompt	promptly
calm	calmly
unusual	unusually

GOOD/WELL

These two words are often confused. **Good** always functions as an adjective and should never be used as an adverb. Remember, adjectives describe nouns.

Examples:　Janelle is a **good** student. (*Good* modifies *student*.)

Gianna feels **good** today. (*Good* describes Gianna's health.)

Well, on the other hand, can function as both an adjective and an adverb. As an adverb, it modifies an action verb and answers how something is done. When *well* is used as an adjective, it means suitable, proper, or healthy. Thus, *good* or *well* can be used to describe health.

Examples: The students worked **well** together. (*Well* modifies the verb *worked*.)
Jake looks **well** today. (*Well* suggests that Jake *looks* healthy today.)

PRACTICE 1

In the blank, choose 'good' or 'well'.

1. Pablo delivered his speech_____ (good/well).

2. Jonathan, Israel, and Robert play the piano_____ (good/well).

3. I feel_____ (good/well) about completing my 20-page project.

4. Joseph looked _____ (good/well) when I saw him at the meeting.

5. Arlene, in my opinion, would make a very_____ (good/well) teacher.

6. How _____ (good/well) do you know the Johnsons?

7. Jacky appears to be getting along _____ (good/well) with her boss these days.

8. Andrea seems to be doing _____ (good/well) these days.

INTERROGATIVE ADVERBS

How, when, why, and *where* are adverbs used to ask questions.

Examples: **How** did you get there?
When did you arrive?
Why is that?
Where is my car?

PRACTICE 2

Using all the rules you have learned, correct the following sentences.

1. Marcie believes she can type more better than Sandra.

2. Eileen is the most intelligentest student in her class.

3. Close the door very soft, please.

4. The salesman believes he is the better of all the salesmen.

5. Mrs. Munoz is a well known individual in her neighborhood.

6. Raymond has a tendency of shouting loud at Manny.

7. Dorothy was rated the most fastest typist in her typing class.

8. The Stewarts are the more dependable individuals in their company.

9. Getting the new position gives Ana better self esteem these days.

10. Arnold walks slower than anyone I know.

11. Arlene is the most selfish of her two sisters.

12. Alfred is a very unique person who does not socialize.

13. The children looked sadly when their mom told them they couldn't go to the park.

14. Annette can complete her job responsibilities quicker than anyone on her team.

15. Natalie's three year old daughter can surely express herself good.

16. She has the beautifulest face.

17. My mother looks as if she is not doing good today.

18. Melissa recites her poem quicker than anyone in her class.

19. This paper is yellower than the one I bought at the bookstore.

20. Of all the guys on the football team, Jonathan is the faster player.

Prepositions

A **preposition** is a word that shows the relationship of a noun or pronoun to some other word in the sentence. Spotting prepositions is simple because they often indicate where something is located (*below, beneath, on, beside, by*), the direction in which someone or something is going (*to, from*), or the time of an occurrence (*at, during, before*).

Prepositions

aboard	behind	from	per
about	below	in	regarding
above	beneath	inside	round
across	beside	into	since
after	besides	like	till
against	between	near	through
along	beyond	next	throughout
alongside	but*	of	to***
amid	by	off	toward
amidst	concerning	on	under
among	despite	onto	underneath
around	down	out	until
as	during	outside	up/upon
at	except	over	via
before	for**	pending	with/without/within

*Use *but* as a preposition only when it means except.
**When *for* means because, it is a conjunction and not a preposition.
***When *to* is followed by a verb (to eat), it is an infinitive and not a prepositional phrase.

A **prepositional phrase** consists of two or more words. It begins with a preposition and is followed by a noun or an objective pronoun (*me, you, her, him, us, them, it, whom/whomever*), which is referred to as the **object of the preposition**.

PREPOSITIONAL PHRASES

according to	in place of	in addition to	
along with	on account of	contrary to	
in front of	on top of	in answer to	
in the middle of	out of	in fairness to	
in spite of	for the sake of	in relation to	

> **phrase:** *during the game*
>
> **preposition**   **noun**
> *during*   *the game*

Note: Some prepositions like *about, after, before, down, in, out, around, near,* and *up* can function as adverbs. Also, the preposition "after" can be a conjunction when it is followed by a subject and a verb.

Example: *After* I left the game, I went to dinner.
("After" is a conjunction because it is followed by a subject and verb.)

After the game, I went to dinner.
("After" is a preposition because it is only followed by a noun.)

PRACTICE 1

*Use the list of prepositions to help you identify prepositions in the sentences below. Put a **P** over each preposition.*

Remember: When *to* is followed by a verb (*to run; to plant*), it is an infinitive and not a preposition.

Example: This book came from Canada.
                                      P

1. Despite Andy's illness, he went to a basketball game.

2. At this time, I am unable to take care of Candy's concerns.

3. During the week, Daniel studies until late for his economics class.

4. In the summer, Jessica will go to New York for orientation.

5. By the end of the day, your report should be placed in my mailbox.

6. Last year I drove to New York to buy parts for my car.

7. A picture of Bob Marley hangs above my bed.

8. Frantically, the young mother screamed for help when her baby fell off the bed.

9. Did you pass alongside me on the highway at 80 miles per hour?

10. At noon, the office will be closed for lunch.

11. Concerning Jonathan's progress in his math class, I am not pleased.

12. Israel made a touchdown after several yards.

13. Tonight I will be home in time for dinner with my family.

14. Immediately after the rain, Luis washed his car.

15. As per our telephone conversation, I am ready to receive the carpet.

16. According to Juan's lab report, he is in good health.

17. Instead of having ice cream, I will have a yogurt.

18. Because of your persistence, I will be at the party with my children.

19. The cake, which is on top of the stove, is for Andy's birthday.

20. In spite of your rude behavior, I will attend tonight's meeting.

PRACTICE 2

Practice finding prepositions and their objects (prepositional phrases).

                   P   **O**
Example: The books are on the table.

Some prepositions have two objects:

              P   **O**   **O**
Example: Between you and me, Marla is getting married.

1. Andrea is going to switch her major from nursing to journalism.

2. The war in Iraq has affected families all over the United States and in Europe.

3. Keith promised to study with me after his art class.

4. Between Robert and Chad, they were able to clean the house spotlessly.

5. Running everyday for two hours has enabled me to lose weight.

6. Susan studied until midnight in order to pass her chemistry test.

7. Olga, by 10 o'clock tonight, I want the office to be closed.

8. Between you and me, I am not going to attend the meeting.

9. Everyone but Felix was present for the graduation ceremony.

10. Lavern has been at the doctor's office since noon.

11. Against all odds, Ana went to college and earned a degree in political science.

12. Someone stole my purse from underneath my desk at about 2 p.m.

13. At my birthday party, many of my friends did not socialize.

14. Are you going to Disney World with us in the summer?

15. Diana's party will be sponsored by Nick and me.

Note: The object of the preposition (a noun or pronoun) does not have to be right next to the preposition. Adjectives and other parts of speech may come in between. Keep in mind, however, that a prepositional phrase begins with a preposition and ends with a noun or pronoun.

$$\text{P} \quad \text{adj} \quad \text{adj} \quad \text{adj} \quad \text{O}$$

Example: The napkins are on the huge black and white table.
(huge, black, and *white* describe the table.)

PRACTICE 3

*Put brackets around all the prepositional phrases in the sentences below. Don't forget to watch out for infinitives (**to** + verb). They are not prepositional phrases.*

Example: Marlon wants to go [to France] [in the summer.]

1. Despite Nora's hard work, she did not pass her exam.

2. The bicycle shop is across the street next to the gas station.

3. During the summer, I go to Jamaica for about two weeks.

4. One of the students missed the unit exam and wants to speak with her teacher.

5. Amidst the huge crowd, my son found me and sat by me and my friends.

6. Most of the children in my neighborhood are between two and eight years old.

7. About 6 p.m., I will go to dinner with my colleagues to eat all I desire.

8. After waiting for my doctor for more than an hour, I finally went home.

9. For Monica, Edwin and Joan, a good diet is paramount in order to stay healthy.

10. Everyone in my family, except Mary, will go to Jenny's wedding.

11. Do you want to play volleyball with me in the afternoon after dinner?

12. By the time you get home, I will be through cooking.

13. As a matter of fact, I made a lot of food for you and your friends.

14. On Sundays, I am against working around the house, especially in the yard.

15. Today, I will be home in time for the 6 o'clock news.

16. I am not thrilled about the present for my birthday.

17. For your silver wedding anniversary, Manny will take you to your favorite restaurant to eat at 7 p.m. on Saturday.

18. Despite my decision to move in six months, I have not notified my job yet.

19. Allan's inheritance will be distributed among his four siblings.

20. Robert is going to the store for his mother.

MISUSING PREPOSITIONS

Avoid ending sentences with prepositions. This is called a **dangling preposition**.

Bad Construction: Whom will you give the gift **to**?
Better: **To** whom will you give the gift?

Bad Construction: Where do you live **at**?
Better: Where do you live?

Remember: Some prepositions can function as adverbs, so a preposition at the end of a sentence does not necessarily have to be a preposition. For example, look at following sentence:

When I went to Carla's house for dinner, her mother invited me **in**.
(*In* is functioning as an adverb and not as a preposition.)

When in doubt, reword the sentence.

Here are four prepositions that are often misused:

1. IN

In can mean beneath the surface:

- The soap is **in** the water.
- Josh burnt a hole **in** the rug.

In can also mean location:

- John said he would meet you **in** front of Burdines.

Use *in* with cities, states, countries, counties and specific areas:

- **City**:   I live **in** Miami.
- **State**:   My Aunt Lucy lives **in** the state of New York.
- **Country**: I have relatives **in** Haiti.
- **Area**:   I live **in** Kendall.

In can also be used to indicate duration of time:

- She has to pick her brother up **in** 30 minutes.
- My mother wants Ana home **in** time for dinner.

2. ON

On means to touch the surface:

- The book is **on** the desk.
- Shirley wrote the address **on** the envelope.

Use *on* with street names when the number is not given:

- My friend lives **on** Fifth Avenue.

On can also be used to indicate days:

- Your mother will pick you up **on** Friday, July 14, 2004.

3. INTO

Into means from outside to inside.

4. AT

At usually indicates a specific location:

- I'll meet you **at** the college.

Use *at* with house or building numbers:

- She lives **at** 6051 N.W. Fourth Court.

Use *at* to indicate exact time:

- I will meet you **at** 6 p.m.

Use *at* to indicate approximate time:_

- I am scared **at** night when I hear strange sounds.

PRACTICE 4

*Fill in the blanks with either **in**, **on**, or **at**.*

1. Two years ago, I lived _____ New York.

2. Will Carl arrive home _____ time for dinner?

3. I will meet you _____ 6 p.m. _____ front of the cafeteria.

4. Wilfred is thinking about living _____ Haiti for a year.

5. The ball is _____ the pool _____ the bottom.

6. Are you still living _____ the same address _____ the same apartment?

7. For the first time, Holly will be _____ time for her class.

8. The books were left _____ top of the table _____ the same area where we studied for the test.

9. Did you write the wrong address _____ the envelope?

10. I often go to the gym _____ Sunset whenever I am _____ the area _____ company business.

10

Conjunctions

There are *two* kinds of conjunctions: **coordinating** and **subordinating**. **Conjunctions** join words, phrases, or clauses. They often help show relationships to the rest of a sentence. A **phrase** is a group of related words (two or more) that does not contain a subject and a verb whereas a **clause** is a group of words that has a subject and a verb. Some clauses are **independent** (can stand alone) while others are **dependent** (incapable of standing alone). Independent clauses are simple sentences; dependent clauses are called subordinating clauses.

> **Independent Clause** = Complete sentence, which makes sense
> **Dependent Clause** = Fragment, needs more information to make sense

COORDINATING CONJUNCTIONS

There are *seven* **coordinating conjunctions,** which are used to join words, phrases, or clauses of the same (parallel) form. An easy way to remember them is to use the acronym **FANBOYS**:

F	=	*for*	=	cause
A	=	*and*	=	addition
N	=	*nor*	=	negative option
B	=	*but*	=	contrast
O	=	*or*	=	positive option
Y	=	*yet*	=	contrast
S	=	*so*	=	result

> **Parallel Form**
>
> Coordinating conjunctions should join nouns with nouns; adjectives with adjectives; and prepositional phrases with prepositional phrases.

Examples: I enjoy milk **and** ice cream. (connecting two words.)
Eileen writes in her journal **and** in her notebook. (connecting two phrases)
Marlon failed math, **so** he has to retake it. (connecting two independent clauses)
I would go to the party, **but** I am tired.   (connecting two independent clauses)

Note: Using the wrong conjunction can drastically change the meaning of a sentence. Thus, make sure you choose the right conjunction that shows logical relationship of ideas:

Incorrect: I am sick, **so** I am going to class. (*"so"* does not show logical relationship.)
Correct: I am sick, **but** I am going to class. (*"but"* shows logical relationship.)

Note: If a noun or subjective pronoun (*he, she, it, I, you, we,* and *they*) does not follow a coordinating conjunction, do *not* use a comma.

Comma: The bicyclist fell, **and** he injured himself. (Subject and verb follow "*and*".)
No comma: The bicyclist fell **and** injured himself.   (No subject follows "*and*".)

PRACTICE 1

Combine these sentences using logical FANBOYS: **for, and, nor, but, or, yet, so**.
For numbers 4 and 7, change the question into a statement.

1. Dorothy wants to lose weight. She does not want to change her eating habits.

2. Today, I don't feel like doing anything. I think I will go to the movie.

3. I like chocolate. I like milk, too.

4. I don't like broccoli. Do I like spinach?

5. I am getting poor eyesight. I need to see an eye doctor.

6. You may submit your homework today. You may turn it in on Monday.

7. Sofia doesn't have a job. Does she try to get one?

8. The speaker forgot his speech. He was truly embarrassed.

9. Marcia usually passes her test. She studies at least two hours per day.

10. Sandra likes to exercise. She likes to do yoga, too

11. Cell phones are convenient. They can be dangerous, too.

12. That intersection is prone to accidents. Several individuals have died there.

CORRELATIVE CONJUNCTIONS

Correlative conjunctions work in pairs and show the relationship between elements that are paired or parallel in structure. These conjunctions include:

- either/or
- neither/nor
- both/and
- not only/but also
- whether/or

Technically, a correlative conjunction is simply a coordinating conjunction (*and, but, or, nor*) coupled with an adverb (*not, only*) or adjective (*both, either, neither*).

Examples: **Neither** Tim **nor** Michael finished his work on time. (joins proper nouns: *Tim* and *Michael*)
         He **not only** wrote the play **but also** starred in it. (joins verbs: *wrote* and *starred*)
         Whether eating **or** sleeping, our bodies burn calories. (joins gerunds: *eating* and *sleeping*)

Remember: Correlative conjunctions cannot be comingled. For instance, ***neither*** and ***or*** cannot combine two parallel elements. ***Neither*** goes with ***nor***, and ***either*** goes with ***or***:

Incorrect: **Neither** Tim **or** Michael finished his work on time.
Correct: **Neither** Tim **nor** Michael finished his work on time.

Incorrect: He **not only** wrote the play **but** starred in it.
Correct: He **not only** wrote the play **but also** starred in it.

Incorrect: **Whether** eating **nor** sleeping, our body burns calories.
Correct: **Whether** eating **or** sleeping, our body burns calories.

PRACTICE 2

Rewrite the following sentences with correlative conjunctions. Make sure that what follows the first correlative is parallel to what follows the other correlative.

                      adj   noun
Example: Marie is **not only** <u>intelligent</u> **but also** a <u>beauty</u>. **(incorrect)**
            adj   adj
Marie is **not only** <u>intelligent</u> **but also** <u>beautiful</u>. **(correct)**

1. Leon **not only** graduated from college with honors **but also** he was given a huge scholarship.

    _____

    _____

2. Jonathan was told by his parents **either** to go to college **or** he should find a job.

    _____

    _____

3. The children liked **neither** the French fries **nor** did they like the fruit punch.

    _____

    _____

4. **Whether** studying **or** to do your job, you should be dedicated.

    _____

    _____

5.   The professor should **either** let the student know if he is passing his class **or** he should notify him to drop the class.

_____

_____

Semicolon as a Connector

A **semicolon** can be used to connect two ideas that are closely related. It is not as strong as the period because it cannot be used as an end punctuation. Consider it a weak period, which can only be used as a connector.

Examples: My sister is a nurse**;** my brother is a doctor.
My parents live in New York**;** I call them regularly.

PRACTICE 3

Use a semicolon to connect the following sentences.

1.   The athlete spent many hours swimming it's time for him to rest.

2.   Weekends are hectic for most people they usually return to work tired.

3.   The robber entered the house through the screen door it was unlocked.

4.   Jessica helped Helen with her biology project she never thanked her.

5.   Most of today's youth are overweight they mostly eat junk foods.

6.   Monica likes to go to the mall on Sundays she does not like to go to church.

7.   I am tired of eating chicken for dinner I will try fish tonight.

8.   The car accident left Manuel depressed he doesn't even leave his house.

9.   My desire is to live in Europe I have lots of family there.

10. That baby cries a lot his mother needs to put him in a daycare.

11. The concert was too lengthy some people in the audience fell asleep.

12. Cristina seems to be happier these days she has been smiling a lot.

13. Tim is a doctor his sister is an attorney.

14. Sergio likes the cold weather his sister likes the warm weather.

Conjunctive Adverbs as Coordinating Conjunctions

Like the FANBOYS, **conjunctive adverbs**, which are also called **adverbial conjunctions**, can join independent clauses. However, do not use them to join words, phrases, or dependent clauses.
Notice the punctuation **before** and **after** the conjunctive adverb:

- Monica has a cold; **therefore,** she called to say she is sick.
- Monica has a cold. **Therefore,** she called to say she is sick.

Note: *Do not* use a semicolon before a conjunctive adverb unless it is connecting *two* independent clauses.

Incorrect: I am grateful for your invitation; **however,** am not able to attend the party.
                  (The subject is missing.)
Correct: I am grateful for your invitation; **however,** I am not able to attend the party.

In order to gain mastery of conjunctions, writers must ensure that they are using the most precise conjunction to convey the correct meaning. Here are common *conjunctive adverbs* and their meanings:

Contrast	Result	Addition	Emphasis	Alternative
however	consequently	in addition	indeed	otherwise
nevertheless	therefore	furthermore	in fact	
still	as a result	moreover		
on the other hand	thus	also		
on the contrary	hence	besides		
instead				

PRACTICE 4

In the space provided, choose the appropriate conjunctive adverb that logically shows the relationship between each sentence. Don't forget to punctuate correctly, and do not use a conjunction more than once. **Answers will vary.**

however	**otherwise**	**moreover**	**indeed**
therefore	**nevertheless**	**as a result**	**thus**
in fact	**consequently**	**in addition**	**besides**

1.   The citrus trees need to be sprayed _____ they will die.

2.   Professor Brown shows favoritism toward Andrew_____ the other students are jealous.

3.   On the weekend, I went to a movie _____ I went to the beach.

4.   Katherine is not prejudice against overweight people _____ she believes they should curtail their eating habits.

5.   The car accident left Miguel depressed _____ he has secluded himself from his family and friends.

6.   Homelessness has become a major problem in some major cities _____ the government needs to do something about it.

7.   For the past week, I have had insomnia _____ I am very exhausted.

8.   Debra likes to listen to gospel music _____ she likes to read religious books.

9.   These cleaning products can be dangerous_____ they can be harmful if they are swallowed.

10.   Ana has poor eyesight _____ she just got a stronger eyeglass prescription.

PRACTICE 5

Combine the following pairs of sentences into compound sentences, using logical conjunctive adverbs.

Example: I worked late last night.
                I am exhausted.
                <u>I worked late last night; **consequently**, I am exhausted.</u>

1.   I invited my friends for Thanksgiving dinner.
      They did not show up.

      _____

      _____

2.   Edward likes to be cold.
      His wife likes the heat.

      _____

      _____

3.   Keith did not understand the instructions for his game.
      He could not play with it for a month.

      _____

      _____

4.   Fanny likes to do gardening.
      She likes to go to the movies.

      _____

      _____

5.   Bill was tired by the time he reached the campsite.
        He immediately crawled in his sleeping bag.

_____

_____

SUBORDINATING CONJUNCTIONS

Subordinating conjunctions are used to create *complex sentences*. To create a complex sentence, there has to be an **independent** clause and a **subordinating (dependent)** clause, which is where the conjunction is located.

Examples: **Because** it rained, many people missed the meeting. (complex sentence)
                 Many people attended the meeting **even though** it rained. (complex sentence)

Unlike an independent clause that can stand alone, a subordinating (dependent) clause cannot stand alone. Although it has a subject and a verb, it is incapable of standing alone. It depends on the independent clause to complete its meaning. The subordinating conjunction may be placed at the beginning or in the middle of a sentence. When it is placed at the beginning, use a comma to separate the dependent clause from the independent clause. On the other hand, if it is placed in the middle, **do not use a comma**:

Examples: **Although** Paula is known to be a procrastinator, she still gets her work done.
                 Paula still gets her work done **although** she is known to be a procrastinator. (no comma)

Commonly used *subordinating conjunctions* and their meanings:

Contrast	Result	Time	Condition	Relative Pronoun
even though	since	as	if	who
although	because	after	whether	which
though	so that	before	while	that
whereas		until	as	
		when(ever)	lest	
		while	unless	

Note: Some conjunctions serve *two* purposes: They can be used as either a conjunction or a preposition. When it is followed by a *subject* and *verb*, it functions as a subordinating conjunction. When **no** *subject* or *verb* follows, it is a preposition:

- **After** I <u>finished</u> dinner, I had ice cream for dessert.
  (**After** is used as a subordinating conjunction because it is followed by a subject and verb.)

- **After** the game, I <u>ate</u> popcorn.
  ("After" is *not* followed by a subject and verb; therefore, it is used as a preposition.)

| Independent Clauses need coordinating conjunctions to join them. |
| **Dependent Clauses** need subordinating conjunctions to begin them. |

Note: An "independent clause" is a sentence.
A "dependent clause" is a fragment of a sentence.

PRACTICE 6

*Punctuate the following complex sentences correctly. If a sentence is correct, write **C** for correct.*

1. When Barbara arrived at work she realized she left her glasses.

2. Barbara realized she left her glasses when she arrived at work.

3. Melissa's parents want her to be an attorney although Melissa wants to be a dancer.

4. Although Melissa wants to be a dancer her parents want her to be an attorney.

5. While I was jogging around the park I ran into an old schoolmate.

6. I ran into an old school mate while I was jogging around the park.

7. Because the woman would not give the robber her purse he shot her in the leg.

8. The robber shot the woman in her leg because she would not give him her purse.

9. After I made my decision about accepting the job I changed my mind.

10. I changed my mind after I made my decision about accepting the job.

11. Since Grace is not working she can't go on the trip with her classmates.

12. Grace can't go on the trip with her classmates since she is not working.

13. As soon as the sun rose the children jumped out of bed.

14. The children jumped out of bed as soon as the sun rose.

Sentence Variations
(Notice the punctuation changes)

1.	Independent Clause,	Coordinating Conjunction	Independent Clause.
	She likes ice cream,	**but**	**she likes cake better.**
2.	Independent Clause	Coordinating Conjunction	Phrase.
	He irons his clothes	**and**	**watches television.**
3.	Independent Clause;	Conjunctive Adverb,	Independent Clause.
	We got lost while hiking;	**nevertheless,**	**everyone had fun.**
4.	Subordinating Conjunction	Dependent Clause,	Independent Clause.
	Because	**the dogs barked,**	**the robber fled.**
5.	Independent Clause	Subordinating Conjunction	Dependent Clause.
	The robber fled	**because**	**the dog barked.**

PRACTICE 7

*In the following sentences, underline the conjunctions; then on the line before each sentence, write **W** if the conjunction joins words, **P** if it joins phrases, **IC** if it joins two independent clauses, and **SC** if it is a subordinating conjunction.*

_____ 1. After I had breakfast, I jogged five miles.

_____ 2. Taking a test is not easy for me because I encounter test anxiety.

_____ 3. My favorite meal is chicken and broccoli.

_____ 4. I studied for my math exam; however, I scored low.

_____ 5. Keith, Robert, and I mowed the lawn on Saturday.

_____ 6. Several ants are in Marcia's kitchen and bathroom.

_____ 7. I am famished although I had two hamburgers for lunch.

_____ 8. In the middle of Jon's speech and toward the end, he apologized for his lateness.

_____ 9. Between me and you, I am not going to Ana's birthday party.

_____ 10. Since you bought your new car, you have not taken a long road trip.

_____ 11. I am willing to tutor you so that you can take the test.

_____ 12. At Steve's house and at his job, he makes the coffee every morning.

_____ 13. I drove my new car slowly, but I still had an accident.

_____ 14. Underneath the chairs and on the floor, chewing gum can be found.

REVIEW

Use coordination, conjunctive adverbs, or subordinating conjunctions to join the following sentences. Don't forget to use the right conjunctions that show logical relationships. **Answers will vary.**

Example: Sofia was arrested.
She stole her mother's purse.

Sofia was arrested because she stole her mother's purse.

1.   AIDS is a phantom killer.
People are still not taking precaution.

_____

2.   Residents are complaining about the new water restriction.
The county is not doing anything about it.

_____

_____

3.   These days a lot of people are shopping online.
It is more convenient.

_____

_____

4.   My mother takes credit for my academic success.
My father is the one who motivated me to go to college.

_____

_____

5.   Gardening is therapeutic for my mother.
Some flowers give her a rash.

_____

_____

6.   Karl's Ford Mustang is a reliable car.
It broke down on the highway last night.

_____

_____

7.   Most New Yorkers ride the train to work.
        It is far more economical than driving.

_____

_____

8.   The fire alarm went off.
        Everyone scurried out of the building.

_____

_____

9.   Professor Martin says he enjoys teaching English.
        He complains about the tons of papers he has to grade.

_____

_____

10.   My computer is always reliable.
        Today, it is broken.

_____

_____

11.   I love to work in my garden.
        It is therapeutic.

_____

_____

12.   Manuel goes to high school.
        His sister goes to a university in North Carolina.

_____

_____

13.   These cleaning products are hazardous and should be stored in a safe place.
        They should be locked away.

_____

_____

14.   These days Carla is exercising.
       She is eating more fruits and vegetables.

_____

_____

DOUBLE NEGATIVES

A *negative* is a word that expresses a sense of "no." The following are negatives:

no	none	nothing	barely
not	nowhere	no one	hardly
never	nobody	ain't	scarcely

CHALLENGE:
Do you know the part of speech for each word?

A **double negative** is the use of two negatives in a single clause. This is unacceptable and should be avoided.

Incorrect
No one can do *nothing* to please you.
Ari can*not* go *nowhere* without his sister.
I didn't (did *not*) talk to *nobody*.

Correct
No one can do anything to please you.
Ari cannot go anywhere without his sister.
I didn't talk to anyone.

Using two negatives in a sentence cancel each other and create a positive. Remember this to help you avoid creating an unintended meaning:

NEGATIVE + NEGATIVE = POSITIVE

Sentence
I *don't* want *nothing* to eat right now.

Meaning
I want something to eat right now.

NEGATIVE + POSITIVE = NEGATIVE

Sentence
I *don't* want *anything* to eat right now.

Meaning
I want nothing to eat right now.

REVIEW

Rewrite each of the following sentences on a separate sheet of paper so that none of them contain double negatives.

1.   You don't need no education.

2.   We ain't got none of those.

3.   Make sure you don't get in no trouble at school.

4.   The students should not do nothing to jeopardize their financial aid.

5.   We can hardly find nobody who is worthy of entering the contest.

6.   The guests could not find nowhere to park their cars.

7.   He has barely no hair.

8.   Hardly no one went to Pat's surprise party.

9.   We don't never go nowhere for the holidays.

10.   The new bill had scarcely no opposing votes.

UNIT III Hammer:
SENTENCE BUILDING

11

Simple Writing

In order to b an effective writer, your sentences need to be clear, consistent and concise. These are skills that you will learn in this unit. Writers of every kind will learn how to construct sentences that conform to basic grammar rules. With this mastery, emerging writers like you will be able to create more interesting prose using sentence variety within their paragraphs, which is covered in Unit 3.

A **sentence** is a set of words that convey a clear, complete idea, containing a subject and predicate. It can consist of one independent clause or include subordinate clauses and phrases. There are different types of sentences, but they must all have *five* important elements:

1. It must begin with a capital letter.
2. It must have a subject (**noun**: a person, place or thing, or a **subjective pronoun**: *he, she, it, we you, they*).
3. It must have a verb (action or linking).
4. It must have ending punctuation (a period, a question mark, or an exclamation).
5. It must make sense!

> **Example:** *Going home.*
>
> This is not a sentence.
> This is a fragment of a sentence.

IDENTIFYING SUBJECTS

The subject of a sentence is either a noun or pronoun. Furthermore, it is one of the five basic elements of a sentence. Without a subject, there is no sentence. What you will have is a sentence fragment. The subject is the person or thing performing the action in the sentence. To find the subject of a sentence, ask **who** or **what** the sentence is about.

In the sentence fragment in the example above, the subject, which is a very important element in a sentence, is missing. It does not answer *who* or *what*.

Look at the following sentence and its subject:

Example: Phyllis sang ~~at the Billy's wedding~~.

Who sang? Phyllis sang. Therefore, "*Phyllis*" is the subject, and *at Billy's wedding* is a prepositional phrase.

The subject is not always going to be the first word of a sentence; however, no matter where the subject is located, if you ask **who** or **what** the sentence is about, you will be able to locate the subject:

Example: Where is the bus **station** located?

What is this sentence talking about? It is talking about *the bus station*. However, in locating the simple subject, do not include adjectives. *Bus* is an adjective that describes *station*; thus, the simple subject is *station*.

Can *one* or *two* words be a sentence? Certainly, they can!

Example: *Go home.* Complete Sentence Subject: *You* (implied)

Example: *Stop!* Complete Sentence Subject: *You* (implied)

Note: If a sentence is giving a command, it does not have to include the word *you* because it is understood:

Examples: (**You**) Go to your counselor for advice.
           (**You**) Tell me what your friends said about me.

Gerunds

A **gerund** is an *–ing* word that functions as a subject.

Example: **Exercising** for fifteen minutes each day can relieve stress.
            Understanding the math formula was very difficult.

PRACTICE 1

In the following sentences, underline the subject once:

1.   Where were you last night?

2.   This semester I have a hectic schedule.

3.   Stop talking so loudly.

4.   Robert likes to study at 4 a.m.

5.   Ebony invited me for Thanksgiving dinner.

6.   Ten students missed my reading class today.

7.   Building a new home will take lots of planning.

8.   Jesus has been the class president for two consecutive years.

9.   The maker of this toy guarantees its safety.

10.   Heart attack is one of the leading causes of death in the United States.

11.   The students are worried about their finals.

12.   Is the governor a republican or a democrat?

13. The playful kids built a castle in the sand.

14. Close the door!

15. Regular exercise helps to reduce stress.

16. Playing basketball is my son's favorite activity.

COMPOUND SUBJECTS

A **compound** subject is typically joined by the conjunction **and**:

Example: **Sherman** and **Elaine** went to school.
            (*Sherman* and *Elaine* are the subjects.)

PRACTICE 2

In the following sentences, underline the compound subjects once:

1.   Nancy and Angelica stayed up late to study for their math class.

2.   Mark and Sam like to play Scrabble.

3.   Baking and cooking are two important skills.

4.   Andrew and Catalina are always together.

5.   Sofia and Mike refused to do the project for extra credit.

6.   Running and drinking lots of water help me to lose weight.

7.   Katia and Felix went on a business trip to Europe.

8.   Are Michael and Tommy going to summer school?

9.   Baseball and soccer are Mike's favorite sports.

10.   Reading and gardening are my passion.

TERMS TO KNOW

Types of Sentence Fragments

Clause: a group of words with a verb and its subject
Phrase: a group of words with a verb form

Remember, it is easy to confuse the object of the preposition with the subject of the sentence since the object of a preposition is a noun or objective pronoun, and the subject of a sentence is also a noun or subjective pronoun. However, bear in mind that a prepositional phrase begins with a preposition and ends with a noun or objective pronoun (*me, us him, her, them, you, it*).

Example: One ~~of my sisters~~ will be moving ~~to Miami.~~

prep noun and *prep noun*

"*Of my sisters*" and "*to Miami*" are prepositional phrases. Who will be moving? Only *one* of my sisters will be moving. Therefore, *one* is the subject and not *sisters*

PRACTICE 3

In the following sentences, cross out the prepositional phrases and then underline the subject or subjects once.

Example: Most ~~of the students~~ failed the exam.

1.   Both Andrea and her sons love math but dislike English.

2.   After the party, I went to Stan's house for ice cream and cake.

3.   Most of Kathy's friends love to study and work on weekends.

4.   Have you seen the recent article about the death toll in Iraq?

5.   Throughout Anne's tenure at Bell South, she was respected by her peers.

6.   Two of my favorite movies will be showing this weekend.

7.   Several of my relatives lived in England and then ended up in Miami.

8.   In my spare time, I do gardening.

9.   A pile of debris has been lying on the side of the road for six months now.

10. Dino plays baseball for his high school.

11. Give me your address so I can visit you when I am in town.

12. Everybody was allowed to leave the building when the fire alarm went off.

13. Have you heard the latest news about the oil crisis in the Gulf?

14. Jogging in the park is a fun exercise for me.

15. Broccoli and spinach are my favorite vegetables.

16. Wind and rain have ruined my tomatoes.

17. The administration plans to suspend the boisterous students who vandalized the principal's office.

18. Lorenzo missed his class over ten times in one semester.

19. Are Israel and his brothers ready for their annual summer trip?

20. Voters are complaining about their congressman.

IDENTIFYING VERBS

The **verb** is another important element of a sentence. It tells the reader exactly what the subject is doing. It does not always show action. As already discussed, there are *three* types of verbs:

Action Verb, *Linking Verb*, and *Helping Verb*

Action: *run, walk, sing, dance, think, know, remember*
Linking: *am, is, are, was, were, feel, seem, be, taste, look*
Helping: *can, could, shall, should, will, would, must, might, may*

Direct Objects

Sometimes an action verb is followed by a noun or an objective pronoun (*me, us him, her, them, you, it*). This is called the **direct object**. Don't confuse the direct object with the subject. The subject of a sentence is either a noun or pronoun, and the direct object is either a noun or pronoun. Therefore, confusing the object of the verb for the subject of the verb is easy. To find the direct object, ask **what** or **whom** after the action verb.

If the noun or pronoun after the verb is a person, it will answer **whom**.
If the noun or pronoun after the verb is a thing, it will answer **what**.

Examples: Mildred received a **gift** for her birthday. (*Gift* is the direct object.)
Manny gave Maria the **money**. (*Money* is the direct object.)
The students gave **Ishak** a card for his birthday. (*Card* is the direct object.)

In sentence *one*, *gift* is the **direct object** because it answers *what* was received.
In sentence *two*, money is the **direct object** because it answers *what* Manny gave Maria.
In sentence *three*, the thing (*card*) that the students gave Ishak is the **direct object**.

Note: Every sentence *does not* have a **direct object** after an action verb:

Example: My car needs [to go] [to the body shop.]

After the verb, there's no noun. *Needs* is the verb. *To go* is an infinitive, and *to the body shop* is a prepositional phrase. The sentence has no **direct object**.

PRACTICE 4

*In each of the following sentences, underline the subject once and the verb twice. Then, put **DO** over the direct object.*

                                         DO
Example: <u>Carlton</u> <u><u>gave</u></u> his wife perfume for her birthday.

1.   Last night my children completed their homework assignments early.

2.   For lunch, I ate a tossed salad.

3.   Maritza sang a solo at Joan's wedding ceremony.

4.   All the students in my class received free books.

5.   Ana's roommate stole her expensive jewelry.

6.   Christian reads more than anyone his age.

7.   Last year, Soraya and her family went to Europe for two weeks.

8.   Kevin took his car to the body shop to be painted.

9.   My daughter sold her house for a lot of money.

10.   Arlene thinks lobster should be eaten for dinner every weekend.

Indirect Objects

An **indirect object** is a noun or objective pronoun (*me, us him, her, them, you, it*) that follows an action verb and comes *before* a **direct object**. To find the indirect object, ask *to what* or *to whom* after the action verb. The indirect object *only* appears between the verb and the direct object.

Examples: I gave **Darla** a dress. (*Darla* is the **indirect object** and *dress* is the **direct object**.)
                   He took **Tom** a cake. (*Tom* is the **indirect object** and *cake* is the **direct object**.)

Tip: An easy way to find the indirect object is to use the verb to ask the following questions:

       (1) **To whom?**   (2) **For whom?**   (3) **Of whom?**

Here's a chart to help you better understand *indirect objects*:

Subject	Verb	Indirect Object	Direct Object
We	gave	[to] Manny	a watch
Marjorie	sent	[to] me	a package
Ciara	made	[for] her mother	a pie.
The tour guide	gave	[to] the guests	poor advice
The reporter	asked	[of] us	three questions

Note: Every sentence does not have an indirect object.

PRACTICE 5

In each of the following sentences, underline the subject once and the verb twice. Then, put IO over the indirect object.

                           IO

Example: <u>Carla</u> <u><u>offered</u></u> him a job.

1.   I baked them a key lime pie.

2.   Was Marlon serious about marrying Rebecca?

3.   Monica went to the University of Miami to study medicine.

4.   That lasagna burned a hole in the table cloth.

5.   Sofia became a teacher after being a secretary for ten years.

6.   The students are very worried about their last test.

7.   The criminal felt that the judge was biased in handing down the punishment.

8.   Those doctors risked their job to save her.

9.   My mother wanted twins instead of just one child.

10.   Anthony donated his comic books to the library.

11.   My children sent me money for Christmas.

12.   Irish and her family moved to North Carolina.

13.   Sally borrowed money from me to pay her rent.

14.   Ellen and Cory made themselves choir robes.

15.   Danny emailed us directions to her house.

COMPLEMENTS

A complement is the part of the sentence that provides more information about the subject (a subject complement) or the object (an object complement) of the sentence.

Subject Complements

A **subject complement**, sometimes called a **predicate complement**, is a *noun, pronoun* or *adjective* that *follows* a **linking verb** to either rename or describe its subject.

Common linking verbs:

Be: *am, is, are, was, were, be, being, been*

Other linking verbs that function exactly as the *be* verbs:

Seem, appear, become, sound, taste, feel, smell, look

Here is a chart to help you identify *subject complements*:

Subject	Linking Verb	Subject Complement
Mr. Lee	is	a doctor (noun)
Anna Maria	seems	worried (adjective)
T.D. Jakes	is	a preacher (noun)

In sentence *one*, the subject *Lee* and the subject complement *doctor* refer to the same person.
In sentence *two*, the adjective *worried* is describing the subject Anna Maria.
In sentence *three*, the subject *T. D. Jakes* and the noun *preacher* refer to the same person.

Object Complements

An **object complement** is a noun or adjective that follows the direct object to complete the meaning of the sentence. It either describes or renames the direct object. Object complements only appear in sentences with action verbs.

Example: He called his dog **Rex**.
              I consider that **wrong**.

Subject	Action Verb	Direct Object	Object Complement
She	called	her sister	a dummy (noun)
I	painted	my nails	green (adjective)
The dye	turned	my hair	purple (adjective)

In sentence *one*, the **object complement** *dummy* (a noun) is renaming the direct object *sister*.
In sentence *two*, the **object complement** *green* (an adjective) is describing the direct object *nails*.
In sentence *three*, the **object complement** *purple* (an adjective) is describing the direct object *hair*.

PRACTICE 6

*In each of the following sentences, underline the subject once and the verb twice. Then, put **OC** over the object complement and **SC** over the subject complement.*

1.   My grandson named his dog Pepe.

2.   Mrs. Fernandez and her husband are professors at a college in Florida.

3.   My neighbor painted his house green.

4.   Cecilia thinks her husband is handsome.

5. That cheese cake certainly tasted delicious.

6. The police officer gave me a ticket for no reason.

7. The Joneses consider their children brilliant.

8. Eleana is a motivational speaker.

9. The doctor considers his patients' feelings important.

10. Mildred appears bewildered after she broke up with her best friend John.

REVIEW

Write a sentence with a **compound subject**.

_____

_____

Write a sentence with a **gerund**.

_____

_____

Write a sentence with a **direct object**.

_____

_____

Write a sentence with an in**direct object.**

_____

_____

Write a sentence with a **direct object** and an **indirect object**.

_____

_____

Write a sentence with an **object complement**.

_____

_____

Write a sentence with a **subject complement**.

_____

_____

FRAGMENTS _____

What is a Fragment?

A **fragment** is an incomplete sentence that cannot stand on its own. A sentence, on the other hand, is an independent clause with both a subject and verb that make sense. Unlike a sentence, a fragment may have a subject and not a verb, or it may have a verb and not a subject. It may also be just a phrase without a subject or a verb. There are *several* types of fragments:

Dependent Clause Fragments

A **dependent clause** is not a sentence. It has a subject and a verb; however, it cannot stand alone because it depends upon the remainder of the sentence to complete its meaning. It often starts with a subordinating conjunction: *since, although, when,* and so forth. Correcting dependent clause fragments sometimes only involves minor changes:

Fragment:	**Because I had no money**. I did not take a vacation last summer.
Correct:	**Because I had no money**, I did not take a vacation last summer.
Correct:	I did not take a vacation last summer **because I had no money**. (**no comma**)

Fragment:	**I communicated with my professor**. Who advised me to change my major.
Correct:	**I communicated with my professor**, who advised me to change my major.

Note: In sentence one, notice that the period after *money* was removed and replaced with a comma. In the second sentence, the period after *professor* was replaced with a comma, and the *w* in *who* was lowercased.

Here is a list of commonly used **subordinating** (dependent) **conjunctions** that begin dependent clauses:

after	even though	though	whereas	who
although	if	unless	whether	which
as/as if	since	until	while	that
because	so that	when(ever)	whether	provided (that)
before	than	where(ever)	lest	now that

Remember: When a subordinating (dependent) conjunction starts a sentence, use a comma to separate the dependent clause from the independent clause. However, when these conjunctions (except for *who* or *which*) appear in the middle of a sentence, no comma is necessary. For example:

Correct: We stayed at home **because** the weather was so bad. (**no comma**)
Correct: **Because** the weather was so bad, we stayed at home. (**comma**)

PRACTICE 1

Correct the following dependent clause fragments by connecting them to the independent clauses.

1. If I were you. I would not go to the park alone.

   _____

   _____

2. You cannot go out with your friends. Until you have completed all your chores.

   _____

   _____

3. Renew your passport as quickly as possible. If you intend to go to Israel with the group.

   _____

   _____

4. The meeting was canceled. Since few people showed up.

   _____

   _____

5. When I drove to New York several years ago. I stopped in several small towns.

   _____

   _____

Participial Phrase Fragments

Participles tell which one, what kind or how many about a noun or pronoun. A **participial phrase** is a group of words that begin with a participle ending in *-ing*, *-ed*, *-t*, *-k*, or *-en* word. There are two kinds of participial phrases: **present** and **past**.

Present Participial Phrase Fragment (*–ing*):

Fragment: **Strolling down the street.** I ran into an old friend.
Correct: **Strolling down the street**, I ran into an old friend.

Fragment: I ran into an old friend. **Strolling down the street**.
Correct: I ran into an old friend, **strolling down the street**.

Past Participial Phrase Fragments (-ed, -t, -k, or –en):

Fragment: **Stopped by the police officer.** I panicked.
Correct: **Stopped by the police officer,** I panicked.

Fragment: I panicked. **Stopped by the police officer.**
Correct: I panicked when **stopped by the police officer.**

As seen in the above examples, the participial phrase can either be at the beginning of the sentence or at the end. When a participial phrase (present or past) begins a sentence, a comma should be placed after the phrase. When a **past participial phrase** appears in the middle of a sentence, no comma is placed before the participle. However, when a **present participial phrase** appears in the middle of a sentence, a comma is placed before the –*ing* word. For example:

Correct: She talked a lot about her past, **sharing** stories from her native country. (**comma**)

PRACTICE 2

Correct the following participial phrase fragments by connecting them to the independent clauses. You may put the phrase at the beginning or in the middle. ***Answers will vary.***

1. Shaken by Michael's rude remarks. Sergio had an automobile accident.

   _____

   _____

2. Spending time with my grandmother. I learned all about my family's history.

   _____

   _____

3. Melissa likes to feed the ducks. Riding her bicycle around the park.

   _____

   _____

4. Dreamt of becoming a teacher from about 6 years old. Monica never gave up on her dreams.

   _____

   _____

5. Chosen for the teacher of the year. Volkan received numerous awards from faculty and staff.

   _____

   _____

The Infinitive Fragments (to + a verb)

An **infinitive** is the form of a verb that is preceded by the preposition *to*. So, an **infinitive phrase** will have the word *to + a verb.*

Fragment: **To ensure that I pass my State Board Exam**. I studied for six months.
Correct: **To ensure that I pass my State Board Exam**, I studied for six months.
Correct: I studied for six months **to ensure that I pass my State Board Exam**. (no comma)

Fragment: **To go to downtown** Miami. It is better to ride the Metrorail.
Correct: **To go downtown** Miami, it is better to ride the Metrorail.

Note: When the infinitive fragment appears **in the middle** of a sentence, do not put a comma.

Fragment: It is better to ride the Metrorail. **To go to downtown Miami**.
Correct: It is better to ride the Metrorail **to go to downtown Miami**. (no comma)

PRACTICE 3

*Correct the following infinitive phrase fragments by connecting them to the independent clauses. You may put the phrase at the beginning or in the middle. **Answers will vary**.*

1. Beverly and Ralph lease their cars. To save money.

   _____

2. To obtain a valid driver's license. Cubby went to driving school for six months.

   _____

3. Determination and motivation are important. To be successful in life.

   _____

4. Last weekend, my friends and I shopped. To go on our trip.

   _____

5. To go to the prom. You will have to get an escort.

   _____

Prepositional Phrase Fragments

Remember, a **prepositional phrase** begins with a preposition and ends with a noun or pronoun. It adds meaning to the sentence in which it appears, but it cannot stand alone.

Fragment: **After eating the salty peanuts at the basketball game**. I was very thirsty.
Correct: **After eating the salty peanuts at the basketball game**, I was very thirsty.

Fragment: I was very thirsty. **After eating the salty peanuts at the basketball game**.
Correct: I was very thirsty **after eating the salty peanuts at the basketball game**.

PRACTICE 4

*Correct the following prepositional phrase fragments by connecting them to the independent clauses. You may put the phrase at the beginning or in the middle. **Answers will vary**.*

1. During Stephen's visit to the photo studio. He met O. J. Simpson.

_____

2. Anne went to dinner with a group of her friends. After her graduation.

_____

3. On a tour of my daughter's first day in college. She met all her teachers.

_____

4. In an effort to get to the airport on time. Stephanie left her passport on her bed.

_____

5. To the surprise of the many viewers of American Idol. Jessica was voted off the show.

_____

Missing Subject/Verb Fragment

Missing **subject/verb fragments** usually lack a subject or a verb. These fragments can be corrected by simply adding the missing subject, verb, or part of the verb phrase that will make the fragment a complete sentence.

Fragment: Went on a trip to the mountains. (Who *went on a trip?*)
Correct: **Tom** went on a trip to the mountains.

Fragment: Awarded the prize for the employee of the month. (*Who was awarded the prize?*)
Correct: **Alisson** was awarded the prize for the employee of the month.

Fragment: Amber did her homework. And then went for a stroll.
Correct: Amber did her homework and then went for a stroll.

Note: A comma is not placed before the conjunction ***and*** because a **subject** does not follow. The only time a comma goes after a ***FANBOY*** conjunction is when a **subject** and a **verb** follow.

Practice 5

*If a group of words is a sentence, write **C** for correct. If a group of words is a fragment, correct it as you see fit.* **Answers will vary**.

1. Yelling for him to stop playing the music so loudly.

   _____

2. Please do not disturb me until I have completed my term paper.

   _____

3. Jumping up and down in the store.

   _____

4. Cooking on weekends. One task I despise.

   _____

5. I cleaned the house and washed the car. But did not water the plants.

   _____

6. Doing the thing he always wanted to do.

   _____

7. Melissa, the bus driver, left several passengers.

   _____

8. Paying the ultimate price for his mistake.

   _____

9. On the table is a cup of coffee.

   _____

10. Steven was going to Atlanta for a conference. But left his ticket at home.

    _____

Added-Detail Fragments

The **added-detail fragment** occurs when a group of words that provides more detail about the main independent clause is separated from the main clause. This type of fragment is corrected by simply **rejoining** the group of words to the sentence from which it is separated. Look at the following fragments and pay close attention to their corrections:

Fragment: I enjoy going to the gym. **Especially early in the morning**.
Correct: I enjoy going to the gym, **especially early in the morning**.

Fragment: Ida loves vegetables. **Such as broccoli, lettuce, and spinach**.
Correct: Ida loves vegetables, **such as broccoli, lettuce, and spinach**.

Fragment: Everyone who is going to the football game. **Including Mildred, needs a pass**.
Correct: Everyone who is going to the football game, **including Mildred, needs a pass**.

Fragment: Some discussions are difficult to win. **For example, politics and religion**.
Correct: Some discussions are difficult to win, **for example, politics and religion**.

Note: In the first example above, the period after the word *gym* was deleted, and the *e* in *especially* was changed to lowercase. The same type of correction was made in examples two, three and four above.

The following words trigger added-detail fragments:

for example	especially	including
for instance	except	as well
such as	like	whether to

PRACTICE 6

In the following sentences, correct the fragments as you see fit. Add commas wherever necessary.

1. Some sports are difficult to win. For example, soccer and basketball.

_____

2. Everyone from the group. Including Kristina, agreed with my comments.

_____

3. It's difficult for Fanny to make a decision. Whether to eat first or take a shower.

_____

4. Everyone sings in the choir. Except Jasmine, who sings like an angel.

_____

5. Regular exercise. As well as proper diet, helps to prolong life.

_____

6. Melissa sings and plays the piano. Like a professional.

_____

7. On my trip to New York, I visited several tourist attractions. Such as the Empire State Building and the Statue of Liberty.

_____

8. Everyone completed the project. Except Manuel and Katrina.

_____

REVIEW

Correct the following groups of sentences, but if a sentence is correct, write "C" for correct above it.

(1) Trying to complete the project by the deadline. Bill inadvertently left out important information. (2) When Michael asked Bill to redo the project. Bill threw it on Michael's desk and walked away. (3) Everyone was surprised that Bill acted the way he did. Because he always had a positive attitude. (4) Two days later, Bill returned to work. And apologized to Michael and his colleagues for the manner in which he behaved. (5) Everyone hugged him and told him how happy they were. That he returned.

(6) Dehydrated from running five miles. Carmen drank half a gallon of water. (7) To be sure this does not happen again. She never forgets to put water in her backpack. (8) During her last marathon. She packed five bottles of water. As well as three bottles of Gatorade. (9) Carmen learned a good lesson. Making sure she never gets dehydrated again. (10) Her friends also learned. To never leave home without a bottle of water!

RUN-ON SENTENCES

A run-on sentence occurs when *two* complete sentences (independent clauses) run together as one sentence. There are *two* types of run-on sentences: *Fused* and *Comma Splice*.

Fused Sentence

In English, every complete sentence needs an ending punctuation. The **fused sentence** consists of two complete sentences (independent clauses) without any punctuation mark.

<table>
<tr><td></td><td>subj</td><td>verb</td><td></td><td>subj</td><td>verb (can go)</td></tr>
</table>

Fused Correct: The weatherman warned of thunderstorms I can't go to work.
Correct: The weatherman warned of thunderstorms. I can't go to work.

Fused Correct: The weatherman warned of thunderstorms therefore I can't go to work.
Correct: The weatherman warned of thunderstorms; therefore, I can't go to work.

Comma Splice (C/S)

The **comma splice** also consists of two complete sentences (independent clauses) joined by a comma. A comma cannot connect two independent clauses. This is a major problem for most writers because they strongly believe that a comma is sufficient to connect two sentences. Think of the comma as a weak period. It simply must not be used as a connector.

Comma Splice: The weatherman warned of thunderstorms, I can't go to work.
Correct: The weatherman warned of thunderstorms. I can't go to work.

Comma Splice: The weatherman warned of thunderstorms, therefore, I can't go to work.
Correct: The weatherman warned of thunderstorms; therefore, I can't go to work

Note: As you can see, the only difference between the fused sentence and the comma splice is that the fused sentence has no mark of punctuation whereas the comma splice is incorrectly punctuated.

Correcting Run-on Sentences and Comma Splices

Both the **fused** and **comma splice** sentence can be corrected in the same way, using *several* methods:

- Drivers are warned that there is a thunderstorm I can't go to work. (Fused)
- Drivers are warned that there is a thunderstorm, I can't go to work. (C/S)

Corrections:

1. **Use a Semicolon (;)**

- Drivers are warned that there is a thunderstorm; I can't go to work.

2. **Use a Period (.)**

- Drivers are warned that there is a thunderstorm. I can't go to work.

3. **Use a comma and a Coordinating Conjunction:** *for, and, nor, but, or, yet, so*

- Drivers are warned that there is a thunderstorm, **so** I can't go to work.

4. **Use a Conjunctive Adverb (*therefore, moreover, however, in addition, thus, etc.*)**

- Drivers are warned that there is a thunderstorm; **therefore**, I can't go to work.
- Drivers are warned that there is a thunderstorm. **Therefore**, I can't go to work.

5. **Use a Subordinating Conjunction (*because, although, after, since, when, until, while etc.*)**

- **Since** drivers are warned that there is a thunderstorm, I can't go to work.
- I can't go to work **since** drivers are warned that there is a thunderstorm. (*no comma*)

PRACTICE 1

Using one of the five methods above, first locate the two main clause; then correct the run-ons and comma splices in any way you desire. **Answers will vary**.

1. The police officer stopped the criminal, he jumped out of his car and ran in the bushes.

_____

_____

2. Alligators are man's worst enemies this year alone 50 people were attacked.

_____

_____

3. Crime in our neighborhood is rampant citizens need to get involved.

_____

_____

4. Ms. Reid was walking down the street, a speeding car hit her.

_____

_____

5. Students in Professor Jones' class must turn in their work on time he deducts points.

_____

_____

6. Joan lives three miles away from her mother, she only visits her mother on holidays.

_____

_____

7. Mike needs to take a vacation he looks very exhausted.

_____

_____

8. Fiona had a bad headache yesterday, therefore, she was grumpy.

_____

_____

9. I did not spray my tomatoes, the spider mites killed the entire crop.

_____

_____

10. Maria says she enjoys playing volleyball it builds muscles.

_____

_____

PRACTICE 2

*Correct the following run-on sentences in **five** ways. Remember, if you do not use the right conjunction, the meaning of the sentence will be changed.*

1. Jonathan enjoys playing basketball his younger brother enjoys playing football.

a. _____

b. _____

c. _____

d. _____

e. _____

2. The movie theater was very cold, the children did not enjoy the movie.

a. _____

b. _____

c. _____

d. _____

e. _____

3. Israel is gifted in math he has a problem with reading.

a. _____

b. _____

c. _____

d. _____

e. _____

4. President Barack Obama was the first African-American president elected, America made history.

a. _____

b. _____

c. _____

d. _____

e. _____

5. Carol's five-year-old son has a passion for reading he likes music too.

a. _____

b. _____

c. _____

d. _____

e. _____

Practice 3

Using only **conjunctive adverbs**, *correct the run-on sentences and comma splices below. Remember to punctuate correctly.* **Answers will vary.**

(1) Frank worked feverishly on his report he received a bad grade. (2) He became despondent and quit school. (3) His teacher saw him several years ago on one of her shopping sprees, he was a cashier. (4) She said he was not angry with her, he offered to give her a discount on an expensive pair of running shoes she had bought. (5) She told him thanks for his generosity she visited the store frequently so she could take advantage of his employee discount.

Practice 4

*Using only **subordinating conjunctions** and **conjunctive adverbs**, correct the run-on sentences and comma splices in the passage below. Remember to punctuate correctly. **Answers will vary.***

(1) Hurricane Andrew struck I was home alone. (2) I had just moved into my new four-bedroom house, I had bought new furniture and decorated every room. (3) All the houses in the neighborhood were damaged only few tiles on the roof of my house got broken. (4) This was a stressful period for everyone the lights were out for several days, very little food could be found in the stores. (5) Most of the neighbors moved away their houses were being repaired. (6) Today, the neighborhood is more beautiful than before the hurricane.

Practice 5

*Using only FAN BOYS, correct the fragments, run-on sentences and comma splices below. Remember to punctuate correctly. **Answers will vary***

1. Ana wants to be a nurse, her mother wants her to be a doctor.

   _____

2. Alex went to the movie theater with Joan today we went to dinner.

   _____

3. Barbara arrived at school she realized she left her books in her car.

   _____

4. Amber's car is always reliable, it broke down today.

   _____

5. Juanita enjoys her new computer, she had her other computer for ten years.

   _____

6. Her friends are now jealous of her, they are asking their parents for a new computer.

   _____

7. Thanks for being a part of this event, it would not be what it is if it were not for you.

   _____

8. She has time neither today nor tomorrow to take the test, graduation is next week.

_____

9. The boys did several projects like mowing the lawn, cleaning their rooms was the hard part.

_____

10. The lights went out in the area, we will not get any work done tonight.

_____

12

Clear Writing

What is the purpose of punctuation?

Punctuation serves to structure and organize writing, as well as regulate the flow of speaking when reading aloud. Knowing punctuation rules is one of the most important aspects in writing. For one, writers will either overuse or misuse some punctuation marks, especially the comma, without knowing the rules. An incorrect use of punctuation can change the meaning of a sentence, which can, no doubt, cause confusion for readers. This chapter covers the common uses of punctuation, which helps to make your writing clear.

PUNCTUATION

Here is a list of the punctuation marks that will be covered in this chapter:

PUNCTUATION	PURPOSE
Apostrophe	Possession/Omission
Bracket	Supplement
Colon	Introduction
Comma	Interruption
Dash	Supplement
Ellipsis	Omission
Exclamation Point	Emphasis
Hyphen	Join
Parenthesis	Supplement
Period	Statement
Question Mark	Inquiry
Quotation Mark	Declaration
Semicolon	Separation

Commas (,)

Independent Clauses

Use a comma to separate two independent clauses joined by a coordinating conjunction (FANBOYS: *for, and, nor, but, or, yet, so*):

- I have a high temperature**, so** I am sweating.

Items in a Series

Use a comma to separate each item in a series of *three* or more:

- Martin went to the store to buy **milk, eggs,** and **bananas**. (nouns in a series)
- Andrea walked **confidently, articulately,** and **quietly**. (adverbs in a series)
- During the **summer, Melissa swims, reads,** and **plays** the piano. (verbs in a series)

Use a comma before the concluding conjunction when collective items appear in a series:

- Martin ate **toast,** *ham* **and** *eggs*, and a banana for breakfast.

Introductory Phrases

Use a comma after an introductory (prepositional, infinitive, or participial) phrase at the beginning of a sentence:

- **Without your help,** I can't finish the project. (introductory prepositional phrase)
- **Looking for someone to do the project,** I ran into my former school mate. (introductory present participial phrase)
- **Determined for me to become a nurse,** my mother bought me all types of medical toys at an early age. (introductory past participial phrase)
- **To be able to afford college,** I worked 16 hours per day for six months. (introductory infinitive phrase)

Note: Whether a **present participial** phrase (a word ending in *–ing*) appears at the beginning or at the end of a sentence, a comma separates it from the independent clause:

- **Hoping my favorite American Idol would win,** I watched every Tuesday night.
  (comma separates introductory present participial phrase **at the beginning**)

- I watched American Idol every Tuesday night, **hoping my favorite idol would win.**
  (comma separates present participial phrase **at the end** of the sentence)

Dependent Clauses

Use a comma to set off dependent clauses at the beginning of a sentence (but not at the end of a sentence):

- **Because I respect you,** I will not respond to your absurd remark.
- I will not respond to your absurd remark **because I respect you**. (**no comma**)

Parenthetical Expressions

Use a comma to set off parenthetical expressions (extra information) that, if removed from the sentence, would not change the meaning:

- Mr. Brown, **in my opinion,** is not a good teacher.
- The students, **however,** think he is a good teacher.
- **As a matter of fact,** I am through with the project.
- **Of course,** I am willing to tell the truth.
- **In fact,** this is a dangerous intersection.

Note: Any expression that tends to interfere with the flow of a sentence must be set off with commas. If the words *in my opinion, however, as a matter of fact, of course,* and *in fact,* were to be removed from the above sentences, they would still make sense. Therefore, they are interferences.

Nonrestrictive Clauses

Use a comma to set off nonrestrictive (nonessential) clauses introduced by words such as *who, whose, whom,* and *which.* Nonrestrictive clauses (like the ones in **bold** below) are not necessary to identify their subjects; therefore, they can be omitted. Clauses that follow *proper nouns* and *specific nouns* are almost always nonrestrictive.

Nonrestrictive: Mr. Andrews, **who was my supervisor,** transferred to the Atlanta office.
Nonrestrictive: The school's bookstore, **which is located next to the pool,** is closed today.
Nonrestrictive: My sister in law, **whom you met yesterday,** went back to England.
Nonrestrictive: Allan, **whose discussions are always about politics,** is going to run for state senator.

Restrictive Clauses

Do not use commas with restrictive (essential) clauses introduced by words such as *that, who, whose, whom,* and *which* because they are *necessary* to identify their subjects, which are *common* nouns (not proper or specific nouns). Because the subjects are common nouns, **commas are not needed before the clauses.**

Restrictive: The man **who was my supervisor** transferred to the Atlanta office.
Restrictive: The woman **whose car I borrowed** is my neighbor.
Restrictive: The ticket **that you received** can cause many problems for you.

Note: If the **restrictive** clauses in bold in the above sentences were set off by commas, they would not make sense; we would not know which *man* transferred, which *woman's car* I borrowed, or *what problems* the ticket could cause. (*Man, woman,* and *ticket* are common nouns.)

Nonrestrictive Appositive Phrases

Use commas to set off nonrestrictive (nonessential) appositives phrases.

An **appositive** is a phrase or word that immediately follows a noun to explain, rename or specifically identify the noun. If a nonrestrictive appositive is omitted from a sentence, the meaning would not change; consequently, the commas are necessary.

- Professor Brown, **a compassionate teacher,** will do anything to help his students pass his class.
- Jamaica, **one of the leading countries that supplies coffee to America,** lost its entire crop as a result of the six-month drought.
- Alfredo is a unique student, **one who will do whatever it takes to achieve his goals.**

Note: If the appositive is short and closely connected to the noun it modifies, there is no need for commas:

Example: My friend Ana now lives in Europe.

Coordinate Adjectives

Use a comma to set off coordinate adjectives, which are equal adjectives that modify the same noun:

- Marlon is surrounded by **loud, boisterous** friends.

Note: In the sentence above, the adjectives *loud* and *boisterous* describe the character of Marlon's friends. The adjectives can also be reversed, and the conjunction *and* can be placed between them and still makes sense. Thus, they are coordinate adjectives:

- Marlon is surrounded by **loud and boisterous** friends. (*and* replaces the comma)
- Marlon is surrounded by **boisterous and loud** friends. (adjectives can be reversed)

Let's test the following sentence to determine if it has coordinate adjectives:

Example: I gave **ten old** blouses to Goodwill.
I gave **ten and old** blouses to Goodwill. (comma cannot replace *and*)
I gave **old ten** blouses to Goodwill. (adjectives cannot be reversed)

Note: The adjectives *ten* and *old* are **not** coordinate adjectives because they would not make sense if they are reversed.

Introductory Expressions

Use a comma to set off introductory expressions such as names, transitional words, interjections, and other words that that are nonessential:

- **Johnny,** where are you going tonight?
- Give me the book, **Frank.**
- **Yes,** I would like to go to dinner with you, **Alfred.**
- **No,** you will not be grounded for not turning in your project on time.
- **You know,** I admire you very much.
- **Well,** I am through with my homework.
- **Cautiously,** I entered my house at midnight.
- **Oh, no,** I forgot about last night's meeting.
- **However,** I am not a perfect individual.
- **For example,** I am aware that you cheated on the test.

Direct Quotations

Use commas in direct quotations (a person's actual words):

- Annette said, **"If you do not stop talking, you will go to your room."**
- **"If you do not stop talking,"** said Annette, **"you will go to your room."**
- **"If you do not stop talking, you will go to your room,"** said Annette.
- He asked the nurse, **"May I see the doctor now?"**

Note: A comma is typically always placed inside a closing quotation.

A comma is *not* used for a partial quote.

- He said he is **"frustrated and angry"** about what happened.

Abbreviations

Use commas in abbreviations that follow names to indicate titles, academic degrees, etc:

- Robert Frances, **Sr.,** lives in Arizona.
- Martin B. Jones, **Ph.D.,** began his teaching career at an early age.
- John Alfred Smith **III** is not a registered voter. (**no comma**)
- Professor Brown, **M.A.,** retired last year.

Note: Commas are placed before and after the titles in sentence one, two, and four. Also, note that in sentence 3, no comma is placed before or after *III*.

Dates and Addresses

Use commas to separate *complete* dates and addresses within sentences:

- Tom and his wife moved to Brooklyn, New York, on Monday, July 10, 2006.
- The letter was mailed to Mrs. Mildred Watson on Thursday, March 27, 2007, at 12 noon.
- S. & R. Roofing Company, Inc., is located at 8 S.W. First Street, Quincy, Florida.

Do <u>not</u> use a comma between the month and the day or the state and the zip code:

- Tom and his wife moved to Brooklyn on **July 10** several years ago.
- I am planning to go to England in **September 2008**.
- The company is located at 2 S.W. First Street, Quincy, **FL 33396**.

"Of" and "From" Phrases

Use commas in *"of"* phrases that follow a person's name:

- Ms. Debra Brown, **of Virginia,** will be the new director of our company.
- Althea Jones, **from Jamaica**, **New York**, was caught with drugs in her luggage.

Do <u>not</u> use a comma in *"from"* phrases that follow a person's name when the info is essential.

- John Smith **from Alabama** is going to start in today's game. (*"from...."* eliminates possible confusion)

Numbers

Use commas with numbers of more than three digits:

- We counted **23,721** people in the arena.
- My neighbors won $**50,000,000**.
- I need $**1,000** to pay for my classes.

Note: Count backward from the last digit on the right and place a comma after every *third* digit.

Reversed Names

Use commas when first names and surnames are reversed:

- **Brown,** Mildred. E.
- **Lucas,** Jonathan F.
- **Martinez-Ferrer,** Olga R.

PRACTICE 1

Insert commas wherever needed in the following sentences. If a sentence is correct, write C.

1. All the participants on American Idol are polite humble and articulate.

2. I could tell you a secret but I am afraid you will tell your friends.

3. At the Miami Heat's game I saw many employees from my company.

4. Hoping to join the police department Luis joined a gym and changed his diet.

5. Skilled in the area of computers Jonathan applied for a job at Best Buy.

6. Mr. Jones a native of Trinidad got his U.S. citizenship on April 11 2007 in Atlanta Georgia.

7. If I were like you I would tell the truth on the application.

8. Jennifer of the Access Department is in a wheelchair so she has a special bus service to take her to and from work.

9. Frank will you be able to paint my house in the summer?

10. "I am tired of your condescending remarks about my weight" said Myrtle to her cousin.

11. The girl who won the Spelling Bee contest is from Jamaica.

12. Monica who is in my photography class had her baby on April 26 2007 at Baptist Hospital.

13. Yes I will go to England with you Manny if you pay my airfare.

14. Because of your dedication motivation and determination I will give you a book scholarship for $5000.

15. Sean Oliver Ph.D. will take over the company as of August 2008.

16. Thankfully I was selected for the secretarial position but I will have to get a new wardrobe.

17. On Monday May 7 I have to go to St. Petersburg Florida to see an old friend.

18. Johnny Johnson Sr. and Emmet Riley III will be visiting the company today.

19. Claudette is a brilliant beautiful woman who will add class to this institution.

20. The rude remark that you made cannot be taken back.

REVIEW

Write one sentence each, illustrating the following rules:

Appositive Phrase _____

_____.

Non-Restrictive Clause_____

_____.

Restrictive Clause_____

_____.

Parenthetical Expression_____

_____.

Coordinate Adjectives_____

_____.

Series_____

_____.

Uses of Semicolons (;)

The **semicolon** is not as strong as the period; however, it has a greater value than the comma. Think of it as a weak period. By itself, it can join two sentences that are closely related whereas the comma cannot join two independent clauses.

Use a semicolon to join two simple sentences if you choose not to use a comma and a coordinating conjunction (*for*, *and*, *nor*, *but*, or*, yet*):

- Marcie is older than I; Johnny is younger than both of us.
- Nina will go to Europe with you; my boss does not mind.
- The students turned in their portfolios; they are above average.

Note: After a semicolon, use lowercase unless it's a proper noun.

Use a semicolon and a comma between two simple sentences joined by a conjunctive adverb, such as *however, therefore, nevertheless, as a result, thus, moreover, furthermore, in addition, in fact, besides, consequently, still, then, also, for example, on the other hand, on the contrary*:

- I admire your dedication to your job**; however**, you have to be on time.
- The meeting will last for two hours**; in addition**, lunch will be served.

Use a semicolon instead of a comma to separate items in a series when there are commas within the items:

- At the meeting, we need Mildred, the notetaker; Anthony, the computer analyst; and Fiona, the CPA.

Note: Place the semicolon *outside* the quotation marks.

PRACTICE 2

Insert commas and semicolons wherever necessary.

1. Marlene the blonde is my sister Monica the petite one is my friend and Olga the chubby one is my sister's friend.

2. I have poor eyesight therefore I avoid driving after 8 p.m.

3. Freda my sister lives in the Dominican Republic Marlon my brother lives in Fort Lauderdale Florida and Audrey my friend lives in Miami.

4. Juanita is a charismatic individual on the other hand she can be low key at times.

5. That is a dangerous intersection in fact 40 accidents occurred there in 2006.

6. Frankie is an avid reader Samantha likes to sing.

7. Donna changed her mind about attending college she now wants to a vocational school.

8. The hurricane season is approaching therefore I need to purchase shutters.

9. Efficient time management is one of the keys to success many people have not grasped this concept.

10. Brian left his house in a hurry as a result he left his lunch box on the kitchen counter.

Colon (:)

The **colon** (:) means "as follows." It is most often used to introduce a list or a block of text.

Use a colon when a list is introduced:

- Cindy went to the store to buy the following items: milk, sugar, banana, and cheese.

Use a colon to introduce a block of text or long quotation (more than one sentence) within a paragraph:

- In Sherry's concluding speech, she said**:** "One day, you never know, Mr. Anderson, I might be the president of this company, and you will have to report me. I want you to know that if I became president of this company, I will treat you the same way you treated me."

Note: The text before the colon should be a complete sentence. If the text that follows the colon is an **incomplete** sentence, *do not* capitalize the first word unless it is a proper noun.

Use a colon after the salutation of a formal or business letter:

- Dear Mrs. Brown**:**
- Dear Sir or Madam:

Use a colon to separate the hour and minute of a time reference:

- It is 10:30 a.m., and you are still in bed.
- The meeting will begin no later than 6:01 p.m.

Use a colon between the chapter and verse of a Biblical reference:

- Proverbs 3:5, 6 are my favorite Bible verses.
- John 1:1-3, 3:16 are helpful to my understanding of the Gospel.

PRACTICE 3

Insert colons wherever necessary.

1. Here are the items that are needed for the party chicken, sodas, potato chips and ice cream.

2. This morning I woke up at 10 25 a.m.

3. Dear Participants Please pay at the front desk before 11 30 p.m.

4. I am afraid I can't meet your demands coming up with $3,000 for the rent.

5. At the Speaker's Tournament, the young woman concluded her speech with some resounding remarks Smoking is the leading cause of lung cancer today, so young and old, stop contaminating your lungs with that cancer stick. If you don't care about your lungs, care about someone else's lungs. Give up the cigarettes today!"

6. John 3 16 is one of the most read scripture verses in the New Testament.

The Apostrophe (')

The apostrophe serves *two* purposes: to show ownership (possession) and to indicate contraction (omission of letters).

To form the possessive case of a *singular* noun, first write the singular spelling of the word, and then add the apostrophe plus *s*.

Example: **student** (singular noun)
            student's book (Add the apostrophe and then *s* to form the possessive.)

To form the possessive case of a *plural* noun, first, write the plural spelling of the word; then add the apostrophe:

Example: **students** (plural noun).
            students' books (Add the apostrophe after the *s* to form the possessive.)

To form the possessive case of a *plural* noun that does *not* end in *s*, first, write the word; then add the apostrophe plus *s*.

Example: **children** (plural noun that does not end in *s*)
            children's toys (Add the apostrophe plus *s* to form the possessive.)

Do *not* add *s* apostrophe to a noun that already ends in *s*; instead, add the apostrophe after the *s*:

<u>Incorrect</u>	<u>Correct</u>
Luis's car	Luis' car
Doris's purse	Doris' purse
Mr. Jones's house	Mr. Jones' house

Do *not* add apostrophe to pronouns that are already possessive: *hers*, *its*, *his*, *theirs*, *yours*.

Below are more examples of **singular** and **plural** possessives:

<u>**Singular Possessive** (one)</u>	<u>**Plural Possessive** (two or more)</u>
girl's toy	girls' toys
Carlos' car	Carlos' and Thomas' cars (own separate cars)*
child's name	children's names
computer's disc	computers' discs
wife's ring	wives' rings
man's idea	men's ideas
cat's paw	cats' paws
lady's purse	ladies' purses
woman's apparel	women's apparel
person's bank	people's bank
Nadia's apartment	Nadia and Grace's apartment (own together)**
the book's cover	the books' covers

*Since Carlos and Thomas own separate cars, apostrophe goes on *both* names.
**On the other hand, Nadia and Grace share the *same* apartment, so the apostrophe only goes on Grace's name.

Also, use the apostrophe to replace an omitted letter or number:

- He loves **rock 'n' roll** music. (rock and roll)
- Sandra recently bought a **'90** Ford. (1990 Ford).

Use the apostrophe plus *s* to form the plurals of letters and numbers:

- Last semester, Keith brought home all **A's** and **B's**.
- Jason's teacher only gave him **4's** and **5's** on his papers.
- There are too many **do's** and **don'ts** in this place.
- In every sentence, there are at least three **but's** and two **and's**.

Use the apostrophe to form contractions (omitted letters).

Here's a list of common contractions:

Note: Contractions should only be used in informal writing and conversation.
Do not confuse the possessive word *its* with the contraction *it's* (*it is*).

aren't	=	are not	he's	=	he is; he has	shouldn't	=	should not
can't	=	cannot	I'd	=	I would	should've	=	should have
couldn't	=	could not	I'll	=	I will	that's	=	that is
didn't	=	did not	I'm	=	I am	they'll	=	they will
doesn't	=	does not	isn't	=	is not	they're	=	they are
don't	=	do not	it'll	=	it will	who's	=	who is; who has
hadn't	=	had not	it's	=	it is; it has	won't	=	will not
hasn't	=	has not	she'd	=	she would	you'd	=	you would
haven't	=	have not	she'll	=	she will	you'll	=	you will
he'd	=	he would	she's	=	she is;	you're	=	you are
he'll	=	he will			she has			

PRACTICE 4

*Correct the following sentences by either adding apostrophes where needed or deleting unnecessary apostrophes. If a sentence is correct, write **C**.*

1. My sister hair is black.

2. Women purses are on sale at Walmart.

3. These suits are yours', and they need to go to the cleaners.

4. Elvis computer is broken, so hes' taking it to a computer technician.

5. The men jobs are dissolved because the company has downsized.

6. Janet and Julio apartments are in the same building.

7. Please remove the orchids new growth, and place them in another pot.

8.   These days, childrens attitude toward education has drastically changed.

9.   Alexis and her mother birthday falls on Fathers Day.

10. These pencils are theirs' and not yours'.

11. In Jeffreys family, only A s and B s are acceptable.

12. Alinas writing assignment consists of several buts and donts.

PRACTICE 5

Rewrite each of the following expressions in the possessive case.

The buttons of the blouse.   <u>**The blouse's buttons**.</u>
—

The cover of the computer   _____

The ideas of the group   _____

The salute of the soldier   _____

The color of the house   _____

The names of the guests   _____

The members of the group   _____

The argument of the men   _____

The truck of Jonathan   _____

The car of the Thomas family   _____

PRACTICE 6

Underline each italicized word; some need apostrophe while others can be converted to contractions.

(1) I *do not* think *I am* going to work this summer because *I am* tired. (2) *It will* be good for me since *I will* get an opportunity to organize my house. (3) While *I am* home, the *citys* garbage container will be delivered to my house. (4) *I have* made several *doctors* appointments. (5)   By the way, *I will* update my *computers* files. (6) *They are* long overdue.

Hyphens (-)

Use a hyphen to avoid ambiguity or confusion:

- We had to **re-cover** the old sofa. (means to cover again, not to get well)
- He tried to **show-boat** during the last debate. (means to brag, not a ship)

Use a hyphen between two or more words that form a compound modifier before the word it modifies:

up-to-date account	six-year-old child
single-parent family	old-fashioned clothes
well-known man	part-time job

Note: Do not use hyphens if a modifier does not follow a compound word:

- My bills are up to **date**. (A noun modifier does not follow the word *date*.)

Use a hyphen with compound numbers from twenty-one to ninety-nine:

- Tim gave Arlene **twenty-one** red roses for her birthday.
- Millie says her son can count up to **fifty-six**.

Use a hyphen in fractions used as adjectives:

- A **two-thirds** majority is required to vote for the project. (The noun *majority* follows)
- **One third** of the voters will decide on the candidate. (No noun follows)

Use a hyphen (not the word "*to*") between numbers that express ratios, odds, and scores:

- The New York Giants beat the Miami Heat **89-69**.
- The odds of Blake winning the American Idol are **6-4**.

Use a hyphen with words that begin with the prefix *self*:

- My neighbors have **self-respect**.
- Females should be **self-conscious** about their appearance.
- The students in my class are **self-reliant** because they complete their projects by themselves.

Exceptions:

- Andy's three-year-old son is **selfish**.
- Austin is always engaged in **selfless** acts.

Use a hyphen to avoid duplicated vowels or consonants:

Anti-American, pre-exist, re-elect

Use a hyphen to divide a word at the end of a line. Be sure to divide words only between syllables:

- knowledge   knowl-edge (not know-ledge)

Note: Avoid carrying over a *two-letter* syllable; the hyphen takes up one space, so it is unnecessary to divide the word.

- pretty   pret-ty (unnecessary to divide)

Parentheses ( )

Use parentheses around material primarily used to further explain a word(s) in a sentence. The material might be important enough to be included, but it is not intended to be a part of the main sentence:

- Sen. Edward Kennedy **(D., Massachusetts)** proposed the bill.
- He used terminology **(jargon)** that seemed foreign to us
- The GOP **(Grand Old Party)** will hold its convention in New York this year.

Use parentheses to enclose your own parenthetical (incidental) material that would normally be set off by commas:

- Brian **(my math student)** did not attend my class today.
- Arlene **(who once worked in the accounting department)** is applying for another position.

Note: Commas and dashes are more effective with parenthetical material.

PRACTICE 7

Add hyphens, dashes, and parentheses to the following sentences:

1. Ms. Marcy who is my English teacher is going to have surgery next week.

2. According to Judge Judy, children who are left by themselves at home are a tailor made prescription for trouble.

3. Angela a busy body gets in trouble at school for talking too much.

4. I paid twenty five dollars for the necklace I am wearing.

5. Mildred is a well known politician in her neighborhood.

6. Mr. Kemp is well known in the Kendall area.

7. Oral Roberts a once fire and brimstone preacher turned over his church to his oldest son.

8. Ike Tina Turner's former husband used to abuse her.

9. I am terrified of high rise buildings especially the Empire State Building.

10. According to a National Public Radio NPR news report, the last individual to leave the burning building was an 87 year old woman.

Period (.)

Use a period at the end of a declarative statement:

- I am working hard to accomplish my goals this year.

Use a period at the end of a slightly imperative statement:

- Go outside.

Use a period at the end of a rhetorical question that functions more as a suggestion than a question:

- Shall we go.

Use a period before a decimal to separate dollars and cents written alone.

- The answer to the math problem is **66.46** percent.
- I paid **$12.50** for the shoes.
- The only change I have is **$0.12**.

Use a period after common abbreviations:

- Mr. Ms. Mrs. Aug. Jan. p.m. a.m.

Acronyms are exceptions: NATO FBI UN FHA

Question Mark (?)

Use a question mark at the end of a direct question:

- Are you ready to go to sleep?
- Did you wonder who showed him how to do that?
- You burned the rag?
- Why me? (rhetorical question)

> A rhetorical question is asked to provoke thought or express emotion, not to obtain an answer. It may be punctuated by a question mark, period or exclamation mark, depending on the context.

Note: A statement that includes an indirect question should be followed by a period and not a question mark:

- Martin asked me if I am interested in buying stocks.

Quotation Marks ("")

Use quotation marks to enclose a person's exact words (direct quote) expressed to others or him/herself:

- The teacher said, "Your project must be turned in by noon."
- "I am tired of walking now," said the child.
- "I will get the stroller," said the woman, "if you stop crying."
- She thought, "He should really be going the other direction."

- Someone watching the scene thought "the main goal is cooperation."

However, do not use quotation marks with an *indirect* quotation using the word "that" to reword a person's direct words.

- The teacher said *that* the project must be turned in by noon. (**indirect quote**)

Use quotation marks to enclose a person's exact question expressed to others or him/herself:

- **"Are you ready to go to sleep?"** asked Sally.
- **"Are you ready"** asked Sally, **"to go to sleep now?"**
- Elsie thought, **"Why would the meeting start so late?"**

When using only part of a source's exact words (partial quote), place quotation marks around only the words the source could have said:

Wrong: They chanted **"their disgust and disrespect of the mayor."**
Correct: They chanted their **"disgust and disrespect"** of the mayor.

Use single quotation marks to enclose a *quote from another source* within a quotation:

- She said, "He would **'rather die'** than eat his peas."
- "He argued **'I will never give up so long as I know that I'm right,'"** said Helen.

When a paragraph ends in a full, not partial, quote that is continued in a second paragraph, do not put an ending quotation mark at the end of the first paragraph. Instead, put an opening quotation mark around the first sentence in the second paragraph:

Senator Thurman said, "We are determined to punish those who needlessly punish the environment by littering in their communities and on their jobs.

"We have organized a special task force to deal with both residential and commercial dumping of toxic substances."

Note: This pattern should continue in subsequent paragraphs if a quote continues to other paragraphs.

When a quote is three lines or longer, it should be set off in a *block* without quotation marks. In a block quotation, the period comes before the parenthetical citation:

The federal court summarized its orders as follows:

> In addition to paralegal training, my orders require the defendants to provide female inmates with post-secondary education; to implement various vocational, and apprenticeship programs; to make use of off-grounds and work pass programs with eligible prisoners; to establish prison industry programs; to pay back wages to a trust fund established for the benefit of the women prisoners; and to re-evaluate and standardize the prisoner wage scale used by the defendants to assure that it is applied to women fairly (Glover 721).

All punctuation, except the colon and semicolon, is placed *inside* a closing quotation mark.

- Tony said these are the "most capable candidates": Jeff, Allan, Tamara, Shawn.
- She said, "Don't tell your friends my secret"; nevertheless, she admitted that she told them something

about me.
- "Give me your honest opinion," said Ernie to his friend.
- Nadia yelled to her son, "Get out of the way! A car is coming"

The dash, semicolon, question mark, and exclamation mark only go inside quotation marks when they pertain to the quoted material:

- We should ask, "How are the purposes of our heart met except by us?" (Johnson 15).
- Drop your gun, and put your hands up!" shouted the police officer to the criminal.
- What a beautiful rendition of "Amazing Grace"!

The period goes outside of the quotation mark when using a parenthetical reference:

- "Get receipts whenever possible" (Poytner 73).

Quotations from music or poetry lyrics of one to three lines should be enclosed by quotation marks. The slash mark (/) should be used to indicate the original separation of each line:

- "I never knew such a day could **come** / **And** I never knew such a **love** / **Could** be inside of one" (Benet).

Put quotation marks around nicknames, ironic words, or unfamiliar terms.

- We voted for Leon **"Sunny"** Waters. (nickname)
- The pastor decided to **"love"** his enemy with a lawsuit. (irony)
- The holy warriors, or **"mujahedeen,"** proposed a treaty. (unfamiliar term)

Brackets [ ]

When quoting a source, enclose any additional information within brackets [ ]. A writer most often includes this information for clarification, but it is not the original words of the source.

- Sandra said, "I was born and raised in Miami [Ohio] and moved to Texas at 13."
- The speaker beckoned, "Ladies and gentlemen, the next voice you will hear is that of Colonel **[Colin]** Powell."

Note: Do not confuse the bracket with the parentheses; the bracket is primarily used to insert a correction within material a writer is quoting.

Ellipses (...)

Use an ellipsis to indicate that one or more words have been omitted from a sentence or quoted material. Be careful not to leave out important information that can distort the meaning:

Original: "I am opposed to the notion of death penalty because it is truly barbaric."

Shortened: "I am opposed to the . . . death penalty because it is . . . barbaric."
Use an ellipsis followed by a period for omissions at the end of a sentence. Use *four* spaced periods:

- "I am opposed to the . . . death penalty . . . ."

Dashes (--)

Use a dash to indicate a sudden change in thought, a sharp break, or a shift in thought. Think of it as an abrupt personal comment in the middle of a sentence:

- Maria – **as you are aware** – my last day at work is Friday.
- My granddaughter – **a social butterfly** – is very dramatic.

Exclamation Point (!)

Use an exclamation point after a word or group of words that expresses strong emotion or surprise:

- Well, that was truly an inappropriate remark you made at the meeting!
- Ouch! You stepped on my toes.
- "Drop your gun, and put your hands up!" shouted the police officer to the criminal.
- What a beautiful rendition of "Amazing Grace"!

Note: The exclamation point is usually placed inside the closing quotation mark. However, it is placed on the outside of an ending quotation mark when it pertains only to the sentence and not the quoted material, such as in the last example.

REVIEW

Add ellipses, period, question mark and exclamation marks to the following sentences.

1. What time are you supposed to leave the office

2. The former prime minister of Jamaica is a female

3. At the concert last month, how awesome was the rendition of His Eye Is on the Sparrow

4. Can I guarantee your arrival at the concert

5. "Do not allow anyone out there   and in here either   until help arrives." These were the words of the ailing victim who was hit by a car.

6. Watch out for the dogs

7. "Listen to me, please," said the student, "I must pass this course to get into school "

8. Who said this would be easy

9. Last week, Anthony only brought home $106 65 for his pay.

10. Oh, no, I am terrified

SENTENCE VARIETY

A good writer will understand how to construct a simple sentence with first a subject, then a verb, and finally a subject/object complement. Great writers, however, understand how to compose sentences based on a desired effect. In other words, they use sentence variety to add interest and precise meaning to their writing. Sometimes passive voice is better than active voice. Sometimes a dependent clause should begin a sentence rather than end it. Sometimes a prepositional or participial phrase may work best to introduce a subject. Knowing when to use sentence variety, moving from a basic to a complex construction, is a powerful tool for writers.

Here are some ways to create sentence variety:

1. **Add a second complete thought to a simple sentence (coordination).**

When you add a second complete thought to a simple sentence, the result is a **compound** (or double) **sentence** that must be joined by a coordinating word (*and, but, for, or, nor, so, yet*).

- He worked all night. (simple sentence)
- We worked all night, **but** we were still able to get up this morning for class. (compound)
- Gary has worked on the car all day, **so** I think he may miss the party. (compound)

2. **Add a dependent clause (subordination)**

When you add a dependent thought to a simple sentence, the result is a **complex sentence**. A dependent clause begins with a subordinating conjunction like (*although, before, until, while*).

- **Although he studied**, he couldn't pass the test.
- **Until you stop jumping**, the boat won't stop swaying.
- **When you get home,** we will begin painting the baby's room.

3. **Add a compound complex sentence**

A compound complex sentence has two or more independent clauses and one or more dependent clauses.

- **Although** the students encountered difficulty completing their homework, they were all able to pass the quiz, **and** some were even able to make 100 percent.
- **When** you get more practice, you will be a better soccer player, **and** your team will have a better chance at winning a championship.
- We made plans to visit several museums next week, **and because** no one except Todd has paid, we may have to cancel the outing entirely.

4. Add a conjunctive adverb

- Employees were asked to leave the building; **however**, they refused to leave.
- The doctor advised Johnnie to exercise; **also**, he told him to stop smoking.
- I have not been resting well; **therefore**, I am exhausted.

5. Add a nonrestrictive clause

A non-restrictive clause uses the relative pronouns *who, which, where*. These clauses are set off by commas and can be removed from the sentence without changing the meaning.

- Mr. Alexander, **who heads the accounting department,** transferred to another department.
- Juan's red car, **which is a target for the police,** causes him a lot of grief.
- Cook County Library, **where I borrowed the DVD,** is the best in the state.

6. Add a restrictive clause

A restrictive clause uses the relative pronouns who, which, that. However, no comma is needed because the descriptive word group is necessary to identify the subject (a person or thing).

- The man **who joined the staff** is out to lunch.
- The news **that my sister sent me** is not good.
- The vice principal **who was hired last year** drives the car **that was parked here**.

7. Begin with a special opening word: preposition, adverb, infinitive, or participial phrase (-ing, -ed)

- **Concerned for his life,** Paul took his medicine regularly. (past participial phrase)

- **Scurrying to get to class on time,** I left my books in the restroom. (present participial phrase)

- **Irrationally,** she begged for an extension to pay for her classes. (adverb)

- **To stay physically fit,** the hurdler practices every day. (infinitive phrase)

- **During the exam,** no one spoke. (prepositional phrase)

8. Add adjectives or verbs in a series

- **Agitated, angry** passengers waited for the police to remove the **dented, silver** car.

- The car **skidded** off the road, **slammed** into a tree, and **split** in half.

- **Determined,** Frank took the graduation test for the second time.

9. **Add an appositive**

An **appositive** is a noun or pronoun that immediately follows another noun or pronoun and tends to describe or rename the noun or pronoun.

- Juanita, **the friendliest person I know**, works for my husband.
- Bradley, **my present doctor**, opened a new office.
- Ryan, **a Grammy-nominated musician**, will during the seminar on Thursday.

Practice

Combine the following sentences into one to demonstrate your knowledge of how many ways sentences can be written. Use the criteria and examples above to label each sentence type. Do not use one example more than once, and omit repeated words or phrases. **Answers will vary.**

Example: The candidate was determined to win the election.
He slandered his opponent on television and on the radio.
He revealed things he had done in his teenage years.

Because the candidate was determined to win the election, he slandered his opponent on television and on the radio, and he revealed things the candidate had done in his teenage years. *(compound complex)*

My father cares about my welfare.
He pays for my gym membership.
He buys fresh fruits and vegetables for me.
He makes sure I get enough rest.

_____

_____

_____

Paris is the most exciting place I have ever visited.
The city hosts an annual jazz festival.
The Tour de France always attracts international attention.
The fashion shows feature premier designs.

_____

_____

_____

My professor was born in London, England.
She came to America when she was 16 years old.
She went to elementary and high school in England.
She attended to college in America.

_____

_____

_____

Adam was not afraid to box.
His opponent has a better record.
He has been boxing since he was 12 years old.
James was favored to win.

_____

_____

_____

The referee signaled no touchdown.
He was standing in the end zone.
This was a very controversial call.
The players were livid.

_____

_____

_____

Andy went to the Dominican Republic.
It was an exciting trip.
It was two weeks ago.
He visited the beaches.
He visited the shopping centers.

_____

_____

_____

The hurricane season is approaching.
Newscasters remind residents to stock up on supplies for two days.
They emphasized the danger of generators.
They said to buy a device to monitor the carbon monoxide.

_____

_____

_____

Keith fell off his bicycle.
He fell to the ground.
He landed on his back.
He screamed for his mother.
His mother immediately called 911.
The rescue arrived in minutes.
He went to the hospital.

_____

_____

_____

_____

MISPLACED AND DANGLING MODIFIERS _____

As you have probably learned, a **modifier** is a word or a phrase that describes something else in a sentence. Sometimes writers get careless and do not place these modifiers close to their modifiers, or the words they describe. When this occurs, it causes illogical sentences that are difficult to comprehend. **Misplaced** and dangling **modifiers** are two such modifiers that create illogical sentences.

Misplaced Modifiers

A **misplaced modifier** is one that is not correctly placed in relation to the word it modifies. Some words in English can have more than one meaning, and their meaning depends on how they are placed in a sentence. Here are four different types of misplaced modifiers:

Misplaced Adjectives
Misplaced: The food **spoiled** made us sick. (spoiled made?)
Correct: The **spoiled** food made us sick. (spoiled food)

Misplaced: Police found the **stolen** man's car. (stolen man?)
Correct: Police found the man's **stolen** car. (stolen car)

Misplaced Adverbs

Misplaced: **Only** I earned $10 for painting. (no one else earned $10?)
Misplaced: I earned $10 **only** for painting. (only for painting and nothing else?)
Misplaced: I **only** earned $10 for painting. (only earned money for painting?)
Correct: I earned **only** $10 for painting. (earned only $10 for painting)

Misplaced: We jogged around the park **vigorously**. (vigorous park?)
Correct: We **vigorously** jogged around the park. (vigorous jog)
Correct: **Vigorously**, we jogged around the park.

Note: Watch out for adverbs (words ending in *–ly*) plus other adverbs like *almost, often, even,* etc. If they are improperly placed, your sentences will be difficult to comprehend.

Misplaced Phrases

Misplaced: The woman hung the pictures for her students **painted in class**. (painted students?)
Correct: The woman hung the pictures **painted in class** for her students. (painted pictures)

Misplaced: Two electricians repaired the ceiling **with new tools**. (a ceiling with tools?)
Correct: Two electricians **with new tools** repaired the ceiling. (electricians with tools)

Misplaced Clauses

Misplaced: He put sheets on the bed **that smelled fresh**. (fresh bed?)
Correct: He put **sheets that smelled fresh** on the bed. (fresh sheets)

Misplaced: The hurricane hit another town **that destroyed everything**.
                (a town destroyed everything?)
Correct: The hurricane **that destroyed everything** hit another town.
                (a hurricane destroyed everything)

PRACTICE 1

Rewrite each sentence, placing their modifiers as close as possible to the words, phrases, or clauses they modify.

1. Mr. Pearson thanked me for my dedication and gave me a trophy without hesitation.

_____

_____

2. We have only two weeks left for the semester to be over.

_____

_____

3. To complete this project by June, it is obvious that I have to work overtime.

_____

4. Martin's briefcase was reported stolen by the police.

_____

_____

5. When my mother called for me to pick her up, I jumped in my car hurriedly to pick her up.

_____

_____

6. I was yesterday asked to speak at a women's retreat.

_____

_____

7. You should stretch thoroughly before exercising.

_____

_____

8. The raccoon ate almost the entire sandwich.

_____

_____

9. I have $2,000 only to buy a used car.

_____

_____

10. Because Angela went to bed late, she slept last night hardly.

_____

_____

Dangling Modifiers

A **dangling modifier** mostly occurs at the beginning of a sentence when the subject of the sentence is missing in an introductory phrase (gerund, infinitive, participle) or at the beginning of the main clause. Unlike a misplaced modifier, a dangling modifier is not typically corrected by moving it to a different place in a sentence.

Two methods for correcting dangling modifiers are:

1. Place the subject (who or what) immediately after the opening phrase or clause:

Dangling: To iron well, an ironing board is needed.
Correct: To iron well, **one** needs an ironing board.

Immediately after the comma, answer who needs an ironing board.

Dangling: Having left the jacket, the bus company had my other bags.
Correct: Having left the jacket, **I** called the bus company that had my other bags.

Immediately after the comma, answer who left the jacket.

2. Add the subject (who or what) to the opening phrase or clause.

Dangling: While ironing, a spot occurred on my blouse.
Correct: While ironing **my** blouse, a spot occurred.

A spot cannot iron, so in the introductory clause, answer who was ironing.

Dangling: Having been left, the bus company had to locate the bags.
Correct: Because the **bags** were left, the bus company had to locate them.

In the introductory clause, include what was left. The bus company had not been left, as the first sentence suggests; the bags were left.

Dangling modifiers can also occur in the middle or at the end of a sentence. Unlike dangling modifiers that commonly occur at the beginning of a sentence, these are corrected by moving them to a different place in a sentence, or closer to the word they modify.

Dangling: **Melissa** paused before saying hello, **looking somewhat puzzled**.
Correct: **Melissa, looking somewhat puzzled**, paused before saying hello.

Looking somewhat puzzled modifies *Melissa*, not *hello*, so place it closer to its modifier.

Dangling: The room was so cold that the *students* couldn't concentrate *taking the SAT*.
Correct: The *students taking the SAT* were so cold that they couldn't concentrate.
Correct: While the *students were taking the SAT*, the room was so cold that they couldn't concentrate.

Taking the SAT modifies *students*, not *concentrate*, so place it closer to its modifier.

PRACTICE 2

Rewrite each sentence, making sure the modifiers are logically placed. In some sentences, you might have to add or delete a word or a phrase.

1. The guy was stalking the celebrity in the red Honda Civic.

_____

_____

2. When buying a new car, the many features and sales tax cause some people to become exhausted.

_____

_____

3. Stopped by a state trooper, the flashing lights frighten many people.

_____

_____

4. Arriving in Santo Domingo, Spanish was understood by the American tourists.

_____

_____

5. Having left the party drunk, a tree hit Dan's car.

_____

_____

6. When a young child, an iron burnt me on my right knee.

_____

_____

7. Tripping over the shoes, blood fell from the man's head.

_____

_____

8. While driving home after midnight, the traffic lights were blinking.

_____

9. Having completed the dissertation, a well-deserved vacation is needed.

_____

_____

10. After returning from the store, burglars showed up at my door.

_____

_____

PRACTICE 3

Rewrite each sentence to eliminate any misplaced or dangling modifiers.

1. By the end of the semester, only 21 credits will be left to graduate.

_____

_____

2. My neighbor nearly cleans his truck for eight hours every Saturday.

_____

_____

3. To get up on time each day, an alarm clock is set to wake me up at 6 a.m.

_____

_____

4. While still in bed, the pajamas were removed from the baby.

_____

_____

5. I found $20 during lunch under the table.

_____

_____

13

Consistent Writing

Consistent writing means maintaining a flow within a sentence and related sentences that will not confuse readers. Thus, writers must use the same form of words or parts of speech to achieve consistent writing. Shifts in verb tense, voice, or person (point of view) affect the logical meaning, as well as flow.

CONSISTENT TENSE

Tense means time (present, past, future, etc.). The verb you use in your writing determines the tense. Consider the following sentences:

- Anita **runs** five miles.   (**present** – action is occurring now)
- Anita **ran** five miles.   (**past** – action is completed)
- Anita **will run** five miles.   (**future** – action will take place in the future)

In your writing, do not shift tense from past to present or vice versa because this can confuse your readers. Unless there is a change in time for each event mentioned in your writing, *do not* shift from one tense to another. Aim at keeping your writing in a consistent tense.

Examples:

- **Inconsistent tense**: Carlos **studied** and **passes** his final exam.
- **Consistent tense**:   Carlos **studied** and **passed** his final exam.

Sentence 1 is inconsistent because **studied** is in the *past tense* and **passes** is in *present tense*.
Sentence 2 is consistent because both **studied** and **passed** are in the *past tense*.

Note: Sometimes a change of tense is necessary to show a normal progression in time:

- I **went** to the store yesterday, but I **must go** again tomorrow.

When you refer to literary works (books, magazines, websites, etc.) and historical events that occurred a long time ago, keep them in the present tense because they are still current.

- King David and Moses **are** two important individuals who **play** important roles in history.

- The Bill of Rights **states** that the government cannot stop any individual from participating in the religion of his or her choice.

PRACTICE 1

Cross out any inconsistent verb you find, and then write the correct verb above the word.

                                                            went

Example: Half of the students went to the museum, and half ~~goes~~ to the library.

1. Last summer, Professor Mason taught five classes and is writing a new textbook for his history class.

2. The pianist played a song with his right hand and directs the choir with his left hand.

3. Manny ran around the track several times before realizing he loses his cell phone.

4. Albert is the type of individual who thought of others before himself.

5. Playing golf is my passion; in fact, I played four nights a week.

6. On Friday in the middle of my final exam, the fire alarm went off. The students grab their belongings, scurried down the stairs, and waited until it was safe for them to return to the classroom.

7. The presidential candidate disparaged his opponent for evading the real issues, but his opponent talks about real issues that caused the public to favor him.

8. Yesterday after church, my family and I cooked. Afterwards, we watch a great movie.

9. When I was growing up, all my teachers encourage reading, and I had to take a book home every weekend so that I got more practice.

10. The athlete finished his warm-up, ran for three miles, and then goes to the gym for an hour.

11. Do you remember when we drove to Canada or sailing to the Bahamas a few years ago?

12. We felt that you were too tired, so trying to go to the movies may be too much for one evening.

13. How do you know who will be entering the contest if you had not checked the registration forms?

14. The company would like to congratulate Ricky Ward for working efficiently and effectively over the last five years.

15. Whitney tried to make a comeback, but her personal demons are destroying her chance.

PRACTICE 2

Read the following paragraphs. Then underline any inconsistency of tense you find, and make the correction above it.

As I was driving to work this morning, I saw a tragic automobile accident. A red Toyota Celica runs the red light and plunged into the back of a bus. The bus driver suddenly stopped, comes out of the bus and calls 911. When the police arrived, they find the driver slumps over the steering wheel. While one officer calls for an ambulance, the other officer questioned the passengers on the bus to see if the passengers could give him an accurate account of what had transpired. Obviously, no one seems to have seen what had really occurred.

Driving in Jamaica is no easy task. I had always heard about some of its narrow roads, but last summer I have an opportunity to witness, firsthand, what driving is really like in that beautiful island. First of all, the taxi driver drove about 80 miles per hour. When he passes loaded buses and trucks while driving around sharp curves and deep bends, some passengers yelled, "Slow down, Mr. Driver." It seemed as if he got angry and increased the speed rather than slowing down. My granddaughter, who was vacationing on the island for the first time, closes her eyes, covers up her face with both hands and screams, "Grandma, I am going to die!" Still, this driver did not care about the screams. All he cares about was taking passengers to their destination and going back to airport to pickup more passengers.

CONSISTENT VOICE _____

Inconsistent voice means shifting between **active** and **passive** voice. In the **active voice**, the subject of a sentence performs some type of physical or mental activity. In the **passive voice**, an action is being done to the subject of the sentence. For more discussion on the **active** and **passive voice**, go to the section titled *Verbs* in the chapter *Parts of Speech*, and look under the subheading *Voice*.

Examples:

	subject	verb	I.O.	D.O.

Active Voice: The **company gave** its employees a bonus.
Passive Voice: A **bonus was given** to employees **by** the company.

                     active voice   passive voice
Inconsistent Voice: He **fought** during the war, but **was discharged** early **by** the Army.

The first part of the sentence is written in **active voice**. The subject *he* performs the action *fought*. The second portion of the sentence shifts to **passive voice**. The sentence is still about him, but something is being done to him by the Army.

active voice   active voice
Consistent Voice: He **fought** during the war, but the Army **discharged** him early.

The second portion of the sentence is now in the same voice as the first part. The Army is performing the action *discharged*.

PRACTICE 3

Cross out any inconsistencies in voice you find, and then write the correct answer above it.

the ending stirred us.
Example: We saw the movie and ~~was stirred by the ending~~.

1.   A child is a precious gift, so the child must be nurtured by his or her parents.

2.   New healthcare benefits were set up for the employees, and they like them better.

3.   The nurse ordered more blood tests and was told by the doctor to schedule another visit this week.

4.   The students completed their projects and was prepared for class.

5.   Everybody seems to have more information about Sally's dismissal than Larry who was hired by her last year.

6.   Everyone wishes to have a debt-free life and peace is desired by all.

7.   When I visited my professor, I was encouraged that I am doing well on my paper.

8.   Each of the witnesses identified the robber who broke into the neighbor's house, so they were given a reward by the police.

9.   People are entitled to voice their opinions and not fear rejection by others.

10. After I found Manny's license, I was told by the officer to bring it to the station.

CONSISTENT PERSON

Inconsistent person usually occurs when a writer changes pronouns, or shifts point of view, from first person to second person to third person. This can certainly cause confusion.

Person	Use
First	*Informal Writing* (personal essays, autobiographies)
Second	*Interactive Writing* (process, quotes, advertising copy)
Third	*Formal Writing* (research papers, reports)

Avoid using second person *you* unless you are writing a process paper (demonstrating to someone how to do something) or quoting someone's direct words.

First person point of view:
- **I** can write from different angles when **I** want to convey who is telling the story.

Second person point of view:
- **You** can write from different angles when **you** want to convey who is telling the story.

Third person point of view:
- **Authors** can write from different angles when **they** want to convey who is telling the story.

Examples:

- **Inconsistent person:** If **one** puts forth enough effort, **you** will surely succeed.
- **Consistent person:**   If **one** puts forth enough effort, **he** or **she** (or **one**) will surely succeed.
- **Consistent person:**   If **people** put forth enough effort, **they** will surely succeed.

In sentence 1, the indefinite pronoun *one* is in the third person, and *you* is in the second person.
In sentence 2, the word *one* is in the third person and *he* or *she* is also in the third person.
In sentence 3, both *people* and *they* are third person plural.

Note: Of all the errors made in shifting from one person to another, the most common occurrence is shifting from third person to second or from second person to third person.

PRACTICE 4

In each sentence, cross out the shifts in person, and then make the correction above the word.

them
Example: The students enjoyed the assignment because it made ~~you~~ think.

1. One should exercise regularly because it will help you to live a longer and healthier life.

2. No one at the meeting was willing to challenge the administration about their raise.

3. Sometimes I like to drink sodas, but they give you pimples.

4. A person who travels often is aware that you should not have certain items in your carry-on luggage.

5. If you have not gone to South Beach in Miami, one needs to go at least once.

6. Every female employee has the right to be treated fairly by your male supervisor.

7. Each individual is entitled to their opinion, but this does not mean that they should abuse that right.

8. According to studies, if one inhales second-hand smoke for a long time, you are more susceptible to cancer than the actual smoker.

9. You should be aware of ambiguous statements in contracts because it contains misleading clauses.

10. My family is health conscious because they are aware of the illnesses that bad diets can cause.

PARALLELISM

Parallelism refers to words, phrases, and clauses in a series that are written in a balanced form. In other words, they are structured in the same grammatical form. When sentence elements do not have similar structured functions, they are considered faulty parallelism, and this can cause your writing to be awkward. Look at the bolded elements of the following sentences:

Faulty parallelism: **Studying** for an hour each day is better **than to cram**.

Revised: **Studying** for an hour each day is better than **cramming**.

Faulty parallelism: Jerry **will either start college** in fall or **to go in the spring term**.

Revised: Jerry **will either start college** in fall or he **will begin in the spring term**.

Sentence 1 is comparing *studying for an hour versus cramming*; remember, comparison always involves two people or two things, and the structure should be the same; in other words, whatever method you use to compare the first element, you should use the same to compare the second element.

In sentence 2, the grammatical structure is parallel: *studying/cramming*.

Sentence 3 has a correlative conjunction (*either ... or*). Whenever correlative conjunctions are used in a sentence, both elements should be structured. *"Jerry will start college in fall"* is structured, but *"to go in the spring term"* is not structured.

In sentence 4, both elements are structured.

Remember: Coordinating conjunctions (*and, but, so, for, or, nor*) should join words, phrases or clauses of the same (parallel) form. Conjunctions should join nouns with nouns; adverb clause with adverb clause; prepositional phrases with prepositional phrases; and so forth.

PRACTICE 5

In each of the following sentences, underline the part of the sentence that is not parallel. Then, on the given lines, rewrite the sentence to make its elements parallel.

gardening

Example: Her hobby is swimming, dancing, and <u>to do gardening</u>.
Her hobby is swimming, dancing, and gardening.

1. John will either do his homework or going to bed early.

_____

_____

2. My mother prefers to do her own ironing, cleaning, and to cook herself.

_____

3. For dinner, she had yellow rice and chicken, mashed potatoes and vegetables, and she ate strawberry ice cream with whipped cream on top.

_____

_____

4. Ted came home from camp with a broken finger, a bruised knee, and his shirt was torn.

_____

_____

5. Julie is the type of individual who likes to read, to do math, and writing.

_____

_____

6. My doctor was not only pleased with my sudden weight loss, but he also mentioned that my cholesterol level is superb.

_____

_____

7. Last year I took several vacations, bought a new car, and my house was painted.

_____

_____

8. Eating at home is a better option than to eat at a restaurant.

_____

_____

9. Professor Brown is not only a qualified teacher, but has several years' experience in his field.

_____

_____

10. I miss going to Jamaica for Christmas because I would visit my parents, go to my old church, and I would go to the market to buy mangoes.

_____

_____

SUBJECT-VERB AGREEMENT _____

Subject-verb agreement means the subject (noun or pronoun) and the verb (action or linking) of a sentence must agree in person and number.

Person is the form that a pronoun takes to distinguish between the speaker (**first person**), the individual or thing spoken to (**second person**), or the individual or thing spoken about (**third person**).

Person	Singular	Plural
First (the person speaking)	I	We
Second (the person spoken to)	You	You
Third (the person or object spoken about)	He, She, It	They

Whenever nouns are used as the subject, the sentence is in the third person:

Example: **Officers Smith** and **Jones** argue every day.

This sentence is talking about two people (*Smith* and *Jones*) other than the writer. However, if the writer talked about his/her activity, the sentence would also be in first person:

Example: Officer Smith and **I** argue every day.

Number is the form taken by a noun, pronoun, or verb to indicate whether something is singular (one) or plural (two or more). Singular subjects need singular verb forms, and plural subjects need plural verb forms.

Adding an *-s* ending to a noun makes the word plural, but this is not the case for verbs. A singular action verb ends in *s*; on the other hand, a plural action verb *does not* end in *s*.

Singular: The boy **runs** to the car. (one boy = *s* on the verb)

Plural: The boys **run** to the car. (more than one boy = no *s* on the verb)

For plural nouns that do not end in *s* (*men, people*), the verb should also **not** end in *-s*.

Example: The **men** **write** well.
Many **people** **like** to fly.

In present tense, third person singular, the verb has an *-s* ending:

Example: Officer Smith **writes** well.
The teacher **records** the grades.

Linking Verbs

A linking verb must also agree with its subject in person and number:

<u>**Singular**</u>	<u>**Plural**</u>
(*he, she, it*) **is/was**	(*we, they*) **are/were**
(*I*) **am/was**	(*you*) **are/were**
(*he, she, it*) **stays**	(*we, you, they*) **stay**
(*he, she, it*) **feels**	(*we, you, they*) **feel**
(*he, she, it*) **seems**	(*we, you, they*) **seem**
(*he, she, it*) **looks**	(*we, you, they*) **look**
(*he, she, it*) **appears**	(*we, you, they*) **appear**

Note: The pronoun *you* (singular and plural) always takes a plural verb (no *s*):

Plural: *You* **<u>are</u>** very punctual in attending your classes.

Plural: **<u>Are</u>** *you* assigned to the night shift?

Plural: *You* **<u>were</u>** not on duty.

Helping Verbs

When a helping verb is added to the main verb, the verb form is always plural (no *-s* ending):

Examples: Officer Smith **<u>can write</u>** well.
            <u>Shall</u> we **<u>prepare</u>** for the storm?
            The officers **<u>must go</u>** on duty at 6 a.m.

Watch out for Prepositional Phrases

Do not be misled by prepositional phrases that appear between the subject and verb. They may confuse you because the object of the preposition (a noun or objective pronoun) may seem like the subject, but it is not. Remember, a prepositional phrase begins with a preposition and ends with a noun or objective pronoun.

Examples: prep   obj
        The caliber ~~of the guns~~ varies. (*Caliber* is the subject, not *guns*.)

            prep   obj
        One ~~of Freddie's sisters~~ likes cheese. (*One* is the subject, not *sisters*)

        Prep   obj
The hotels ~~in the downtown area~~ change rates often. (*Hotel* is the subject, not *area*)

Common Prepositions

aboard	behind	from	per
about	below	in	regarding
above	beneath	inside	round
across	beside	into	since
after	besides	like	till
against	between	near/next	through

along	beyond	of	throughout
alongside	but	off	to
amid	by	on	toward
amidst	concerning	onto	under
among	despite	out	underneath
around	down	outside	until
as	during	over	up/upon
at	except	pending	via
before	for	with	without/within

PRACTICE 1

Underline the subject once and the verb twice._

1. Your apple (is/are) sweeter than mine.

2. The war in Iraq (seems/seem) like it will never be over.

3. The windows in the back of my house (is/are) cracked.

4. Juan (play/plays) the piano well.

5. The constant arguments among the basketball players (cause/causes) them to lose most of their games.

6. Wearing seat belts in Florida (has/have) become mandatory.

7. One of my professors (appear/appears) to be willing to change his grading policies to accommodate struggling students.

8. Not one of my friends (was/were) present at my graduation.

9. The students in my class (prefer/prefers) to take tests than to write essays.

10. The new employees (work/works) well in groups.

Sentences Beginning with *Here* and *There*

Most times, the subject of a sentence is placed *before* the verb. However, whenever the adverbs **here** and **there** start a sentence, the verb is placed *after* the subject. Remember, the subject of a sentence is always a noun or pronoun. Therefore, *here* and *there* cannot function as subjects.

Examples: There are **grounds** for the decision.
(*Grounds* is the subject, not *there*.)

Here is the **dictionary** for your daughter.
(*Dictionary* is the subject, not *here*.)

Note: When in doubt, ask **who** are **what** is doing the verb.

PRACTICE 2

Underline the subject once and the verb twice.

1.   There (was/were) a thumbing sound outside my door last night.

2.   Here (is/are) the shower curtains for your bathrooms.

3.   On the second floor of my apartment, there (is/are) some strange individuals.

4.   There (was/were) several protesters at the abortion clinic near my house.

5.   There (has/have) been numerous robberies at the jewelry store in Dadeland Mall.

6.   Here (is/are) the book you loaned me.

7.   (Is/Are) there any job-related problems in your department?

8.   Here (is/are) my homework assignments.

9.   Over there (is/are) the tax reports.

10. Right now, there (is/are) no time for negative comments.

Interrogative Sentences

An **interrogative sentence** is one that asks a question. Like sentences beginning with *here* and *there*, the verb comes before the subject in interrogative sentences. Most times interrogative sentences can be turned into declarative sentences (statements) by just reversing the order.

Interrogative	**Declarative**
Are you going to the prom?	You are going to the prom._
Is Manny nervous?	Manny is nervous.
Were they in favor of the decision?	They were in favor of the decision.
Should I turn in my project now?	I should turn in my project now.

PRACTICE 3

In the following sentences, underline the subject once and the verb twice.

1. Where (was/were) you when I called last night?

2. (Is/Are) your parents going to allow you to go to the party?

3. How (do/does) your friends tolerate your snobbish attitude?

4. Why (is/are) your decision so sudden?

5. What (seems/seem) to be the matter with you these days?

6. Who (is/are) those individuals in the picture?

7. (Is/Are) the women aware of their failing grades?

8. Where (has/have) she been for the past six months?

9. How (is/are) your bizarre ideas different from mine?

10. Why (isn't/aren't) they ready for the bus to pick them up?

11. Who (has/have) been responsible for the failure of the company?

12. (Was/Were) they able to complete their projects on time?

Verbs with Indefinite Pronouns as Subjects

Some indefinite pronouns are always singular whereas others are always plural. On the other hand, some could be either singular or plural, depending on the antecedent to which they refer. The chart below will demonstrate their categories:

Singular (-s on verb)			**Plural** (no -s on verb)	**Singular** *or* **Plural**
anybody	one	anything	both	all
nobody	no one	nothing	few	any
somebody	anyone	something	many	none
everybody	someone	each	others	some
either(of)	everyone	much	several	more
neither (of)	another			most

Singular: **Anybody** ~~who resists~~ is under arrest.
Singular: **Everyone** <u>respects</u> an officer who is fair.

Singular: **Neither** ~~of the boys~~ <u>is</u> guilty.
Singular: **Either** ~~of the girls~~ <u>is</u> not aware of his or her job responsibilities.

Plural: **Several** ~~of my friends~~ <u>find</u> it difficult to study in silence.
Plural: **Both** ~~of you~~ <u>need</u> to be reprimanded.

Plural: **All** English students <u>are</u> required to go the Lab. (*All* is referring to students.)
Singular: **All** the furniture ~~in the living room~~ <u>is</u> mine.   (*All* is referring to furniture.)

Singular: **Most** ~~of the equipment~~ <u>is</u> in the storage room.   (*Most* is referring to equipment.)
Plural: **Most** ~~of Janet's ideas~~ <u>are</u> taken.   (*Most* is referring to ideas.)

Note: *Either and neither*, followed by *of*, are *always* singular. (-s on verb)

PRACTICE 4

Cross out all prepositional phrases between the subject and the verb; then underline the subject once and the verb twice. Don't forget to look out for the pronouns that could either be singular or plural.

1. Neither of the dresses (fit/fits) my children.

2. No one in the class (like/likes) Ana because she talks too much.

3. Some of your ideas (is/are) excellent.

4. Most people in the North (likes/like) to come to Miami during the winter months.

5. Most of the mail (belongs/belong) to Marcie.

6. Some of the equipment in the storage room (has/have) been there for years.

7. Everything in the pantry (need/needs) to be thrown out.

8. None of the three cars (is/are) working.

9. All of Larry's clothes (was/were) damaged by the storm.

10. Few on the team (know/knows) each other.

11. Several of Tina's colleagues (doesn't/don't) work during the summer.

12. Neither of those two friends (respect/respects) each other.

13. Everybody from Caleb's hometown (know/knows) his parents.

14. Either of these dresses (suit/suits) the occasion.

15. Nothing (seem/seems) to be going well with Althea these days.

Compound Subjects

Either/or and *Neither/nor* Combinations

A compound subject (two or more subjects) with *either/or* or *neither/nor* could either be singular or plural. In these combination constructions, there are always *two* subjects. However, only use the subject *closest* to the verb. This means that if the subject closest to the verb is singular, use a singular verb *(s* on verb). If the subject closest to the verb is plural, use a plural verb (no *s* on verb).

Singular: **Either** the <u>captain</u> **or** the <u>lieutenant</u> <u>is</u> on duty tonight.
                 (*Lieutenant* is closest to the verb.)

Plural: **Neither** the <u>women</u> **nor** the <u>men</u> ~~at the massage parlor~~ <u>were</u> happy about being   arrested.
                 (*Men* is closest to the verb.)

Plural: **Neither** the <u>sergeant</u> **nor** the <u>cadets</u> <u>remember</u> the case.
(*Cadets* is closest to the verb.)

Singular: **Several** <u>deputies</u> **or** one state <u>trooper</u> <u>is</u> needed.
(*Trooper* is closest to the verb.)

Plural: **One** state <u>trooper</u> **or** several <u>deputies</u> <u>are</u> needed.
(*Deputies* are closest to the verb.)

Plural: <u>Are</u> **either** your <u>parents</u> **or** <u>siblings</u> <u>going</u> to the graduation ceremony?
(*Parents* are closest the verb.)

Singular: <u>Is</u> **either** your <u>mother</u> **or** <u>father</u> <u>going</u> to the graduation ceremony?
(*Mother* is closest to the verb.)

Practice 5

In each of the following sentences, underline the subject once and the verb twice.

1. Neither the doctor nor the nurses (has/have) arrived yet.

2. Either Zenia or the choir members (needs/need) to sing at the concert.

3. Neither Frances nor you (has/have) ever seen a bull fight.

4. (Are/Is) either the coach or team members aware of the dangers of not wearing proper attire?

5. Neither Jonary's parents nor Quanricka's parents (was/were) on time for their graduation ceremony.

6. (Has/Have) the guests or the host arrived yet?

7. Several volunteers or parents (are/is) needed for the bake sale.

8. Neither Jerry nor Stephanie (believe/believes) that Peter is ready for the hot dog contest.

9. Either you or your siblings (is/ are) guilty of fraud.

10. Neither the surgeon nor his assistants, in my opinion, (has/have) the expertise to do the surgery.

Not/only and *But/also* Combinations

This combination is much like the *either/or* combination. If the subject closest to the verb is singular, use a singular verb. If the subject closest to the verb is plural use a plural verb.

Singular: **Not only** the <u>audience</u> **but also** the <u>director</u> <u>admits</u> that the movie was horrible.

Plural: **Not only** the <u>audience</u> **but also** the <u>directors</u> <u>admit</u> that the movie was horrible.

The Positive and Negative Construction

When there are two subjects and one is positive and the other is negative, the verb must agree with the positive subject.

Singular: The <u>mayor</u>, **not** the commissioners, <u>has</u> investigated the charges.

Plural: The <u>commissioners</u>, **not** the mayor, <u>have</u> investigated the charges.

Subjects Joined by *And*

Subjects joined by *and* take plural verbs (no *s* on verb)

Plural: A **car** and a **plane** <u>are</u> needed.
            (*Car* and *plane* = *they*. **They** <u>are</u>.)

Single Units Joined by *And*

Occasionally, two nouns joined by *and* are used to name a single unit.

<u>Synonyms</u>:

Singular: The **noise** and **shouting** <u>is</u> endless.

<u>Logical units</u>:

Singular: The **horse** and **cart** <u>is</u> still popular in Britain.

<u>Nouns modified by *each, every, no,* or *many a*</u>:

Singular: **Each** and **every** <u>individual</u> <u>has</u> to take care of his or her responsibilities.
Singular: **Every** <u>child</u> and <u>adult</u> <u>knows</u> what is right from wrong.
Singular: **Many a** <u>thought </u> and <u>effort</u> <u>was</u> put into this project.

Practice 6

Draw a single line under the subject, and double underline the verb.

1. Both the employees and the managers (are/is) planning to go to Janice's wedding.

2. Andrea and her friends, not their parents, (run/runs) their household.

3. Peanut butter and jelly (are/is) an energy booster.

4. Each child and every parent (needs/need) to be at tonight's meeting.

5. Not only the team members but also the coaches (agree/agrees) that their opponents are immature.

6. The workers, as well as the supervisors, (insults/insult) Hilda.

7. The sales clerks and their managers (has/have) been aware that the janitors are stealing.

8.   Ham and cheese (are/is) an on-the-go meal for many children.

9.   My sister and her father (is/are) planning to have the first dance at the reception.

10. Brittany, not her employees, (has/have) the difficult task of closing the store tonight.

11. Any one of the boys who (is/are) interested may register for the weekend basketball tournament.

12. Who (is/are) the best student-athletes this semester?

Collective Nouns

Collective nouns refer to a group of people or things. When they act as a unit (together), they take singular verbs. When they act separately, they take plural verbs.

Singular: The **audience** <u>affirms</u> its satisfaction of the performance by clapping.
Plural: The **audience** <u>are</u> going in their separate directions.
Singular: The **committee** <u>is</u> ready to give its report.
Singular: A **group** ~~of people~~ <u>is</u> standing outside.

Collective Nouns

group	audience	fleet	*number
class	herd	squad	congregation
crowd	tribe	staff	company
team	flock	faculty	Congress
choir	panel	army	Senate
committee	board	school	government
family	college	jury	crew

Note: *When you use **the number**, it is always singular.
         When you use **a number**, it is always plural.

Plural: **A number** ~~of workers~~ <u>have</u> changed their minds about quitting their jobs.
Singular: **The number** ~~of union members at last night's meeting~~ <u>was</u> scanty.

Special Cases of Singular and Plural Nouns

Some nouns that end in *s* have plural forms, but they are singular in meaning; others, on the other hand, are plural:

Singular: On Saturdays, the **news** <u>comes</u> on at 6 p.m.
Singular: **Mathematics** <u>is</u> a bore to many students.
Plural: The **pliers** <u>are</u> ~~in the garage on a shelf~~.

Plural: The **scissors** <u>have</u> not <u>been used</u> for many months.

Here's a list of special singular and plural nouns:

<u>Singular</u>	<u>Singular</u>	<u>Plural</u>	<u>Plural</u>
news	mathematics	scissors	shoes
athletics	wages	pants	socks
economics	phonetics	jeans	goods
civics	species	trousers	tweezers
politics	measles	shears	pajamas
semantics	mumps	pliers	binoculars

Amount (money, distance)

When an amount or distance is expressed as a single unit, it is singular.

Singular: <u>Five dollars</u> *is* the amount I owe you.
Singular: <u>One hundred dollars</u> <u>is</u> all I have in my account.
Singular: <u>Fifty yards</u> ~~of cloth~~ <u>is</u> all I need for the draperies.
Singular: <u>Five miles</u> <u>is</u> a long distance to walk.
Plural: <u>One hundred books</u> <u>were</u> shipped to me last week.

Mathematical Expressions

Depending on the meaning, fractional expressions can either be singular or plural. However, sums and products of mathematical problems are singular and require singular verbs.

Singular: **Two-thirds** of the bouquet **is** roses.
Plural: **Two-thirds** of the flowers **are** roses.
Singular: A small **percentage** of the toast **is** burned.
Plural: A small **percentage** of the students **are** voting today.
Singular: **Five and five is** always ten.
Singular: **Twelve times 12 is** 144.

PRACTICE 7

In each of the following sentences, draw a single line under the subject and double underline the verb.

1. The army (has/have) just invaded Iraq.

2. The basketball team (practice/practices) at 4 a.m. seven days per week.

3. Congress (have/has) just passed a new tax law.

4. Fifty dollars (is/are) all I have in my purse.

5. These days measles (is/are) not common in the United States.

6. A large number of students (does/do) not like to study.

7. Mathematics (are/is) a subject my grandson enjoys.

8. At least two-thirds of the students (was/were) missing today.

9. The number of people at last night's frog-jumping contest (was/were) fewer than last year.

10. Phonics (has/have) become very popular in the United States.

Relative Dependent Clauses

A relative dependent clause must begin with a relative pronoun: *who, which, that,* followed by a verb. If it refers to a singular noun, a singular verb must be used. If it refers to a plural noun, plural verb must be used.

Singular: The **man** ~~who is my neighbor~~ **is** very private.
Plural: The **Martins**, ~~who are from Santo Domingo~~, **are** my neighbors.
Plural: The **pictures** ~~that are hanging in my bedroom~~ **have** been there for five years.
Singular: One ~~of the cars~~, ~~which I sold to Maria~~, **needs** a new engine.

In sentence 1, *who* is referring to *man*; in sentence 2, *who* is referring to the *Martins;* in sentence 3, *that* is referring to *pictures,* and in sentence 4 *which* is referring to cars, but one is the subject because "of the cars" is a prepositional phrase.

PRACTICE 8

In the following sentences, cross out the relative dependent clauses between the subject and the verb. Then underline the subject once and the verb twice. You may also cross out any prepositional phrases that appear between the subject and the verb.

1. The song that was sung by Kelly Clarkson, the first American Idol, (is/are) number one on the radio.

2. Sandy, who sang at Manny's wedding, (has/have) found her soul mate.

3. The car, which is usually occupying my parking space, (was/were) towed away yesterday.

4. One of the women who (has/have) been taking me to work (has/have) just resigned.

5. Lewis, who is a new employee at Burger King, (know/knows) how to charm customers.

6. The book and video that Ana checked out (has/have) been long overdue.

7. This class is not for people who (is/are) not willing to study.

8. Mario, who is the lead singer of the rock band, (decide/decides) to quit.

9. The ideas, which were thrown out at the meeting, (has/have) been adopted by the congregation.

10. Have you heard from the students who (is/are) supposed to do their presentation?

REVIEW

Revise the following sentences by crossing out the incorrect verb form and writing the correct form above it. If a sentence is correct, write C.

1. Neither the teacher nor the students likes the six-week classes.

2. Some styles that is favorite among American women is despised in other cultures.

3. Most college students who works don't do well in their studies.

4. There has been numerous calls for my black Toyota that's for sale.

5. All the equipment are ready to be placed on the shelves.

6. None of the students were missing today although it rained heavily.

7. Is Soraya and Manny going to register for their classes today?

8. Most of the mail on the table belongs to me.

9. Neither of my colleagues has agreed to meet with me.

10. The audience is going their separate ways.

11. Over there is the bills that must be paid this month.

12. (Has/Have) either the principal or the teachers come to an agreement regarding cheating.

13. Where is the dress and coat that I should take to the cleaners today?

14. The study that was done by the scientists prove that people who exercise live longer.

15. Gender discrimination in the corporate world have not been a big problem these days.

16. Some of your ideas seems logical, but I have to discuss them with my supervisor.

17. The jury have been deliberating for three days now.

18. Politics are the one thing I don't discuss.

19. The scissors is lying on my bed.

20. All I have in my purse are $60.

14

Concise Writing

Writing concisely means eliminating every word, phrase or sentence that is unnecessary, confusing or weak. In fact, eliminating wordiness should be a main goal for writers, especially for those writing for the general public (i.e. ads, newspapers). Using only a few words to say something simple is a challenge for some writers because some people think that using long sentences and words is impressive to readers. However, just the opposite is true. Readers want to understand your point, and lots of words may distract them rather than impress them. On the other hand, sentences should not be too elementary, so use vocabulary that is appropriate for your audience without being vague, repetitious or pompous.

SEVEN THINGS TO AVOID

Here are *seven* things to avoid to keep your writing concise:

Vague Expressions

Avoid **vague expressions** like the word *thing*. These words have no specific meaning for the reader. They are especially useless in descriptive writing. The word *thing*, in particular, is useless. It indicates that the writer was too lazy to use a word that is specific. Other useless words: *good, bad, nice, fine, okay, normal, typical, interesting, beautiful, definitely, extremely, quite, really, somewhat, very.*

For example, instead of saying, "One must do three *things*," write, "Three steps are required."

Passive Voice

Avoid **passive voice** expressions like: *there is, there are, there was, there were, there will be.* These words have no function; they say nothing. Reword the sentence for tighter, more effective wording.

For instance, instead of saying, "There are three reasons one should improve his or her English," write, "One should improve his or her English for three reasons." Or, instead of saying, "There is hope," say, "We have hope."

Run-ons/Long Sentences

Avoid **run-ons** and **long sentences** in which the meaning is lost, confused, or buried. If possible, do not use more than 25 words in a sentence.

Wordy Phrases

Avoid **wordy phrases.** Say exactly what you want to say in the fewest possible words. Here are examples and corrections of wordy phrases:

Wordy	Concise
as a result of	because
in order to	to
whether or not	if
at this point in time	now
due to the fact	because
end result	result
two different kinds	two kinds
new innovation	innovation
in spite of the fact that	although
serious crisis	crisis
small in size	small
free gift	gift
fewer in number	fewer
as a general rule	as a rule

Avoid the following phrase in your writing:

"*In my opinion*, we should allow mercy killing; that is what I think."

Instead, say the following:

"Mercy killing should be allowed."

Saying "In my opinion," "I think," or "I believe" is unnecessary because the statement — as corrected — clearly gives the writer's opinion.

Redundancy

Redundancy is a form of wordiness. Writers often unknowingly convey the same meaning twice.

Replace the modifier with the opposite to see if the rephrase makes sense. If the change makes no sense, the original modifier was unnecessary.

Redundant	Opposite	Correct
Past History	Future History (incorrect)	History
True Fact	False Fact (incorrect)	True
Kneel Down	Kneel Up (incorrect)	Kneel
Crouched Down	Crouched Up (incorrect)	Crouched
Sad Frown	Happy Frown (incorrect)	Frown

Personal Feelings	Impersonal Feelings (incorrect)	Feelings
6 a.m. in the morning	6 a.m. at night (incorrect)	6 a.m.
Quick Second	Slow Second (incorrect)	Second

PRACTICE 1

Rewrite the following sentences to get rid of the wordiness or redundancies.

1. I have lived in the city of Miami all my life.

   _____

   _____

2. Manny shrugged his shoulder when I confronted him about cheating on the exam.

   _____

   _____

3. Sage received a free gift at the doctor's office.

   _____

   _____

4. My job is in close proximity to where I live.

   _____

   _____

5. Although Sharlene came to a complete stop at the four-way intersection, the police officer still accused her of not stopping.

   _____

   _____

6. I have never seen a tiger before in my life.

   _____

   _____

7. The car reversed back and hit Sharon's car.

_____

_____

8. The fall semester begins in the month of August.

_____

_____

9. Sydney will not know whether or not he will pass the GRE in order to go to graduate school.

_____

_____

10. Because of Alan's past criminal history, he is unable to get a job in law enforcement.

_____

_____

Clichés

A **cliché** is an overused (trite) expression that has been worn out through constant use. Clichés are common in speech, but they make your writing seem unoriginal and stale. Also, they are often an evasion of the specific details that you must work to provide in your writing. You should, then, avoid clichés and try to express your meaning in fresh, original ways.

Typical Clichés

short but sweet	last but not least	tried and true
drop in the bucket	work like a dog	a death trap
had a hard time of it	all work and no play	as buck would have it
word to the wise	it goes without saying	in the nick of time
it dawned on me	at a loss for words	add insult to injury
sigh of relief	taking a big chance	better late than never
too little, too late	took a turn for the worse	go with the flow
singing the blues	easier said than done	between a rock and a hard place
in the nick of time	on top of the world	a drop in the bucket
too close for comfort	time and time again	easier said than done
saw the light	make ends meet	calm, cool, and collected
a heart of gold	cream of the crop	too good to be true
apple of my eye	dead as a doornail	crystal clear

at the drop of a dime	eat like a bird	under the weather
burn the midnight oil	fit as a fiddle	break the ice
busy as a beaver	flat as a pancake	happy as a lark
handwriting on the wall	through thick and thin	sick as a dog
happy as a clam	on thin ice	powers that be
blind as a bat	strong as an ox	drop dead gorgeous

Practice 2

Write five cliches that you regularly use.

1. _____

2. _____

3. _____

4. _____

5. _____

Jargon

Avoid jargon, which is specialized words or phrases used by a group of people in the same trade or profession (medical, sports, technology, etc.). For example, people who work in the media might say, "We had a remote broadcast." For everyone to understand, they should say, "We had to film on location." Today, people who use social media and text messaging create their own jargon (i.e. LOL). This is referred to as "coined jargon," or newly developed terminology. Jargon is only acceptable if you are writing for or to a specific group, such as computer technicians or sports enthusiasts who have the same level of understanding of that specialized terminology.

Here are examples of jargon in different professions:

Field	Jargon
Advertising	blast, brand, CPC, CPM
Broadcasting	dead air, cue, trailer
Banking	APR, prime rate, stop order
Education	AYP, categorical aid, dropout
Legal	breach, casualty, liability
Medical	EMT, PRN, bolus, stat
Military	ground force, intelligence, ammo
Political	lobbyist, left/right wing, soap box
Journalism	lead, graph, teaser, cutline
Religious	born again, salvation, outreach
Sports	trade, Hail Mary, brick, shutout

Euphemisms

A **euphemism** is another form of jargon. A euphemism is an expression intended to be less offensive, disturbing, or troubling than the word or phrase it replaces. In other words, it is sometimes regarded as a more polite way of saying something.

Common Term	**Euphemism**
drugs	illegal substances
drug addict	substance abuser
old person	senior citizen
police	law enforcement officer
poor	underprivileged
fired	removed from duty
old age	golden age; golden years
money	funds
toilet	restroom
prison	correctional facility
used cars	pre-owned vehicles
died	passed away

Note: When a word or phrase is deliberately used to hide or distort the truth, it is called **doublespeak**. For example, phrases like *layoff*, *downsizing*, *right-sizing*, and *headcount adjustment*, may be used instead of *firing* in the corporate business arena.

REVIEW

On a separate sheet of paper if necessary, revise the following sentences by getting rid of wordiness, including redundancies, clichés, and jargons:

1. I have lived in the state of California for several years.

2. Now that I am through with my 20-page project, I can certainly breathe a sigh of relief.

3. When I reversed back, I hit a light pole.

4. Alden, the last point that I am trying to make is that your paper has too many mechanical errors.

5. There are several reasons why the government should fix the homeless problem in this society of ours.

6. The thing I have been trying to get across to you is that justice is too slow.

7. My friend's three children are retarded.

8. As a general rule, I eat breakfast at 7 a.m. in the morning.

9. My brother's girlfriend is as dumb as an ox.

10. On Sunday, I had an unexpected surprise from a woman who used to attend the same church as I did.

11. My uncle Robert is as blind as a bat.

12. A lazy individual is always quick to make excuses.

13. The police gave me a ticket this morning because I did not come to a complete stop at the stop sign.

14. In my personal opinion, the student cheated on the test.

15. My grandson plays several different kinds of sports like soccer, football and baseball.

16. At this point and time in my life, I should stop working so much.

17. My friend Ana had a big smile on her face when I ran into her while shopping.

18. The adulterous woman was shot and killed by her husband.

19. The 15-year-old boy was holding a pistol in his right hand when the police approached him.

20. The new semester will start in the month of January.

21. Althea is a very unique individual.

22. Andrea moved her mother from the hospital to an old person's home.

23. I live in close proximity to my job.

24. There are a whole lot of people who never read a book from cover to cover.

25. I have not decided whether or not I will go to Europe this year.

UNIT IV

Building Blocks:
PARAGRAPH AND ESSAY DEVELOPMENT

15

The Writing Process

Writing effectively means writing for your audience. Thus, this unit is organized to develop specific forms of writing. First, in Unit 3, you'll learn the five steps to the writing process and how missing critical steps can affect the outcome of your work. Then you will learn how to write for your target audience or identify your audience; how to determine the purpose of your message to properly classify your writing; and how to determine the most effective tone of your writing.

Effective writing cannot be done in a hurry. It takes time and good planning. In fact, good writers are never satisfied with their writing because they are always seeking ways to make their writing better. The art of effective writing might be lengthy; however, in the end, you will produce better pieces of writing. No matter what type of writing you are doing, use the following four steps to help you generate ideas on the topic:

1. **Prewriting**
2. **Drafting**
3. **Revising**
4. **Editing**

PREWRITING

Prewriting refers to whatever writing technique you use before you write the first draft of your paper. Writing is definitely a journey, and good planning is the key to aid you in your journey to become a better writer. The following prewriting steps will aid you in your journey to become a better writer:

- Freewriting
- Questioning
- Brainstorming
- Clustering or Mapping
- Keeping a Journal
- Outlining

Freewriting

Freewriting is a technique that is used to jot down ideas about your given topic. For about five to ten minutes, you would quickly jot down anything that comes to mind about your topic without stopping or thinking about grammar, punctuation, or spelling. Once you are through jotting down your ideas, you would sort through them and identify the ones that pertain to your topic. If you got stuck, you would repeat an idea you have already written. Whatever the case may be, the idea is not to stop writing.

Questioning

Questioning is a technique journalists use to cover the important elements in a news story. It is known as **the five *Ws* and one *H***: *Who? What? Where? Why? When? How?* Many writing teachers also use this technique to make sure students cover the important elements in the topics about which they are writing.

Brainstorming

Like freewriting, brainstorming is another simple prewriting technique that helps writers to overcome the writers' block they encounter during writing. It involves jotting down whatever comes to mind on a specific topic. The one difference between free writing and brainstorming is that with brainstorming, you can pause and think about ideas that deal with your topic whereas with free writing, you should not stop.

This technique is not only used for college papers, but it is also used in large or small group settings to generate ideas on specific topics. At times, we all encounter writers' block, so brainstorming is a useful technique to break through that barrier.

To brainstorm, you should follow these simple steps:

1. First, get a blank sheet of paper.
2. Next, write your topic on the paper.
3. Then, jot down everything that comes to mind about the topic.
4. Don't worry about grammar, punctuation, spelling, or editing. Just write.
5. Once you are through, look at the list and organize the points you would use in your paper in a logical manner.

Clustering or Mapping

Clustering or mapping is still another common prewriting technique that helps writers to organize their thoughts. It is an easy technique because there is no right or wrong way to do it:

To cluster or map, you should follow these simple steps:

1. First, get a blank sheet of paper.
2. In the center of the paper, draw a circle.
3. Write the name of your subject in the circle.
4. Then draw lines from the center circle to connect to new circles that relate to your subject.
5. Continue connecting new circles using lines to show how they relate to each other.
6. Don't be afraid to draw new circles because there is no wrong way.

Keeping a Journal

Writing in your journal for about ten to 15 minutes everyday is one way to improve your writing skills. For one thing, it builds your confidence because the more you write, the better you will become. Since it is freewriting, you don't have to worry about the mechanics of writing.

Use a small notebook and write about those innermost secrets that you don't want to discuss with others. It will free your mind, and in the meantime, you will be developing a good habit of writing everyday, which will eventually help you become a better writer. If you don't have secrets, write about family, friends, school, or daily encounters. Whatever you do, write!

Many authors will tell you that their journals are always close to them because as soon as a thought creeps into their minds, they jot it down. Several authors testify that they use their journals to write the stories of their lives and then publish them.

Outlining

An outline is a detailed plan that can make the writing of a composition or report much easier. There are *two* types: a **topical outline** and a **sentence outline**.

A **topical outline** has no main idea or subtopics, and the details are expressed in a single word or phrases. Also, it has no ending punctuation. The topical outline is most times used for paragraphs.

Here's an example of a **topical** outline:

The Internet

    I. Information
        A. Dictionary/Encyclopedia
        B. News
        C. Weather

    II. Entertainment
        A. Games
        B. Music
        C. Videos
        D. Shopping

    III. Communication
        A. Email
        B. Social Networking Websites
            1. Facebook
            2. My Space
            3. Twitter

Note: Here are some important points about a **topical** outline:

- The first word of the numerals, letters, and numbers begin with a capital letter.
- The Roman numerals, letters, and numbers are followed by a period.
- If there is an A, there must be a B.
- If there is a 1, there must be a 2.
- The points in your paper must be presented exactly as they are written in the outline.

A **sentence outline**, on the other hand, is expressed in complete sentences. It has a topic sentence, and all the sentences support the topic sentence.

Here's a sample **sentence** outline:

The Most Important Person in My Life

My mother is the most important in my life because she is caring, supportive and loving.

I. Caring

    A. She always wants to know where I am going and with whom I am going.

    B. Whenever I am studyding, she prepares my meals.

    C. When I am out with my friends, she constantly texts me to find out what time I will be arriving home.

II. Supportive

    A. When I received my acceptance letter for college, she drove me to the campus to see an advisor.

    B. She loaned me money to purchase my books until my financial aid was approved.

    C. Before classes started, she offered to go to the college with me to locate my classrooms.

III. Loving

    A. Every night before I go to bed, she hugs and kisses me.

    B. Every year she gives me a surprise birthday party.

    C. Whenever she goes shopping, she buys me gifts, writes me notes telling me how much she loves me, and then she places them in the middle of my bed.

IV. Unquestionably, my mother cares about my welfare, she supports me in all my endeavors, and she loves me beyond measure. Certainly, she is one of a kind.

Note: Here are some very important points about a sentence outline:

- The three main supporting points to be covered in Roman numerals I, II, and III must be parallel. For example, in the above outline, the first point, "caring," is an adjective, so the other two points, "supportive" and "loving," are also adjectives. In other words, they are the same part of speech.
- The topic sentence for each paragraph could be written out or expressed in one word.

DRAFTING

Drafting simply means writing the first draft of your paper. Bear in mind that good writing takes time and that you might change your mind about a piece of writing several times before you feel satisfied. That's the main purpose of the draft. It will go through several changes or revisions, so try to get all your ideas down in the first draft. There will be plenty of opportunities for improvement in subsequent drafts. Some writers will even go back and revise their outlines after the first draft.

Revising

Revising occurs after writing the first draft of your paper. It is the key to writing well because this is where you make changes to your paper to make sure it communicates to the reader exactly what you intended it to say. This means you might have to delete ideas, add ideas, switch ideas, or even paragraphs.

Before you do so, however, it is always best to read your paper aloud. Doing so will enable you to hear some of the obvious errors. Asking someone to read your paper is also a good idea because others can most times see what you can't see.

Watch out for the following:

- Wordiness and long sentences that could be shortened. Long sentences can create fragments or run-on sentences.
- Passive construction:

> **Passive Construction**: My car **was hit** by a tree. (The action is done to the subject.)
>
> **Active Construction**: My car **hit** a tree. (The subject did the action.)

Let the subject do the action rather than the action be done to the subject. Passive construction will certainly make your writing assignments dull.

Editing

Editing is a term that is confused with revision. However, editing only involves finding and correcting errors you have made in grammar, punctuation, and spelling after you have revised your writing for content or information. This represents the last phase of the writing process.

Some people hire professional editors or proofreaders. Meanwhile, others will get assistance from relatives, friends and associates who have an elevated level of knowledge in the topic and/or English. Writers who skip the editing phase typically regret it after getting feedback from instructors or employers. No one is perfect, so having a second pair of eyes to review your work makes sense for even the best writers.

Based on what you're writing, editing may need to conform to specific standards for writing and designing your document. In other words, certain occupations or fields may require how the writing is presented, including how a source is referenced or margins are set. Here are some examples of style guides or manuals:

Type of Writing	Style Guide
News Articles	*Associated Press Stylebook*
Books	*Chicago Manual of Style*
General	*The Elements of Style*
Research Papers	*MLA Handbook for Writers of Research Papers*
	Publication Manual of the American Psychological Association
	Manual for Writers of Research Papers, Theses, and Dissertations (Turabian)

Editing marks are another consideration. Each style guide may have slightly different marks, but by in large, all the marks serve the same function. The following are commonly used editing marks when proofreading writing:

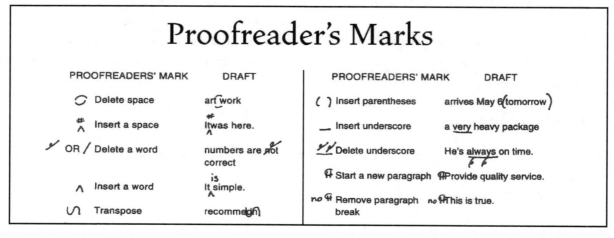

Proofreader's Marks

PROOFREADERS' MARK		DRAFT	PROOFREADERS' MARK		DRAFT
◯	Delete space	art work	( )	Insert parentheses	arrives May 6 (tomorrow)
#	Insert a space	Itwas here.	___	Insert underscore	a very heavy package
OR /	Delete a word	numbers are not correct		Delete underscore	He's always on time.
∧	Insert a word	It simple. (is)		Start a new paragraph	Provide quality service.
∽	Transpose	recommend	no	Remove paragraph break	no This is true.

From the Society of Writers, Editors & Translators

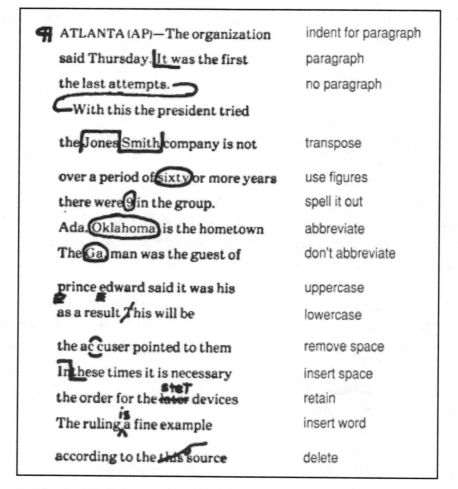

Text	Mark
¶ ATLANTA (AP)—The organization	indent for paragraph
said Thursday. It was the first	paragraph
the last attempts.	no paragraph
With this the president tried	
the Jones Smith company is not	transpose
over a period of sixty or more years	use figures
there were 9 in the group.	spell it out
Ada, Oklahoma is the hometown	abbreviate
The Ga. man was the guest of	don't abbreviate
prince edward said it was his	uppercase
as a result This will be	lowercase
the ac cuser pointed to them	remove space
In these times it is necessary	insert space
the order for the later devices (stet)	retain
The ruling a fine example (is)	insert word
according to the this source	delete

Proofreaders' Marks from the Associated Press Stylebook

REVIEW

FREEWRITING

Write non-stop for 10 minutes on one of the following subjects:

- Good study habits
- What makes you a unique student
- Someone who has made a great impact on your community or family
- An electronic device that has revolutionized the world

_____

_____

_____

_____

_____

_____

_____

_____

_____

_____

_____

_____

_____

_____

_____

_____

_____

_____

_____

_____

_____

Prewriting

QUESTIONING

Generate ideas and details by asking questions about your subject. Choose one of the topics from the list below, pose questions about the topic that a reader would want to know, and then answer the question.

- Good study habits
- What makes you a unique student
- Someone who has made a great impact on your community or family
- An electronic device that has revolutionized the world

Who? _____

Answer_____

_____

What?_____

Answer_____

_____

When? _____

Answer_____

_____

Why? _____

Answer_____

_____

Where?_____

Answer_____

_____

How?

_____

Answer_____

_____

Prewriting

BRAINSTORMING

In no special order, brainstorm on the following topic: ***the effects of poor diet***.

_____

_____

_____

_____

_____

_____

_____

_____

_____

_____

_____

_____

_____

_____

_____

_____

_____

_____

_____

_____

_____

Prewriting

CLUSTERING or MAPPING

Here's a simple sample cluster. This could be expanded by connecting new circles.

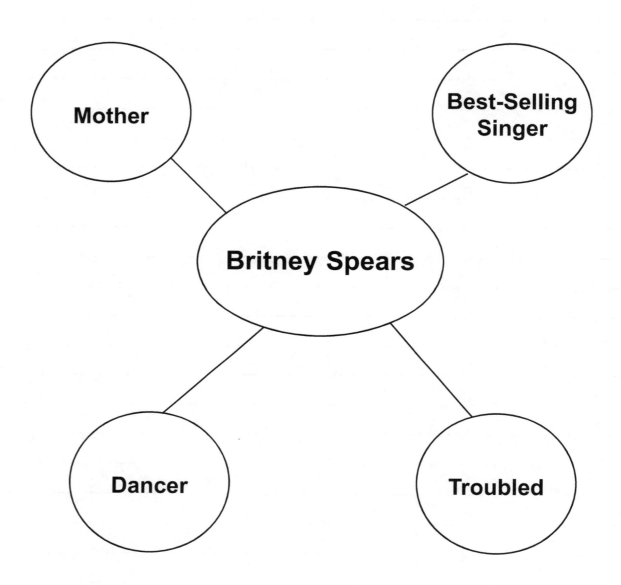

CLUSTERING or MAPPING

Now, do a cluster on the following topic: ***A Public Figure Whom You Admire.*** *Write the name of your subject in the circle below. Then draw lines from the center circle to connect to new circles that relate to your subject. Continue connecting new circles using lines to show how they relate to each other. There is no wrong way to do this.*

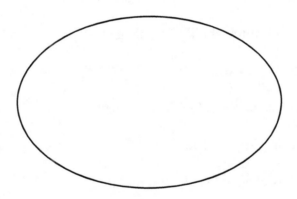

Prewriting

KEEPING A JOURNAL

Each day, write on one of the following topics. You do not have to write them in order.

1.   Significant historical events of your time (Sept. 11, etc.) and how they affected you.

2.   Your favorite family event.

3.   What do you do in your spare time?

4.   Where would you like to be five years from now?

5.   What do you like or don't like about college?

6.   A modern technological device that has changed your life.

7.   A social problem that you think should be changed.

8.   The most important person in your life.

9.   Three characteristics of a successful college student.

10.   The happiest or worst day of your life.

11.   A habit of yours that has changed since you matured.

12.   A place you enjoy visiting.

13.   Your ideal mate.

14.   The characteristics of a good parent.

15.   A habit of someone that has annoyed you.

16.   A celebrity or public official whom you think is a positive or negative role model.

17.   Should smoking be banned from public places?

18.   If you were president of United States, what laws would you change or put in place?

19.   An important quality or skill that everyone should possess.

20.   Three important traits a friend should possess.

Prewriting

OUTLINING

*Compose a **topical outline** on one of the following topics or choose your own:*

- A person who has made a great impact on society
- A historical event of your time
- Benefits of good customer service

_____

_____

_____

_____

_____

_____

_____

_____

_____

_____

_____

_____

_____

_____

_____

_____

_____

_____

Prewriting

OUTLINING

*Compose a **sentence outline** on one of the following topics or choose your own:*

- An electronic device you cannot live without
- Something in the news about which you feel strongly
- An animal that fascinates you

_____

_____

_____

_____

_____

_____

_____

_____

_____

_____

_____

_____

_____

_____

_____

_____

_____

_____

_____

_____

_____

_____

16

The Paragraph

What is a Paragraph?

A paragraph is comprised of a sequence of related sentences, which focus on one topic. In a five-paragraph academic-style essay, the paragraph is the building block. If you know how to write the first paragraph well, the other paragraphs should be quite simple to write. Therefore, learning how to write an effective paragraph is one of the keys to good writing.

A well-written, academic-style paragraph consists of several elements:

- Topic sentence
- Supporting details
- Conclusion
- Unity
- Coherence

THE TOPIC SENTENCE

The topic sentence introduces the paragraph and discusses the main point or topic of it. This sentence must be general enough to summarize the details in the paragraph. It could be placed anywhere in the paragraph. However, it is always a better choice to place it at the beginning of the paragraph. When it is placed at the beginning of the paragraph, it alerts the reader of what is to come.

A good topic sentence has the following:

- Presents the main idea, point or topic of a paragraph or essay
- Is the first sentence in a paragraph or essay (beginning writers), but it can be placed anywhere in a paragraph (advanced writers)
- As the first sentence of an essay, it complements the title directly by using words from the title (beginning writers) or it reintroduces the title indirectly by implying about its topic (advanced writers)
- Establishes the subject matter and tone for subsequent sentences in a paragraph
- Provides a transition from the previous paragraph within an essay.
- Never simply state a fact or an opinion

PRACTICE 1

Revise the following sentences to create effective topic sentences. For example:

Weak: Henry Ford created the Model T automobile.

Revision: Henry Ford popularized the assembly line concept used for mass production of automobiles.

1.   I think dogs make better pets than cats.

_____

_____

2.   The country is still divided along party lines.

_____

_____

3.   Having children changes people.

_____

_____

4.   Cooking is a great way to relax and bond with the family.

_____

_____

5.   Flowers make the best gifts.

_____

_____

SUPPORTING DETAILS

The job of the supporting details is to develop the topic sentence. Supporting details consist of specific details, examples, or reasons that relate to the main point of the paragraph. When writers make a point in the topic sentence, they use supporting details to clarify or prove their point. There are *two* types of supporting details: *major* and *minor*. The major details focus on the topic sentence whereas the minor details further explain the major details. In essays and longer works like books and extended articles, various types of details like statistics and studies are included.

PRACTICE 2

Based on the topic sentences that you wrote in Practice 1, write at least two (2) supporting details that correspond with each one. For example:

Topic Sentence: The Model T revolutionized transportation and American industry.

Support: (1) Simple and inexpensive to drive, becoming the first affordable car for the masses

(2) First mass produced automobile on an assembly line with all interchangeable parts

1.

_____

_____

2.

_____

_____

3.

_____

_____

4.

_____

_____

5.

_____

_____

THE CONCLUSION _____

The conclusion is simply a summary of the main points in the paragraph. Do not introduce any new ideas in the conclusion. While summarizing the main points is one way to conclude, writers may also end with a powerful quote. Whatever ending you choose, try to leave the reader with a lasting impression rather than introducing new material or new ideas on the subject.

UNITY

Unity means that no supporting details that are not related to the topic should appear in the paragraph. A paragraph should only contain pertinent details that are significant to the topic. For instance, if you are writing about oranges, do not include peaches or bananas. Every sentence should be about the orange. The following paragraph has unity because all the details are related to the topic sentence.

> **My sister Carla is a model student**. As soon as she arrives home from school, she reads over her class notes. Afterward, she types her notes. Then, she will read and take notes on her assigned homework. Before every test, she goes to library to review all her notes. At the crack of dawn the next day, she will review her notes again. **It's no wonder she gets all A's in her classes.**

COHERENCE

Coherence refers to the smooth arrangement or organization of the supporting details in a paragraph or essay. The sentences must be arranged in a manner so that they are not confusing and make clear sense as one reads.

You can arrange information according to:

- **Chronological order** – how events occurred or would occur in time (hours, days, years, etc.).
- **Spatial order** – where things are physically placed or their spatial relationship (left to right, north to south, etc.)
- **Emphatic order** – their importance, meaning you can begin with the least important idea and build upon it until you get to the most important idea (inverted pyramid) or you can begin with the most important idea and end with the least important idea (pyramid)
- **Topical order** – how something naturally occurs (problem-solution, classification, cause-effect, etc.)

Various techniques can be used to help achieve coherence, including:

- Transitional expressions (see chart below)
- Repeating key words from previous sentences
- Using synonyms to refer to key words in previous sentences
- Using words that are opposite to key words in previous sentences
- Using pronouns to refer to nouns in previous sentences

ORGANIZATIONAL METHOD	TRANSITIONS
Time/Process (Chronological)	*first, next, then, before, after, later, suddenly*
Location/Place (Spatial)	*above, below, behind, near, beside, next to, on the left/right*
Importance (Emphatic)	*more/most importantly, mainly, primarily, first and foremost*
Subject (Topical)	*therefore, consequently, as a result, as such, in addition, moreover, furthermore, besides*

Look again at the above paragraph about Carla. It is both unified and coherent.

Practice 3

The following paragraph contains sentences that are irrelevant or unnecessary to the main point of the paragraph. To maintain paragraph unity, eliminate all such sentences by drawing a line through them.

The human body is made up of a number of different systems that have separate functions but work together. Each system is made up of organs. The skeletal system supports the body and protects the internal organs such as the lungs, which is part of the respiratory system. The respiratory system enables us to breathe and take oxygen into the blood. The circulatory system is made up of the vessels and the muscles that help to control the flow of the blood around the body. The heart is an organ in the circulatory system. The muscular system is less complicated than the other systems. The digestive system breaks down and processes food. Digestion begins in the mouth. The liver functions as part of the digestive system and other systems. The lymphatic system consists of organs, ducts, and nodes that transport a clear fluid called lymph. This fluid distributes immune cells called lymphocytes, which protect the body against antigens (viruses, bacteria, etc.). The reproductive system works for the purpose of reproduction. Some of these organs are internal while others are external. This is unique. The nervous system controls the other systems and enables human beings to think, feel, hear, see, smell and taste. Some systems in the human body work against each other.

Practice 4

In the spaces below, arrange the sentences into a coherent paragraph.

(1) Once blood travels through the pulmonic valve, it enters your lungs, where the blood gets oxygen.
(2) Blood flows from your left atrium into your left ventricle, which pumps blood through the aortic valve to the aorta and out to the body.
(3) Blood enters the heart through two large veins, the inferior and superior vena cava, emptying oxygen-poor blood from the body into the right atrium.
(4) The pulmonary vein empties oxygen-rich blood, from the lungs into the left atrium.
(5) Blood flows from your right atrium into your right ventricle through and leaves the heart through the pulmonic valve into the pulmonary artery.

_____

_____

_____

_____

_____

(1)   Gordon arrived at the store at 7 a.m., according to a witness, and left five minutes later with a "swollen schoolbag."

(2)   Doug Gordon says he was hungry when he decided to stuff five packs of gum, six packs of licorice, and nine packs of lollipops in his backpack.

(3)   Local officials want to pass a law that prohibits unaccompanied youth under 16 in retail stores.

(4)   An 11-year-old stole 20 packs of candy yesterday from a gas station convenience store in downtown Detroit.

(5)   Det. Karen White says she believes the boy was trying to take the candy to sell at school that day.

_____

_____

_____

_____

_____

_____

(1)   Start the engine and let it idle for about five minutes, looking for leaks.

(2)   Slip the oil filter wrench over oil filter. Turn it counterclockwise to loosen it and then do the rest by hand.

(3)   Now jack up the car if necessary to slide under the car and locate the oil drain plug, which may be labeled "drain plug.' Use a socket that looks about the same size as the nut to loosen it, turning counter-clockwise. Get the oil drain pan and slide it under the drain plug.

(4)   Drive around the neighborhood to get the engine warm. Drive the vehicle far enough and long enough so that the temperature gauge begins to register.

(5)   After allowing the oil to drain, install the filter and then use a funnel to add three to four quarts of oil.

_____

_____

_____

_____

_____

_____

THE TITLE

The title of a paper is typically created once your writing is revised at least once. This is done because writers tend to change the theme, direction or even the subject of a paper once they begin writing. Because titles are often drawn directly from the text, waiting until the content is finished or almost finished makes the most sense. Sometimes writers will initially create what's called a **"working title"** until they decide on a final version. For instance, a working title may be "Pets Make the Best Friends." The writer may decide that writing about pets is too broad and change the title to "Cats Make the Best Friends."

The title's purpose is to:

- Announce the topic of the paper
- Imply the type of paper, as well as its tone
- Create interest in the paper or grab the reader's attention

Titles can be divided into two types: (1) explicit or concrete; and (2) implicit or abstract. *"How to Change a Tire"* is explicit, meaning the subject is clearly understood. *"Keeping It Moving"* is implicit, meaning the subject would have to be deduced. Titles that are abstract are done for reader appeal and usually have a **subtitle**, which is almost always explicit. Explicit titles clearly announce the subject and theme of the paper.

Steps to writing a title:

1. Use a sentence or phrase from your paper that could serve as a title
2. Remove extraneous words that don't help to convey the subject
3. If possible, use action verbs that create an image in the reader's mind
4. Write both an explicit and implicit version of the title
5. If applicable, write the title as both a question and a statement
6. Decide which version is best by reading them aloud and also asking others' opinion

Practice 5

Create titles based on the following topic sentences. Answers will vary.

1. Finding a topic is the most difficult part of writing.

_____

2. Attention Deficit Hyperactive Disorder (ADHD) is a mysterious condition.

_____

3. Teaching has become more about testing than learning.

_____

4.   Where are the "weapons of mass destruction?"

_____

5.   My favorite place has always been my grandmother's house.

_____

Practice 6

*Create a title **with a subtitle** based on the following topic sentences. Answers will vary.*

1.   American media has had a great impact on other cultures, especially young people.

_____

_____

2.   According to a Gallup poll, just 39% of Americans say they believe in evolution, but that number increases as people attain more education.

_____

_____

3.   New technology has changed marketing techniques.

_____

_____

What should be the length of a paragraph?

This is a common question for most writers. Don't agonize over the length of a paragraph. Except for newspaper writing, which uses one or two sentences in a paragraph for style and readability purpose, use at least five sentences in a paragraph. It can be monotonous if your paragraphs are too short or all the same length. It might be that they are lacking proper development. On the other hand, if your paragraphs are too long, they can cause the reader to lose focus and interest. Overall, make sure the central point of your paragraph is well developed. Of utmost importance, make sure each paragraph in your essays or longer works focus on a new idea.

17

The Essay

What is an essay?

An essay, also called a composition, typically consists of *five or more* paragraphs. Just as a paragraph is comprised of a sequence of related sentences that focus on one topic, the essay is also a group of paragraphs that focuses on a single topic. It has three parts: an introduction with a thesis, the body paragraphs and a conclusion. If you have studied the preceding chapter on how to write a good paragraph, you should have no problem writing an essay. Here's an outline of what the essay should look like:

I.   Introduction + thesis
II. Body Paragraph 1
III. Body Paragraph 2
IV. Body Paragraph 3
V.   Conclusion

THE INTRODUCTORY PARAGRAPH _____

The **introductory paragraph** is one of the most important paragraphs in an essay. It is the paragraph that introduces the topic and holds the key to what will be discussed in the three body paragraphs. Think of the introduction as someone whom you would introduce to speak at a special function. The audience would want to know some background information about this individual and the main points of his or her discussion. So it is with the introduction of an essay. As soon as the reader looks at the introduction, it should give him or her a preview of the writer's focal points of the essay.

Here's a caution about the introduction: Do not make announcements. Your reader will determine the purpose of your writing in the thesis without you announcing what the paper will be about. Avoid the following statements:

- *In this essay, I will [talk about]...[discuss]...[prove]...*
- *In the following paragraphs, I will [talk about]...[discuss]...[prove]...*
- *I have chosen to talk about ...*

How Do I Begin the Introduction?

This is a common question that writers ask, but there is no right answer to this question. Depending on your topic, you may use one of the following methods:

- anecdote (story that illustrates a point)
- interesting, relevant quotation
- question for which you will provide an answer
- definition of the intended topic
- dialogue that illustrates a point
- background information of the topic

The arrangement of sentences in an introduction can move from general to specific. Begin the introduction with general references to the topic and then break it down into specific examples. For instance:

Footwear $\longrightarrow$ shoes $\longrightarrow$ casual shoes $\longrightarrow$ sneakers $\longrightarrow$ Air Jordans

Practice 1

Using a couple of sentences, write an introduction to an essay on the following topics. First, name the type or method of introduction you will use, and then write one introduction for each topic. Don't use the same method twice or forget your topic sentence.

Topics:

       Benefits of Exercise

       Money Can Be a Blessing and/or Curse

       High School Cliques

       What is Love?

       Learning from Parents

       Deciding on a Career

1. Topic _____

Method _____

Introduction _____

_____

_____

_____

_____

_____

2. Topic _____

Method _____

Introduction _____

_____

_____

_____

_____

_____

3. Topic _____

Method _____

Introduction _____

_____

_____

_____

_____

THE THESIS STATEMENT _____

The thesis statement is the most important sentence in an essay. It is the main or controlling idea of your essay. It must state your opinion about your chosen subject or topic, and it is usually placed at the *end of the introductory paragraph*. Its main purpose should aim at doing *three* things:

- Convince readers of something, change their minds about something, or urge them to do something
- Address a problem for which no easy solution exists, or ask a question to which no absolute answer exists
- Present a position whereby readers could disagree

Overall, a good thesis statement will accomplish all three goals.

For beginners, the thesis should be a *single sentence* with three parts:

Topic: identifies the writer's subject, usually the topic of the paper itself
Point: identifies writer's position
Slant: provides a distinct reason for writer's position

	Topic	Point	Slant
Broad:	Reading	is the most enjoyable leisure activity	because it stimulates the mind.
Specific:	Mysteries	maintain readers' interest better than any other genre of books	because they generate mental pictures of the characters and places, offer suspense, and have a surprise ending.

You may decide to write a **stated thesis statement** in parallel form with *three* points, which are called the *points of orientation*. These three points should be developed to prove or defend your opinion. The three points in the thesis statement should be discussed in body paragraphs 2, 3, and 4, respectively.

Example: Reading is my favorite activity because it **relaxes me**, **challenges me**, and **motivates me**.
(Each of these points of orientation will become a paragraph.)

Note: Notice that in the thesis statement above, all three points have the same parallel structure. This means that all three points are phrases: *relaxes me*, *challenges me*, and *motivates me*.

A perfect parallel structure is not always possible. In this case, you may decide *not* to list the points and use the **unstated** method.

Example: Reading is my favorite activity for several reasons.

Practice 2

Using the three goals stated previously, write your position on each of the following subjects:

1. GUN CONTROL - Automatic rifles should be banned in the United States.

2. IMMIGRATION -

3. SMOKING -

4. DRUGS -

5. CAPITAL PUNISHMENT -
A thesis statement can be based on a known fact or personal observation.

Examples:
Topic Sentence (Fact):   LeBron James was drafted to the NBA from high school as a number one pick.
Thesis (Opinion):   LeBron James is the best basketball player in the NBA.
Thesis (Observation):   Many people from Cleveland say they will never forgive LeBron James for leaving.

Practice 3

Use each of the following topic sentences to create a "related" thesis.

Topic Sentence: Couples are being counseled while dating as much as they are in marriage.
Thesis:

_____

_____

Topic Sentence: Because of the economy, many unemployed people are going back to school.
Thesis:

_____

_____

Topic Sentence: Pop music is difficult to define.
Thesis:

_____

_____

Topic Sentence: Stem cells are seen by many researchers as having virtually unlimited capabilities in treating and curing many diseases and disorders.
Thesis:

_____

_____

Topic Sentence: Everyone has an equal voice in electing the people who serve in public office.
Thesis:

_____

_____

THE BODY PARAGRAPHS _____

The body paragraphs consist of specific details or examples or reasons about the topic in each paragraph. Remember, each of the body paragraphs will have a different topic. In a five-paragraph essay, the body consists of three supporting paragraphs that must be presented in the same order as they are written in the thesis statement.

Using **transitions** to move from one body paragraph to another is very helpful for the reader of your paper. It signals to the reader that the previous paragraph ends and a new paragraph begins. Within the paragraph, it is also helpful to use transitions to move from one idea to another. However, do not use too many within the paragraphs.

THE CONCLUSION _____

The conclusion is the last paragraph of an essay. The concluding paragraph is just as important as the introductory paragraph. It says to the reader, "I have completed the job." The conclusion is your last chance to persuade the reader, so make sure it's effective in creatively recalling the main points, as well as ultimately convincing the reader.

As with the introduction, there is no one way to conclude the essay. However, most writers first restate the thesis statement; then they summarize each of the body paragraphs in one sentence each and then give an overall summary. Some writers even end with a powerful quote. Whatever you do, however, do not introduce any new material or new ideas on the subject. Aim at leaving your reader with a lasting impression on your topic.

A good conclusion has the following characteristics:

- Complements the introduction, sometimes ending something introduced in the beginning
- Summarizes the content and purpose of your essay, not simply repeating points
- Provides a sense of completion
- Ends with what the reader should learn from your essay or a final impression

Note: Avoid phrases such as "finally," "in conclusion," "to conclude," and "in summary"

To conclude an essay, you may use of the following methods:

- Anecdote (story that illustrates a point) that completes one that had been started in the introduction
- Redefine one of the main arguments or points
- Answer the central question in the essay
- Challenge reader to take action or begin thinking a different way
- Quotation that leaves readers with a closing message about the topic or amplifies the main point
- Outlook or possible implication of the writer's position taken in essay

Remember, the conclusion should be at least four sentences.

Here's a rough draft of a student's illustrative essay:

A Place I Would Like to Live

A place I would like to live is Venezuela, a country located in the coast of Latin America. **I would love to live in Venezuela because of its warm weather, the exotic beaches, and because my family lives there.**

To begin with, a place I would like to live in is Venezuela because of its warm weather. Unlike other countries around the world, Venezuela has only two stations— rainy or dry climate. Since Venezuela is located near the equator, the temperatures are mostly high. As a result, you are welcome to visit the beach any time of the year. For example, I went to Margarita Island during my Christmas vacation. I dedicated most of my time tanning and swimming on the beach. However, when the rainy season comes, it lasts a couple of months.

As well as the weather, I would like to live in Venezuela because of the Venezuelan exotic beaches. In support, Venezuelan exotic beaches are almost like being in paradise. Most of the pretty beaches are far away from the capital, but it is always worth the ride. Sometimes, going to the beach takes a four-hour ride. One of the beaches that I like the most is Morrocoy which has several islands that people can visit. The local fisherman offer boat rides to the islands for an affordable price. Morrocoy and its crystal-clear waters make me feel in a relaxing mood. As I tan under the bright Venezuelan sun, island workers walk by the shore selling oysters, pina coladas, and lobsters. What can be better than to lie on the warm sand and eat a fresh lobster? Another beach I like is Rio Chico, , which is a two-hour ride. My family bought a beach house there because of the number of golf clubs available. Our house is located in front of the beach. As soon as I wake up, I put on my bathing suite and scurry to the beach. I guess I never get enough of it.

Another reason why I would like to live in Venezuela is because my family lives there. Regardless of the current political situation, my family decided to stay in Venezuela and fight for their rights. I, on the other hand, moved to Miami to seek a better future. My mother and my sister live in Caracas, which is the capital of Venezuela. It is also the biggest city. Some of my mother's relatives live in Caracas too. My uncles and cousins live there also. Family is very important to me, so I like spending as much time as I can with them. In spite of the distance, we still keep in touch.

To sum up, Venezuela is a beautiful country to live in. According to each and every positive quality that Venezuela has, this country is the place I would like to live because of its warm weather, the exotic beaches, and because my family lives there.

Note: The thesis statement is not parallel. Points 1 and 2 have the same structure, but point 3 is different. Each paragraph is indented and starts with a transition.

Here's a revised copy of the same essay:

A Place I Would Like to Live

A place I would like to live is Venezuela, a country located in the coast of Latin America. **I would love to live in Venezuela because of its warm weather, the exotic beaches, and ~~because my family lives there.~~ my family ties.**

To begin with, a place I would like to live is Venezuela because of its warm weather. Unlike other countries around the world, Venezuela has only two ~~stations~~ seasons — rainy or dry climate. Since Venezuela is located near the equator, the temperature ~~are~~ is mostly high. As a result, ~~you are~~ one is welcome to visit the beach any time of the year. For example, I went to Margarita Island during my Christmas vacation. I dedicated most of my time tanning and swimming on the beach. However, when the rainy season comes, it only lasts a couple of months.

In addition to ~~As well as~~ the weather, I would like to live in Venezuela because of the Venezuelan exotic beaches. In support, Venezuelan exotic beaches are almost like being in paradise. Most of the exotic beaches are far away from the capital, but it is always worth the ride. Sometimes, going to the beach takes a four-hour ride. One of the beaches that I like the most is Morrocoy, which has several islands that people can visit. The local fisher~~man~~men offer boat rides to the islands at an affordable price. Morrocoy and its crystal-clear waters ~~make me feel~~ put me in a relaxed mood. As I tan under the bright Venezuelan sun, island workers walk by the shore selling oysters, pina coladas, and lobsters. What can be better than lying on the warm sand and eating a fresh lobster? Another beach I like is Rio Chico, which is a two-hour ride. My family bought a beach house there because of the number of golf clubs available. Our house is located in front of the beach. Therefore, every morning as soon as I wake up, I put on my bathing ~~suite~~ suit and scurry to the beach. I guess I never get enough of it.

Another reason I would like to live in Venezuela is because of my family ties. Regardless of the current political situation, my family decided to stay in Venezuela to fight for their rights. I, on the other hand, moved to Miami to seek a better future. My mother and my sister live in Caracas, which is the capital of Venezuela. It is also the biggest city. Some of my mother's relatives live in Caracas too. My uncles and cousins live there also. Family is very important to me, so I like spending as much time as I can with them. In spite of the distance, we still keep in touch.

~~To sum up,~~ Venezuela is undoubtedly, a beautiful country in which to live. According to each and every positive quality that Venezuela has, this country is the place I would like to live because of its great weather, the beautiful coast, and ~~because my relatives live there~~ nearby relatives.

Note: The three points in the thesis now have the same parallel structure.

THE FORMAT OF THE ESSAY

Here is a summary of the components of a five-paragraph essay. Next, you will be asked to compose your own five paragraph essay.

Title

- The name you give to your essay
- Try not to use more than five words
- Should not be a complete sentence
- Should not be underlined or placed in quotation marks
- Capitalize the first and last words and all other words except articles (*a, an, the*) and prepositions that have less than 5 letters

---

Introduction

- Begins with an interesting opening sentence
- Ends with a thesis statement that expresses the main idea of your paper

---

First Body paragraph

- Begins with a topic sentence that introduces the first point
- Presents examples and specific details that develop the first point

---

Second Body Paragraph

- Begins with a topic sentence that introduces the second point
- Presents examples and specific details that develop the second point

---

Third Body Paragraph

- Begins with a topic sentence that introduces the third point
- Presents examples and specific details that develop the third point

---

Conclusion

- Creatively or indirectly restate the main points made in the essay (at least four sentences)
- Do not introduce any new points

REVIEW

Using the above model as an example, write a five-paragraph essay on one of the following topics:

- A place you would like to visit
- The most beautiful place you have ever visited
- If you could be a celebrity for a day, who would you be?
- If you could relive one day, which one would it be?

Introduction _____

_____

_____

_____

_____

Support 1_____

_____

_____

_____

_____

Support 2_____

_____

_____

_____

_____

Support 3_____

_____

_____

_____

_____

Conclusion _____

_____

_____

_____

_____

18

Types of Paragraphs and Essays

To whom are you writing? This is an important question in writing because this will determine many factors, including your choice of words or style of writing.

AUDIENCE

You need to keep your prospective reader in mind both before and during the writing process. In college, you will basically be writing for your instructors. However, you might have to do other types of writing like business letters or even personal letters. Whatever type of writing you do, you need to know your audience. Knowing this will enable you to decide on the type of details you want to convey to your readers. Suppose you were writing on a topic about which your reader has little or no knowledge? How would you present this material so that your reader would not have to write notes all over your paper, indicating that your details are unclear? Well, your job would be to present the material as clearly as possible, give illustrations and define unfamiliar terms.

Your audience will fall into one of three categories, which are called the 3 Ps:

1. **Professional** (outside groups, organizations, etc.)
2. **Peers** (people from school, work, church, etc.)
3. **Personal** (family and friends)

The type of audience will dictate the tone of your writing.

TONE

If you are aware of the audience to whom you are writing, then you will want to use certain details, which will project a certain tone to your audience. Determining the tone in an essay is similar to detecting someone's tone of voice when speaking. The tone in writing can be humorous, sarcastic, serious, and so forth. Even punctuation signals the tone. For instance, contractions are used only for informal writing.

Suppose you were writing to your congressman or congresswoman about a dangerous intersection in your neighborhood. You would probably choose one of the following words to convince him or her that this intersection needs immediate attention:

Words That Signal Tone

amazed	doubtful	rude
angry	friendly	sarcastic
arrogant	insulting	shocked
confident	outraged	skeptical
critical	passionate	sympathetic
cynical	regretful	worried

PURPOSE

Forms of writing are classified by their purpose. Determining the purpose for which you are writing will enable you to select support information accordingly. It will also help you to make a choice as to how you will deliver your purpose to your reader. There are several purposes for which one might want to write. However, most of the writing you will do in college will be **PIE**: to persuade, to inform, or to entertain.

Persuasive writing expresses an opinion about a certain issue, idea or topic, using facts **to persuade** the reader to think, act or believe a certain way. It usually gives reasons why the writer's opinion is valid and should be favored by others. During the general election period, for example, the candidates write lots of letters to voters, giving a plethora of reasons as to why voters should vote for them. That's persuasive writing.

Informative writing, also called expository writing, is primarily used **to inform** readers about a specific topic, person, idea, or issue without giving a personal opinion. Although informative writing deals with facts, it might give readers one's personal opinion without taking sides. It is strictly objective. You will most often find this form of writing in articles and reports. On your jobs, you might receive emails or memos to inform you about changes or additions to your company. You might also receive letters from your insurance companies, informing you of changes or deletions to your policies. The information in expository writing develops the main idea and provides additional details as support, including facts and quotes.

Writing **to entertain** is quite different from informative and persuasive writing. Its main purpose is to entertain or appeal to readers' emotion. Descriptive writing is used to entertain and is found in fiction literature and advertisements. It includes lots of adjectives and figurative language, which we will cover in Unit 4. The writing is often used to produce a feeling or visual experience, allowing the reader to imagine seeing, hearing, feeling, touching, or smelling what is being described.

Some forms of writing can serve multiple purposes depending on *how* it is written. For instance, narrative writing tells a story, and it can be non-fiction (i.e. autobiographies, biographies) or non-fiction (i.e. fables, short-stories). As a form of fiction, narrative writing serves to inform. However, it serves to entertain when written as a form of non-fiction. Non-fiction narratives have a beginning (character development and introduction to the plot line), middle (conflict and climax of the story) and end (resolution of the story).

PRACTICE 1

Read the paragraph below to determine the tone of the passage. You can use the most appropriate tone from those listed in the box or you may choose your own. Then underline the words in the paragraph that best illustrate the tone.

Because Todd Davis' mother abandoned him when he was only 4, he ended up in the state's overrun foster care system. Today, at 26, Davis advocates changing public policy that affects children in foster care. Darla Smith says her mother chose to pursue a professional singing career over raising her three children 60 years ago. At 71, Smith says she understands parental abandonment and is in her 20th year of opening her home to children in the state's foster care system. Davis and Smith are encouraging individuals with a caring heart and any amount of time to make a difference in the life of a foster child.

Tone _____

Writing Tones	
Angry	Humorous
Apologetic	Motivational
Apathetic	Melancholy
Biased	Pompous
Condescending	Romantic
Cynical	Retrospective
Dogmatic	Satirical
Emotional	Sarcastic
Ethical	Serious

PRACTICE 2

Read each title and identify the author's purpose (persuade, inform or entertain).

1. "Where to Find the Best Scholarships and Grants" _____

2. "How to Dress for an Interview" _____

3. "Maybe We Should End Primary Elections" _____

4. "Mother Auctions Baby on Internet" _____

5. "Doctors Speculate about the New Health Crisis" _____

6. "Is Studying Really the Best Way to Pass a Course?" _____

7. "Is Now the Time to Buy GM Stock?" _____

8. "Boy Trains Turtle to Dance" _____

9. "The Benefits of Alternative Medicine" _____

10. "Latest Tax Hike Hurts Consumers" _____

11. "Lindsay Lohan Gets Sentenced to 90 Days in Jail" _____

12. "Investing in Real Estate is Always the Best Bet" _____

13. "Successful Writers Who Failed English" _____

14. "Who Says Carbs are Bad for You?" _____

15. "Judge Finds His Bailiff in Contempt of Court" _____

TYPES OF WRITING

In this chapter, *eight* types of paragraphs and essays will be explored.

Illustration

Illustrative writing is often used to explain a concept or situation. This type of writing requires examples to clarify the point the writer is trying to make. Here's a sample of an <u>illustrative paragraph</u>:

A Sports Figure I Admire

A sports figure I admire is John Thompson, Jr., who was the first African-American head coach to win the NCAA Men's Division I Basketball Championship in 1984 when the George-town University Hoyas defeated the University of Houston with an astounding win of 84-75. To begin with, Thompson is responsible for several black NBA stars, but two of the most notable ones are Alsonso "Zo" Mourning and Patrick Ewing. Thompson was a coach at Georgetown University where Zo played college basketball for the Georgetown University Hoyas. With the great skills Thompson instilled in Zo, he was able to play center for the NBA's Miami Heat. Moreover, Zo's perseverance on defense won him the NBA Defense of the Year twice. Another individual Thompson influenced at Georgetown University was Jamaican-born Patrick Ewing, an NBA all-Star, who played for the New York Knicks as their starting center. He also briefly played with the Seattle Superonics and Orlando Magic. In a 1997 poll when the NBA celebrated its 50th anniversary, Ewing was selected as one of the 50 greatest basketball players of all time. Undoubtedly, Thompson used his success as head coach to influence two of America's greatest athletes.

<u>**Transitions That Signal Illustration**</u>

to begin with	*to illustrate*
for example	*specifically*
for instance	*to be specific*
as an illustration	*as proof*
a case in point is	*another example of*

Now, write your own **illustrative** *paragraph on one of the following topics:*

- Smoking is dangerous.
- Education is the key to success
- Celebrities should or should not be considered role models.
- "Honesty is the best policy."
- the main reason for failure in college.
- a modern-day invention that changed your life
- a significant invention of your time.

Narration

Narrative writing tells a story, typically listing the events in chronological or time order. Narrative can be true or fictional and includes characters, a setting, plot (fiction), and theme. Within these story elements, the following questions should be answered:

> Who is involved?
> What happened?
> Where did the event occur?
> When did the event occur?

Here's a sample <u>narrative paragraph</u>.

A Childhood Memory

At 18 years old, Monica entered a beauty pageant in Jamaica. She remembers that photographers from several newspapers were taking pictures of her almost 25 years ago. As her family and friends gazed at her strutting for the camera, she felt a sense of accomplishment. What she sensed was that she had as good a chance of winning as other contestants. She could smell the victory as she walked down the runway and posed for the camera. The thought of representing her district and holding the prize money in her hand made her mouth water. She could taste the victory dinner her mother would prepare for her to celebrate this glorious victory. Her intelligence soared higher than other contestants because she was able to answer all the questions that were posed to her. So, she knew her chances of winning were great. As she floated down the runway to collect the first-prize, she could hear the victory cheers from her family and friends. As she exited the hall, she could see the cheerful crowd running up to her to hug and congratulate her.

<u>Transitions That Signal Time Order</u>

after	*finally*	*soon*	*ultimately*
as (soon as)	*later*	*subsequently*	*upon*
before	*meanwhile*	*then*	*when*
during	*next*	*now*	*while*
first (second)			

Look at the above **narrative** *paragraph and see if you can answer the following questions:*

Who is involved? _____

What happened? _____

Where did the event occur? _____

When did the event occur? _____

Using a speaker's direct words in a narrative will help to bring your story alive. Look at the following statements which are written in **direct** and **indirect** quote and see which one would be more powerful for a story:

Direct Quote
When Anthony returned from his six-week mission trip**,** his mother exclaimed, "Oh, son, I am so happy your trip went well."

Indirect Quote
When Anthony returned from his six-week mission trip, his mother told him that she was happy his trip went well.

Remember, a person's own words can convey a deeper meaning than your own words.

*Write a **narrative** paragraph on one of the following topics:*

- A significant event in your life
- The most traumatic incident in your life
- The happiest or worst day of your life
- The first day you went to high school or college
- An incident you will never forget
- A family tradition you cherish or despise

Description

Descriptive writing aims at describing a person, an object, or a place. To bring this type of writing alive, use **sensory images** (*smell, sight, touch, taste,* or *hearing*) to help readers visualize what is being described. Rather than telling your reader about the person or object that is being described, use strong *action verbs* to show your reader what the person or object looks like or is doing.

Description falls into *two* categories:

1. *Objective*
2. *Subjective*

Objective description only deals with facts. It does not add or subtract from what you are trying to describe. The facts are presented as they exist. There is no room for your opinion. Objective description is formed by using *sensory images*. On the other hand, **subjective** description, which is also known as **emotional** description, may describe the facts as the writer sees them, but he or she can inject his or her opinion about the details.

1. *Objective*:   The dogs barked until 5 a.m.
2. *Subjective*:   The insensitive dog owners allowed their dogs to bark loudly all night.

In descriptive writing, transitions play an important role. Suppose you were describing your remodeled bedroom to a friend, you would use transitions that signify *space* to show your friend where the furniture and other items in the room are located. However, if you were describing your teenage years, you would use transitions that signify *time* order.

Remember, in descriptive writing, your aim is to show and not tell. Here are examples of showing and telling:

- Jerry is in the big tree. (*telling)*
- Jerry climbed up the 15-foot elm tree. (*showing)*

Here's a sample <u>descriptive paragraph</u> using spatial order:

My Brother's Messy Room

My brother's bedroom is a mess. As soon one enters the door, he or she can see his tattered greasy, tar-looking white sneakers a few inches from the door. Near his sneakers are several pairs of dirty white socks with holes in the toes. In the middle of the room is his twin-size mahogany bed with half of the sheets on the bed and half on the floor. Behind the bed are chewing gum papers, dirty towels, jeans and shirts. To the right of his bed before the television stand on the floor are popcorns, empty beer bottles, video tapes and humungous roaches gnawing away at the moldy leftover pizzas in paper plates. To the left is his dusty four-drawer mahogany dresser with all four drawers open. On top of the dresser are his car keys, bills, his cell phone, loose change, cigarette butts, shampoo, and countless other items. Hanging from the top and bottom drawers are tee-shirts of all colors. Then in the top drawer are numerous cassette and video tapes. Surely, I have seen a lot of messy rooms, but my brother's room tops them all.

<u>Transitions That Signal Location or Order</u>

above	*in front of*	*to the right*
across from	*inside*	*to one side*
adjacent to	*in the distance*	*to the front*
before me	*nearby*	*to the rear*
below me	*next to*	*to the left*
behind	*on my left*	*to the center*
beside me	*opposite to*	*to the middle*
beyond	*beneath*	*toward*

*Now, write your own **descriptive** paragraph on one of the following topics. Be sure to use strong action verbs to show your reader what you are describing:*

- a place you visited
- your best friend's house
- your favorite teacher
- your classroom environment
- a club you frequently visit
- a restaurant you would recommend to someone

Definition

The definition paragraph consists of a key term to be defined. Its main purpose is to help readers see what the key term is. If possible, avoid using the dictionary's definition. In your own words, define the term, using examples or illustrations to make the meaning clear. You might even want your readers to know how the word came in existence.

The types of terms that are defined can include:

1. **Concrete terms**, which have a definite meaning (i.e. motorcycle, grass, knot)
2. **Abstract terms**, which depend upon an individual point of view (i.e. love, happiness, success)
3. **Phrases** (i.e. idiom, slang, slogan)
4. **Sayings** (i.e. proverb)

To ensure that readers understand what is being defined, writers will have to use lots of facts, examples or anecdotes.

Here's a sample <u>definition paragraph</u>:

What it Means to Write Your John Hancock

Have you ever heard of the term "writing your John Hancock?" Well, your John Hancock simply means to write your name. In 1737, there was a man named John Hancock, and his wife Mary had an only son whom she named John. The Hancocks lived in a small town near the city of Boston, Massachusetts. John's father died when he was a young boy. Since his mother was very poor, she asked John's uncle, Thomas Hancock, who was a rich man, to help her. Uncle Thomas took John. When John was 27 years old, his uncle died and left his fortune for him. John became well known in Boston. When Thomas Jefferson wrote the Declaration of Independence in 1776, John Hancock was the first person to sign his name in very large letters. So, the term John Hancock was named after a real man!

<u>Transitions That Signal Definition</u>

means	*consists of*
defined as	*refers to*

Define one of the following terms:

- anorexia nervosa
- bulimia nervosa
- family
- pop music
- mercy killing

Before you start, use one of the prewriting techniques to jot down what you know about the term you choose.

Comparison

In a comparison paragraph, the writer demonstrates how two people, events, objects, or ideas are alike.

Here's a sample comparison paragraph:

> My cousins Gillian and Audrey are similar in several ways. First of all, they were both cheerleaders at their high schools. Then, they both love the same types of gospel and pop music. When they go to a restaurant, they will choose the same type of food and drinks. What's even more peculiar about them is that they both majored in business administration although they went to different colleges and did not consult each other about their majors. When Gillian went to Atlanta to try out for the American Idol Show, she saw Audrey trying out, too. When Audrey had her birthday party in February, Gillian was clad in a black outfit like Audrey. It is almost scary to know that two people could be so much alike.

Transitions That Signal Comparison

another	*equally important*
as if	*in the same way, manner*
as though	*in comparison*
at the same time	*like, likewise, just like*
by the same token	*similarly*

Contrast

In a contrast paragraph, on the other hand, the writer demonstrates how two people, events, objects, or ideas are opposite to each other.

Here's a sample contrast paragraph:

> Today's family is much different from when I was growing up. When I was in elementary school, right after I reached home and said hello to my mother and put my books down, I would have to set the table as if a very important person were coming to dinner. No matter how hungry I was, I could not eat until my father arrived home and cleaned himself up. He had a special seat, and as soon as he sat, either one of my sisters or I would ring the dinner bell to signal my siblings to come to the table. As soon as the bell rang, we would scurry to the table and sit quietly with our elbows off the table until my mother served my father first and then others. We could not even talk at the dining table. Presently, however, when a child arrives home from school, he or she heads to his or her room to watch television, talk on the telephone or go on the Internet. Few families bother to sit at a table together to dine. In fact, a lot of parents do not even cook. In some households, also, every individual has to fend for himself or herself. The families of today are certainly different from the families of my era.

Here's a <u>comparison/contrast paragraph</u>:

My Two Best Friends

My two best friends Jean and Denise share several similarities but have differences. For one thing, they both have good study habits. To illustrate, Jean studies every day for about six hours; similarly, Denise studies six to eight hours per day. They both want to major in criminal justice and later go to law school. In addition, they are both from the same country, Peru. When it comes to sports, Jean likes football whereas Denise likes basketball. Also, their eating habits are completely different. While Jean is always conscientious about what she eats, Denise will eat just about anything, including raw meat! Without a doubt, the two look quite different. Jean is tall and very slender while Denise is about five feet nine inches and is grossly overweight. One last difference they share is their religious beliefs. Jean is Baptist whereas Denise is Catholic. Although these two friends share differences and similarities, they both get along very well.

Comparison or contrast can be organized in two ways:

1) Point by point: the writer addresses a series of characteristics shared by two subjects by stating one point, relating them, and then immediately moving on to the next point. This point-by-point format is like going down a checklist.

Example:
Sarah's eyes are brown, but Tom's eyes are blue. She has a degree in art, and he is a business major. Her family is from the West Coast, so she doesn't always understand his family's Southern dialect.

2) Subject by subject: one subject is thoroughly discussed before the writer moves on to the second subject. This is like writing two separate, comparative or opposing essays about the same topic.

Example:
Sarah's idea of relaxation is being away from everything in her everyday life. After work, she goes straight home, turns off her phone, and reads a book or watches her favorite TV show. She searches for travel deals online to exotic destinations where she can explore new lands and experience different cultures.

Tom, on the other hand, prefers to relax with family and close friends. Sometimes after work, he will meet some of his colleagues at a local sports bar. On holidays, he invites people to his home for elaborate parties. Everyone he knows has come to look forward to these regular events.

<u>Transitions That Signal Contrast</u>

although	*in contrast*	*still*
but	*nevertheless*	*whereas*
conversely	*on the contrary*	*yet*
however	*on the other hand*	*even though*

COMPARING and CONTRASTING

Think about two friends about whom you would like to write. Write about how these friends are both alike and different.

Friend A: _____   Friend B: _____

Before you write about your two friends, fill in the chart to describe their similarities and differences.

CHARACTERISTICS	FRIEND A	BOTH	FRIEND B
1.			
2.			
3.			
4.			
5.			

Use the completed chart to answer these questions:

6. In what two ways are your friends alike?

_____

_____

_____

7. In what two ways are they different?

_____

_____

_____

COMPARING and CONTRASTING

Use the circle diagram to help you describe the similarities and differences between:

- high school and college
- employed and unemployed
- single and married
- no car and car

Topic Sentence:

_____

_____

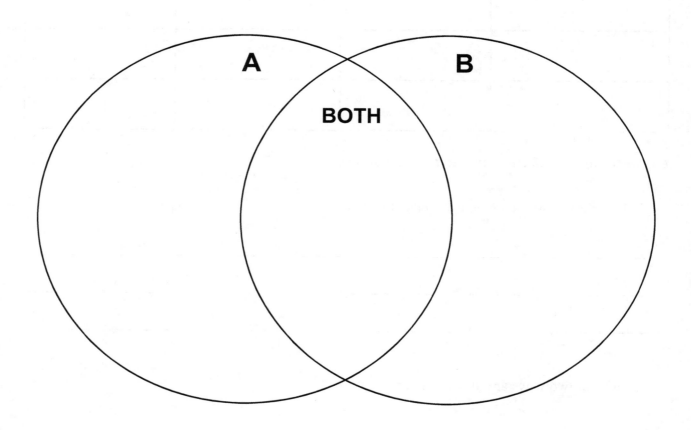

Classification

Classification writing is used to explain, describe or prove how certain groups can be broken down or divided into smaller categories. Whatever the category, each should be clearly broken down into its component parts.

Here is a sample of Joseph's <u>classification paragraph</u>:

Types of Students

       Just as education has many different outcomes, it also gives birth to various types of students. One type of student is the classic overachiever. This type of student is very intelligent and sometimes comes off as being arrogant. His or her study strategy comes to him or her as second nature, and he or she accomplishes the tasks at hand effortlessly. Another type of student is the hardworking student. This group of students studies two hours for each hour he or she is in class. Moreover, he or she is always challenged to do better. The third type of student is the one who just does enough to get by. This type of student is usually very knowledgeable about his or her subject; however, he or she is simply lazy. All he or she cares about is getting a grade without earning it. If he or she ever failed a test, he or she would blame his or her failure on his or her teacher. Life gives one many choices, and the first step to academic success is deciding what type of student you want to be.

Answer the questions in the following outline.

How many types of students are being classified?_____

List the details for the first group._____

_____

_____

List the details for the second group. _____

_____

_____

List the details for the third group._____

_____

_____

Transitions That Signal Classification

category	*first type or kind*
classified	*second type or kind*
divided	*final or last type or kind*

*Write a **classification** paragraph on one of the following topics:*

- teachers
- students at your school
- friends
- music

Persuasion

Persuasive writing is used to persuade others to change their minds or take an action about a certain issue. Most readers are only interested in their own opinion; therefore, persuasion requires strong arguments to enable others to change their minds about the issue you are trying to present. To convince your readers to change their minds about an issue, it is always helpful to use certain words like *should, should not, must, must not, ought,* and *ought not* in the topic sentence or thesis statement.

Here's a student's persuasive paragraph:

Ban Cell Phones in Classrooms

Students should not be allowed to bring cell phones to class. To begin with, cell phones are distracting. Most students will either turn them off before they get to class or keep them on silent. There are some, however, who will disrespect their professors by allowing the phone to ring during important lectures or discussions. Some will even have the audacity to walk out of the classroom and answer them. Not only should students not be allowed to bring cell phones to class because they are distracting, but they should also not bring them to class because they can be used to cheat on tests. For example, if two students have the same teachers at different times and one student took a test before the other, one may text the other friend in the middle of the test to get answers to test questions. To maintain the integrity of the learning environment, students should either keep their cell phones in their cars or not be allowed to bring them to class. Certainly, cell phones are just as distracting and inappropriate in a classroom as they can be in other public places.

*Write a **persuasive** paragraph one of the following topics:*

- Education is one of the keys to success.
- Marijuana should or should not be legalized.
- Healthcare in the United States should be free.
- Illegal aliens should or should not be returned to their countries.
- Smoking is detrimental to one's health.

Here's a student <u>persuasive essay</u>:

Capital punishment is the execution of an offender sentenced to death after conviction by a court of law of a criminal offense. Capital punishment for murder, treason, arson, and rape was widely employed in ancient Greece, and the Romans also used it for a wide range of offenses. It also has been sanctioned at one time or another by most of the world's major religions. In 1794, the U.S. state of Pennsylvania became the first jurisdiction to restrict the death penalty to first-degree murder. I believe in capital punishment because it sends a clear message to others who may want to repeat the same criminal activities, it always cuts crime down by great percentages, and it makes citizens feel safe in their community.

Capital punishment should not only be used as a punishment, but as a standard. I say this because it allows others the opportunity to reevaluate their lives, their situations, and their standing before they commit heinous crimes. Georgia law on capital punishment was challenged in Gregg v. Georgia (1976). The Court decided that the death penalty for people convicted of first-degree murder is constitutional. Similarly, the Bible advocated capital punishment as a means to eradicate people in the community who may taint or harm others. Criminals would even be left hanging or lying dead as an example. I believe capital punishment will certainly make offenders think twice after they hear about a few people being given the death penalty for the crime they committed.

It has been shown and proven that capital punishment has cut down a great deal of crime. Between 1965 and 1980 when executions were either eliminated or drastically reduced, the number of annual murders in the United States went from 9,960 to 23,040, a 131 percent increase, according to researchers. Studies show that between 3-18 lives would be saved by the execution of each convicted killer. There were 37 executions in 2008. That is the lowest number since 1994 (largely due to lethal injection). There were 52 executions in the United States in 2009, 51 by lethal injection and one by electric chair in Virginia. Texas has the largest number of executions. Texas executed 24, followed by Alabama with 6; Ohio with 5; Virginia, Oklahoma, and Georgia with 3; Florida, South Carolina and Tennessee with 2; and Missouri and Indiana with 1. In the states where capital punishment is legal, the crime has gone down tremendously.

Sentencing someone to life rather than death means these criminals will return to the community they harmed in the first place. Sometimes these criminals get out in less than ten years for serious crimes that warranted death, and many times, these criminals repeat their initial offense or commit greater offenses. Since most crime happens in poor communities, we can stop the cycle by not allowing criminals back into the community. Two forms of capital punishment are mentioned directly in the Bible, the more common being stoning, which consisted of all the people hurling stones at the condemned until he died. Furthermore, people would line up to throw stones at the offenders after a crime. There was no waiting 20 years on death row or the possibility of parole. As some may call the death penalty immoral, it allows citizens to feel at ease when they know the law is going to be carried out quickly and to the fullest to protect the innocent.

I know as the years go b y and different persons are elected into office, views of capital punishment will change, and some will try to vote to abolish capital punishment. Still, I know and believe that this severe form of punishment has benefits for even those unaffected by an offense. Some may think it is going too far by taking the life of a person, and they may be justified in their beliefs; however, the benefits outweigh the objections for sure. It will send a clear message to others, reduce crime and bring some peace back into to homes of the troubled, afflicted, poor, handicapped and anywhere else.

Process

The process paragraph is the simplest type of paragraph to write. It explains how something works, functions, or develops. This is also known as the "how to" paragraph.

Here's a sample process paragraph:

Buying a Home

Three steps are essential when buying a home. The first step in buying a home is preparing the budget. To prepare the budget, think about a down payment of at least five percent of the cost of the home. Also, think of the monthly mortgage payment and maintenance on the home and other unexpected situations. The second step is choosing the right location. In choosing the location, consider a clean neighborhood with good lighting. Also, think about proximity to your job, church, your children's school and doctor. Thinking about relatives and friends, shopping centers and banks are also important. Next is finding the right house. This step requires a lot of time. Your realtor might show you several houses, but some might not have suitable backyards or front yards. The roof and plumbing might even have defects, so take as much time as you need to find the right house. Certainly, buying a home requires preparing a budget, choosing the right location, and finding the right house after carefully considering the available options.

Answer the following questions about the above paragraph:

1. What's the first step in buying a home? _____

_____

2. What's the second step?_____

_____

3. What's the third step?_____

_____

What specific details did the writer use to develop the three steps?

Details for step 1: _____

_____

_____

Details for step 2: _____

_____

_____

Details for step 3: _____

_____

_____

Here's a student <u>process essay</u>:

How to Organize Your Room

Cleaning anything, especially a room where you sleep or work, is simple if you start out right. What you'll need to learn is how to begin the process rather than how to clean. If you are a junky person and feel comfortable in clutter, learning how to organize and clean a room is going to be a project instead of a regimen. No matter how you feel about cleaning, organizing any space can be easy once you play the right music, have the right mindset, and get the right tools.

Music can enhance or change someone's mood, so while organizing a room, first play good music that will uplift your spirit. Cleaning is therapeutic, so popping in a great tape or CD will allow the job to get done faster, thoroughly, and more effectively. When I am in my cleaning mode, I prefer to listen to a mix that I made or a Beyonce CD. While many songs talk about fixing and leaving damaged relationships, I use that to inspire my cleaning. Even if the space or room has no power outlets available, a portable CD player, or MP3 with some headphones/earphones should work fine.

Next, when organizing or simply cleaning a room, you must be prepared to throw away and let go of some old, useless or sentimental items or knick-knacks. Perhaps the easiest thing to part with is old paper. Thus, the first step to cleaning any junky room is going through all the paperwork and filing papers that are important and things that will be needed for reference in the next five-year span. Find a 13-gallon trash bag to get started throwing away any papers you haven't used or won't need in five years. The next major focus should be on organizing your clothes. The saying goes, "If it doesn't fit (your body or modern fashion), acquit it." Always try to donate them to a Salvation Army or Goodwill near you before you trash them. Maybe someone wants to wear your 10-year-old suit, but you shouldn't. Next, throw away smaller items, such as scratched CDs, outdated calendars, and broken or cheap jewelry.

Although cleaning supplies and tools may vary depending on the space or room you are cleaning, there are some basic cleaning tools that most everyone can use, such as an old rag, detergent, and a good air freshener. Get plenty of washing detergent because you probably have lots of "stuff," not just clothes, to clean. Wash the sheets on the bed if they have been there for too long (more than 30 days), or if they smell like sweat or you can see the traces of slob you left from the previous night's slumber. It's a great habit to wash your sheets every two weeks. Next, you are going to separate all dirty clothes into four piles: white, light, dark, and delicates. Some people wash jeans in a pile of by themselves, but that is solely up to you. After the clothes are separated, start washing. I like to start with the whites first. With the clothes out the way, use a rag to dust the furniture and clean the windows or glass. Vacuum the floor and spray the room with an odor blocking scent that is not too loud or perfume smelling. I prefer to use Fabreeze to Glade, but that is your choice too.

While organizing a messy room can be tedious and seems like huge job, it is actually a great outlet for stress and a time to get things updated. The actual cleaning of the room should not be your main focus. Instead, it should be on getting prepared for cleaning, which, in turn, makes the task seem easier and smoother. Be prepared to have all the tools needed for the job, including a CD with some good upbeat music. Always remember, the best tools for organizing are an open mind, proper cleaning tools, and great music.

*Now, choose one of the following topics to write a **process** paragraph:*

- how to change the tire on a car
- how to bake a cake
- how to shop for items on line
- how to develop good study habits
- how to maintain a good relationship with your parents, friends, or fiancé

Transitions That Describe a Process

after	*following*	*once*
at this point	*in the beginning*	*immediately after*
before	*in the early stages*	*shortly*
by	*in the end*	*after*
during	*last*	*soon*
eventually	*later*	*then*
finally	*meanwhile*	*today*
first	*next*	*within*

Informative

The informative paragraph or essay attempts to educate the audience on a given topic. The information is objective, so no opinions should be included. While this may seem rather simple, this type of writing can be difficult because writers have to act as experts on their topics (i.e. cancer, alternative fuel, illegal drugs).

Here's a sample informative essay:

Coronary Heart Disease

Coronary heart disease is the most common form of heart disease. In fact, it is the leading cause of death in the United States. Many people suffer from it and 500,000 Americans die from it each year. It is much more common in males in their 40s and older. However, women tend to be older and sicker when they are first treated for a heart attack. The symptoms, cause, and treatment of heart disease vary from person to person.

Coronary heart disease occurs when some of the arteries that carry blood and oxygen to the heart muscle become narrowed with fatty deposits. In this condition, fatty deposits called plaque, composed of cholesterol and fats build up on the inner walls of the coronary arteries. When arteries are narrowed, the heart is not fully supplied with the oxygen and other nutrients it needs. If an artery is completely blocked, a heart attack occurs. Chest pain or discomfort (angina) is the most common symptom. You feel this pain when the heart is not getting enough blood or oxygen. Symptoms may be very noticeable, but sometimes you can have the disease and not have any symptoms.

The tendency to develop heart disease can be genetic and can increase your risk. You are more likely to develop the condition if someone in your family has had a history of heart disease, especially if they had it before age 50. Certain lifestyle factors such as diet and stress make a big difference in reducing the risk of heart disease. Smokers have a much higher risk of heart disease than nonsmokers. Certain illnesses, including diabetes and high blood pressure, also increase your risk of coronary artery disease and heart failure.

Treatment depends on your symptoms and the severity of the disease. Lifestyle changes are typically prescribed, including reducing and avoiding salt (sodium) intake; eating foods low in saturated fats, cholesterol, and trans fat; getting regular exercise; maintaining a healthy weight; keeping your blood sugar strictly under control if you have diabetes; and giving up smoking. Doctors may prescribes medicines, such as Beta-blockers to lower the heart rate, blood pressure, and oxygen use by the heart, or suggest surgery, including angioplasty.

Because some people have different symptoms, doctors suggest people with a family history or suspicions should take an electrocardiogram (ECG), an echocardiogram, angiography or exercise stress test. As people age, doctors also suggest that they reduce or avoid known lifestyle triggers for the disease. While treatments vary as much as recovery, heart disease doesn't have to be fatal. Many people are able to live productive lives after being diagnosed and treated.

Now, choose one of the following topics to write an informative paragraph:

- donating blood
- immunization
- getting a passport
- a political party
- a specific type of cancer
- online marketing

<u>**Transitions That Introduce Information**</u>

However	*In addition to*	*Furthermore*
More importantly	*Similarly*	*Therefore*
Despite this	*In the future*	*As a result*

19

Using Sources

All information has a source. While some comes from our own ideas, other information comes from outside documents and people. Examples of sources include books; encyclopedias; websites; official records; news publications; radio and television broadcasts; government officials; and people involved with, affected by or knowledgeable about an event or issue.

Attribution means identifying the source of information. The purpose of attribution is to:

- **Distinguish Fact from Opinion**: shows that the information is subjective or questionable.
- **Protect Writer**: proves that information is derived from a source other than the writer.
- **Establish Credibility**: verifies the extent of work and quality of sources. The better the source, the more readers will trust the information.

Identifying or attributing, the source of information, is especially important for writers in avoiding plagiarism or even libel. Thus, writers must understand *when* to use attribution and *how* to use the methods of attribution (**citations** and **quotations**). Not every fact used in a story needs attribution. For example, well-known or verifiable facts need no attribution. However, use attribution when information is:

- **Debatable**: different opinions exist
- **Controversial**: could cause negative responses
- **Unverifiable**: doubtful about origin or existence
- **Literal**: exact replication used
- **Derivative**: based on another person's idea or work

COPYRIGHTED WORKS

A copyright legally protects an original artistic, literary, dramatic, or musical work from being reproduced and distributed in various forms. A **citation** is material that writers use in their own work from copyrighted sources. Writers must identify or attribute the source of the citation in order to avoid **plagiarism**. A writer can quote, summarize, or paraphrase the information, and he or she must legally identify the source of copyrighted material. Writers can quote up to 300 words from a copyrighted source freely (without having to pay the source) as long as the source gets credit. This is called "Fair Use."

STYLE GUIDES AND MANUALS

A style guide or manual is a set of standards for writing and designing documents either for general use or for a specific publication, organization or field. A style guide provides uniformity in style and formatting. Here are five such manuals:

APA: **American Psychological Association**
            psychology, education, and other social sciences

MLA: **Modern Language Association**
            literature, arts, and humanities

AMA: **American Medical Association**
            medicine, health, and biological sciences

Turabian: designed for college students to use with all subjects

Chicago: used for publishers of books and journals

Note: Copyright protection covers both published and unpublished works.

If you were asked to write a report and to use either **APA** or **MLA** style to give credit to the sources you use, here's a quick guide:

Book – One Author

APA   Johnson, A. (2005). What's Your Motivation? Atlanta: Allwrite
                Advertising and Publishing.

MLA   Johnson, Annette R. What's Your Motivation? Atlanta: Allwrite
                Advertising and Publishing, 2005.

Book – Two Authors

APA   Brown, R. L & Andrews, L. T. (1998). Successful Working Mothers.
                New York, NY: Spalding Press.

MLA   Brown, Robert L. and Larry T. Andrews. Successful Working Mothers.
                New York, NY: Spalding Press, 1998.

Internet Document

APA   Wikipedia Free Encyclopedia. (2007). Wikipedia.org. Retrivied
                August 13, 2007, from http://www.wikipedia.org

MLA   Wikipedia.org.   2007. Wikipedia Free Encyclopedia. 13 Aug. 2007
                <http://www.wikipedia.org>.

ORIGINAL WORKS

Original works are based on a writer's own observations and interviews, not from an outside source. Reporters, for instance, will gather their own information from witnesses, experts, or official documents in order to compose a story. While these writers don't use a style guide like APA or MLA for citations, they still must follow guidelines in reporting statements in order to avoid *libel*, which is harming someone's reputation in writing. Here are some considerations:

- If a direct quote is more than one sentence long, place attribution at the end of the first sentence. That one attribution is sufficient for an entire paragraph. (Do not put attribution at the end of the second sentence also.)

    "We helped all the homeless in Atlanta this year," said Mayor Thomas. "We hope to do the same next year."

- If *two* different speakers follow each other, you should start the second quote with attribution to avoid confusion.

    "We helped all the homeless in Atlanta this year," said Mayor Thomas. "We hope to do the same next year."
    A homeless woman said: "I didn't know what I would do without the help of the Red Cross. This city is the best place to live without a home."

- Do not follow a partial quote with a complete quote.

    The mayor said the city spent $100,000 to help "all the homeless in Atlanta this year. We hope to do the same next year."

    Correct it like this:

    The city spent $100,000 to help "all the homeless in Atlanta this year," said the mayor. "We hope to do the same next year."

- The first time you identify a speaker use the full name. On second reference, use only the last name or title, depending on how well known the individual is.

- Don't attribute quotes to more than one person.

    "Everyone was jumping out of the window to avoid the fire," said witnesses.

- Place the source name or pronoun before the attributive verb.

    "...," the police said.

- If you are a witness to damages or injuries, do not name yourself as a source. Use official reports instead. Attributing information to police or other officials helps to establish credibility.

- If you are unsure of the facts and there are generalities involved, you should attribute to a source who officially speculates or approximates information, such as a coroner or weatherman.

Writers of original works will use attributive verbs (*said, asked, stated, alleged,* etc.) rather than reference notes. For example, journalists, unlike creative writers, prefer forms of the verb *to say.* They do this because *said* is neutral. It has no connotations, appearing more objective than other verbs. This is especially true for hard (fact-driven) news stories, such as crime and politics, where *said* is used almost exclusively. Meanwhile, soft (emotion-driven) news stories, such as human interest feature stories, use more colorful attributive verbs that convey a deliberate tone. Here is a list:

Added	Declared	Promised
Asserted	Exclaimed	Quipped
Averred	Explained	Recalled
Avowed	Insisted	Remarked
Cautioned	Maintained	Revealed
Charged	Maintained	Snapped
Claimed	Noted	Stated
Commented	Observed	Warned
Complained	Opined	Went On
Continued	Pointed Out	

Some of the attributive verbs, such as *continued* and *added,* in the list are neutral, but others have strong connotations. Using *claimed,* for instance, instead of *said* means the speaker's statement is questionable.

Note: Use *according to* with summarized or paraphrased source information, not with a direct quote.

Attributive adverbs, such as *allegedly, reportedly or apparently,* also work to identify the source of facts and information. However, they should be used only after an official source has been named.

SUMMARIZING

A summary is a brief description that states the main ideas of an original text. In many classes, your teachers will ask you to write a summary of an article or even a speech. When you write a summary, do not rewrite the article or the speech. A summary is meant to condense the content using your own words.

When you summarize, do the following:

- Write the summary in your own words
- Do not add your own ideas
- Keep the ideas in the same order as the original
- Include only the main ideas or points
- Use fewer words than the original text (about one-third of the original)
- Do not delete major details.

PRACTICE 1

Write a summary for the original source material below.

The most remarkable invention ever is the computer because it serves several purposes. First, the computer can be used for word processing. When I took typing in 1974, for example, I used to use a manual typewriter. It would take me a long time to correct errors accurately, plus it was visible that errors were made. Sometimes I would get so annoyed after making several errors that I would just yank the paper out of the typewriter and start over. The keys had to be hit hard, and sometimes they would get stuck. When I was a secretary, I used an electric IBM typewriter, which was much better than the manual typewriter because it had self-correction ribbon. However, when the computer came into existence, the lives of secretaries and other users became easier. I could type pages and pages of documents and save them either on the hard drive or on a disc. Before I got my master's, I had to type a 20-page practicum. When my professor suggested some changes, all I had to do was whip out my disc, stick it into the disc drive and call the document up. Once I made the corrections, I resubmitted an errorless copy. The computer even underlines misspelled words in red and underlines sentence structure and grammatical errors in green. The computer has, no doubt, changed my life for the better.

_____

_____

_____

_____

_____

_____

_____

_____

_____

PARAPHRASING

Paraphrasing means to restate another person's ideas in your own words without changing the meaning.

When you paraphrase, do the following:

- Rephrase the paper step by step.
- Use synonyms for the more difficult vocabulary words.
- Do not add or delete information.
- Do not interject your own opinion.

PRACTICE 2

Paraphrase the following paragraph:

The Internet is a very useful source. Today, people hardly go to the library for whatever they need because they can find it on the Internet. Students who work and go to school find the Internet to be very convenient for research because most of them have personal computers at home. The Internet can even be used for entertainment. One can find out where a movie is playing, what time it is playing, and how much it costs. Frankly, I don't buy the newspaper anymore because I can read the local news and news from around the world on the Internet. If I didn't have time to read a specific newspaper, all I have to do is go to Herald.com, select the date and read it online. Lots of people also do shopping on the Internet. There are also numerous games for one to play. Certainly, the Internet has revolutionized the world.

_____

_____

_____

_____

_____

_____

_____

_____

_____

_____

_____

_____

_____

_____

_____

UNIT V

Paint:
WRITING CREATIVELY

Expanding the Writing Process

Writing is a creative expression done with printed words. Some writing involves more creativity than other types, but it always involves some level of thought or imagination. Nonfiction writing, for example, may use metaphors or similes to make a point, but poems typically involve lots of creativity and can be so abstract that their meanings can be obscure. In this unit, you will learn how to make your writing more interesting by using colorful words and descriptive phrases.

Writing will be about either of the following:

- an *actual* person, place or thing (non-fiction)

Examples: Biography, Self-Help, Reference, Cooking, Travel

- an *imagined* person, place or thing (fiction)

Examples: Mystery, Science Fiction, Romance, Fantasy

No matter the form, all writing should aim to maintain reader interest.

WRITING FOR INTEREST

Have you ever talked to someone who gave only short, vague answers to your questions? Although you may try to coerce the person into saying more, this individual is unable or unwilling to elaborate. Similarly, some people write using the same uninteresting verbiage. They fail to move beyond basic words and sentence structure to use strategies to help them develop or expand their ideas.

Here are some strategies to create clearer, more interesting writing:

- **Use descriptive nouns, verbs and adjectives to create a picture in the reader's mind.** For example:

    Hector <u>closed</u> the door.
    Hector <u>slammed</u> the <u>10-foot</u> door. (We know exactly *how* he closed the door and the amount of force it must have taken.)

- **Use words that create a precise image in the reader's mind.** For example:

    Diana <u>spoke</u> to her <u>teacher</u> after class.
    Diana <u>confronted</u> her <u>math professor</u> after class. (We have a better idea about the *type* of discussion that she had and what it was about.)

- **Use examples, anecdotes, statistics, analogies and quotes to make the meaning as clear as possible in the reader's mind.** For example:

> Wilma had a <u>bad accident</u> in the <u>city</u>.
> Wilma had a <u>head-on collision</u> on <u>Park Street</u>. <u>The police officer said, "If she had not been wearing a seat belt, she would have flown through the front window."</u> (Because we were given more information, we had a better idea about the *extent* of the accident and the area where it occurred.)

As you see, giving the reader a precise idea or picture of your point is not only important, but it also adds interest.

PRACTICE 1

Change the underlined words in each sentence to more precise words that add interest and appeal. Answers will vary.

1. Lauren <u>went</u> <u>outside</u>.

   _____

2. David had a <u>bad</u> <u>day</u>.

   _____

3. She is a <u>great</u> singer.

   _____

4. He <u>made</u> a <u>nice</u> <u>meal</u>.

   _____

5. I <u>saw</u> her <u>reaction</u>.

   _____

6. We <u>ate</u> the <u>ice cream</u>.

   _____

7. Our teacher requires <u>references</u> for the <u>work</u>.

   _____

8. That <u>car</u> will be mine <u>someday</u>.

   _____

9. Mother Teresa was a <u>good</u> <u>person</u>.

   _____

10. The <u>man</u> cleans the office <u>everyday</u>.

   _____

11. Look at the <u>bug</u> <u>on</u> the wall!

_____

12. Please add <u>seasoning</u> to the <u>food</u>.

_____

PRACTICE 2

Read the following paragraph. Cross out words and phrases that are vague. Replace the words you eliminated with more precise, vivid words.

In the past, being fit, having the physical and mental capacity, was necessary for survival. Hunters went out to harvest or slaughter their food. Then they had to prepare the food to be cooked for that day. This was a regular, labor-intensive activity. In our modern society and culture, fitness and health is not necessarily a required component of survival or even daily functioning. For instance, the modern version of a hunter/gatherer may entail working overtime in a cubicle followed by a drive-through at a fast food place to bring home a "value-packed" supersized meal. The other option is going to a local supermarket to buy frozen foods or meals that can be "cooked" in less than 30 minutes. Neither activity requires nor leads to personal fitness. Likewise, with the explosion of medical and surgical options, especially as of lately, it is quite feasible to stay alive even if it means taking a myriad of medications for cholesterol, diabetes, high blood pressure and/or undergoing surgical interventions for heart disease, kidney failure, and so forth. All the while, society in general tends to move toward being more sedentary, passive, and frail, dependent on outside, often quick, fixes.

WRITING TO THE POINT _____

When a person makes a point or takes a position, it should be supported by evidence. Providing supporting evidence establishes a writer's credibility, but it can also provide greater reader interest or appeal. Using examples, anecdotes, statistics, and quotes as support are means to gain both writer credibility and reader interest.

Point: High school dropout rates can improve drastically with special focus on those at risk.
Example: A 17-year-old in Athens, GA, who had planned to dropout last year is set to graduate next year after attending an in-school intervention program.
Anecdote: At 3:30 every afternoon in the school cafeteria, a team of administrators, counselors, social workers and graduation coaches worked exclusively with students, like 17-year-old Roger

Stewart, who was at risk of dropping out of high school. Each week, a member of the team was assigned to provide snacks, which some of the participants came to enjoy as much as the program. After getting a cup of homemade lemonade and pound cake, Roger would sit and speak to his social worker, Carol King. She helped Roger get a youth job training and placement program. Roger liked to cook, so King was able to help him find a part-time job at a nearby restaurant. Roger said it was King's interest in helping him more so than the job that helped him decide to take his future more seriously and stay in school.

Statistic: Clarke County witnessed a 35 percent decrease in the high school dropout rate during their first year of its program.

Quote: The teen said, "I never thought my parents, who never finished high school, would ever see me graduate, but one of my teachers decided she wanted to help. She would walk me to the dropout program every afternoon."

PRACTICE 3

Finish each statement. Then for each point you are attempting to establish, provide support in the form of an example, anecdote, statistic or a quote.

1. *Point*:   Voting…_____

    _____

    _____

    _____

    _____

2. *Point*:   The most beautiful feature on a person's face…_____

    _____

    _____

    _____

    _____

3. *Point*:   Dating…_____

    _____

    _____

    _____

    _____

4. *Point*:   Family…_____

_____

_____

_____

_____

_____

5. *Point*:   Working and going to school…_____

_____

_____

_____

_____

_____

21

Literary Devices

Language is a means of communication by audible sounds and written symbols. While basic sounds and symbols are enough to communicate a message, literary devices produce a specific effect during communication. Effective speakers and writers have always used literary devices to enhance, illuminate, and embellish their communication. Writers mainly use literary devices in creative writing forms, which include:

- Autobiography/Memoir
- Personal & Journalistic Essays
- Epic
- Novel
- Playwriting/Dramatic writing
- Poetry
- Screenwriting
- Short story
- Songwriting

By definition, creative writing expresses the writer's thoughts and feelings in an imaginative, often unique, or poetic way. It goes beyond the scope of most academic and professional writing.

Here is a list of common literary devices:

Alliteration
An alliteration is a repetition of the initial sounds of neighboring words. The repetition may be at the beginning of successive words or inside the words. Alliteration is often used in tongue twisters.

Example: Millionaire Milton mailed a mangled mitten   (successive *m* sound)

Example: frowned...around...town   (internal *ow* sound)

Allegory
An allegory is a story that teaches a lesson or shows something about life by having the characters or events stand for ideas, people or moral principles. It can be incorporated into any type of story or even poem.

Example: In the *Pilgrim's Progress* by John Bunyan, concepts like hope and mercy become real-life characters in this tale of a man named Christian searching for salvation.

Allusion

An allusion is a short, indirect reference to a well-known person or event from history, geography, literature, or religion. Many of our songs contain allusions. For instance, "Please, let's not part the Red Sea," makes an allusion to the biblical parting of the Red Sea.

Analogy

An analogy is a form of comparison between two objects or ideas. They are very helpful in both written and oral communication because they enable one to explain technical or unfamiliar information to something more familiar. There are several types of analogous relationships: antonyms, synonyms, homonyms, part to whole, item to category, part to part, or activity to result. So, in figuring out analogies, you must first find the relationship between the first set of relationship and then find that same relationship between the second set. Analogies are written in one of two ways: "hot is to shorts as cold is to coat" or "hot : shorts :: cold : coat. The single colon (:) represents "is to" whereas the double colon (::) represents *as*.

Connotation

Connotation is the emotional suggestions or other associations connected to a word. For example, the word "snake" has a connotative (secondary) meaning of evil. Also, all words do not have a secondary meaning.

Denotation

The denotation of a word is its literal (dictionary) meaning. For example, the word "snake" means a scaly, legless reptile.

Emblem

An emblem is a tangible, pictorial image, or object used to represent an abstract moral or spiritual quality, such as a crown for royalty or a scepter for sovereignty. It represents something intangible.

Hyperbole

A hyperbole is a deliberate exaggeration of a statement. It overstates a point and goes beyond the limits of truth in order to give greater emphasis to meaning. In our everyday conversations, hyperbole is common. When we say, "The room was so cold that I froze to death," or "He turned as white as a sheet," we are using hyperbole.

Irony

Irony involves implying the opposite of what one means, often for the purpose of ridicule, mockery or laughter. It takes three forms:

- **Verbal irony** is when a writer or speaker intentionally says one thing and means something else (i.e. sarcasm).

- **Dramatic irony** is when an audience knows something that a character in the literature does not know.

- **Situational irony** is an unexpected discrepancy between the expected result and actual results. In irony of situation, the result of an action is the reverse of what the actor expected. Macbeth murders his king hoping that in becoming king he will achieve great happiness. Actually, Macbeth never knows another moment of peace after the king's death, and finally, Macbeth is beheaded for his murderous act.

Metaphor

A metaphor is a figure of speech that compares two dissimilar things without using comparative words like *as* or *like*. In other words, it makes the comparison indirectly by stating that one thing *is* something else rather than being alike. Most often used in poetry, a metaphor makes a comparison using a form of the verb *to be*. You can form a metaphor by comparing nouns to make a point. For example:

Concrete Noun to Abstract Noun: "Books *are* lasting friendships."
                                           (*Point*: Books bring long-term comfort or support.)

Concrete Noun to Concrete Noun: "You *are* my sunshine."
                                           (*Point*: You bring me joy or happiness.)

Abstract Noun to Abstract Noun: "Life *is* misery."
                                           (*Point*: Daily living is difficult.)

Note: We can experience concrete nouns with our five senses (see, touch, taste, hear, smell), but abstract nouns are intangible (concepts or ideas).

Metonymy

A metonymy substitutes a term for another that is closely associated with that term. For example, the whole may be substituted for the part, the part for the whole, the container for the thing contained, a substance for the thing made of it, or one thing is substituted for another. Let us note these separately:

- **Whole for the part:** "Every creature" is often used for the human race, not animals. "All the world" may mean only a known area.
- **Part for the whole:** The Golden Rule, "Do unto others…" only characterizes the intent of our laws.
- **Container for what it contains:** A cup is mentioned to indicate its contents.
- **Substance for the thing made of it:** "We are water."
- **One word for another closely associated with it in meaning:** "Breaking bread [eating food]."

Onomatopoeia

Onomatopoeia is a word whose sound echoes the sound it is describing. The words *splash, knock, roar, bang, growl* and *roar* are examples of onomatopoeia.

Oxymoron

An oxymoron is putting two contradictory words or phrases together. For example: *jumbo shrimp, soft scream, pretty ugly,* or *exact estimate*.

Paradox

A paradox reveals a kind of truth that at first seems contradictory. For example, "Stone walls do not a prison make, nor iron bars a cage" (Richard Lovelace).

Pathetic Fallacy

Pathetic fallacy is the description of inanimate natural objects in a way that gives them human feelings, thoughts, and sensations. For example, "Nature abhors a vacuum" says that nature *abhors* (hates) something.

Personification

A story in which animals or inanimate (nonhuman) objects or ideas function as if they were humans, such as by walking, talking, or being given arms, legs, facial features, human locomotion or other anthropoid form. This was used in *Alice in Wonderland*.

Prolepsis

A prolepsis is a figure of speech in which a future event is referred to in anticipation. In other words, the event or name is referred to in the future as if it had already existed or occurred.   For example, a person who is about to die might be described as "a dead man" before he or she is actually dead.

Pun

A pun is a humorous use of a word(s) in such a way as to suggest different meanings and applications. Simply put, it is a play on words. For example, "A plateau is a high form of flattery" or "Santa's helpers are subordinate Clauses."

Sarcasm

Sarcasm involves a cutting humor in which the user may actually say the opposite of what he or she means. After a series of disastrous basketball games, one may remark, "What a great team we have! Maybe they'll even make it to the championships if the league gives credit for participation!"

Satire

Using humor, irony, or ridicule to attack or make fun of human faults. Satire could be compared to comedy; however, comedy entertains while satire aims at attacking or ridiculing the incompetence (shortcomings) in a person or thing in order to bring about some kind of change. Mark Twain used satire in Huckleberry Finn to criticize racism.

Simile

A simile is the simplest and most commonly used literary device in which one thing or idea is compared to another by using the words *as, like* or *than*.

Examples: No one can beat Eddie at the game Hide-and-Seek.

Eddie	hides *as*	well as a chameleon in danger.
Eddie	hides *like*	a chameleon in danger.
Eddie	hides better *than*	a chameleon in danger.

Examples: She is such a talented writer that a pen in her hand is *like* a paintbrush on canvas.
At age 85, Dr. Turner's mind is still as sharp *as* a university scholar.

Symbol

A symbol is an object or action that represents something more than its literal meaning. It represents something tangible. For example, a red octagon is a symbol for a stop sign.

Tricolon

A tricolon is a sentence with three clearly defined parts of equal length, usually independent clauses. For example, "She conquered shame with passion, fear with audacity, reason with madness" (Cicero, Pro

Cluentio VI.15).

Zeugma

A general term describing when one part of speech (most often the main verb, but sometimes a noun) governs two or more other parts of a sentence (often in a series). For example, saying, "He played first base, second fiddle, and *Three Blind Mice.*" The verb *played* refers to three varying activities.

PRACTICE 1

Create a metaphor by writing a <u>concrete noun</u> *on the first line and an* <u>abstract noun</u> *that you compare to it on the second line. Be careful not to form a cliché. State your point for each in the space to the right.*

1. _____ is/are _____

2. _____ is/are _____

3. _____ is/are _____

4. _____ is/are _____

Create a metaphor by writing a <u>concrete noun</u> *on the first line and a* <u>concrete noun</u> *that you compare to it on the second line. Be careful not to form a cliché. State your point for each in the space to the right.*

5. _____ is/are _____

6. _____ is/are _____

7. _____ is/are _____

8. _____ is/are _____

Create a metaphor by writing an <u>abstract noun</u> *on the first line and an* <u>abstract noun</u> *that you compare to it on the second line. Be careful not to form a cliché. State your point for each in the space to the right.*

9. _____ is/are _____

10. _____ is/are _____

11. _____ is/are _____

12. _____ is/are _____

PRACTICE 2

Create a simile by writing a noun on the first line and a word or term that compares to it on the second line. Be careful not to form a cliché.

1. _____ works on it like _____

2. _____ drinks as _____

3. _____ explains it like _____

4. _____ dances as _____

5. _____ thinks like _____

6. _____ operates like _____

7. _____ is valuable as _____

8. _____ is prettier than _____

9. _____ runs like _____

10. _____ understands it like a _____

–

REVIEW

Read each example below and determine which literary device it best represents from the list. Then write the corresponding letter to the example of the literary device.

A = Alliteration	**H** = Irony	**O** = Prolepsis
B = Allegory	**I** = Metaphor	**P** = Sarcasm
C = Allusion	**J** = Onomatopoeia	**Q** = Satire
D = Connotation	**K** = Oxymoron	**R** = Simile
E = Denotation	**L** = Paradox	**S** = Symbol
F = Emblem	**M** = Pathetic Fallacy	**T** = Tricolon
G = Hyperbole	**N** = Personification	**U** = Zeugma

Letter

1. The old doors are groaning.   _____

2. Sizzling sausage   _____

3. Police pick on paupers.   _____

4. Living dead   _____

5. A smiling moon   _____

6. Dante represents all people who are in search of their purpose.   _____

7. "I came, I saw, I conquered."   _____

8. "They have ears, but do not hear."   _____

9. The wall protects us from our enemies.   _____

10. His simple invention destroyed the Goliath company.   _____

11. A pyramid represents wisdom.   _____

12. These tires are perfection.   _____

13. An animal poacher gets killed in a trap.   _____

14. "We keep the wall between us as we go."   _____

15. He's as tall as a skyscraper.   _____

16. Terry entered the contest and the room.   _____

17. A headline titled "The Impotence of Proofreading"   _____

18. Saying "this is great" after something bad happens   _____

19. I miss him like air.   _____

20. A skull and crossbones represents poison   _____

21. "We're going to starve on this deserted island."   _____

Appendix

A. CAPITALIZATION _____

What should be capitalized? Among other things, proper nouns or formal names (names of specific persons, places, and things) should be capitalized.

Proper Nouns

Proper Nouns	**Common Nouns**
President Clinton	He was **president** for two terms.
Professor Jones	He has been a **professor** for ten years.
Killian Senior High School	Margie will graduate from **high school** soon.
The Blue Mountains	This is a very high **mountain**.
Captain Reid	He has only been a **captain** for four years.
Golden Gate Bridge	I drove by a **bridge** to get to Miami Beach.
Empire State Building	Every one had to evacuate the **building**.
Pacific Ocean	I have a passion for the **ocean**.
Georgia State University	My daughter went to a **university** in Florida.
Miami Dade College	Liz is now a **college** student.
Dr. Edwards	I need to see my **doctor** soon.
Highway 12	The **highway** is busy during the holidays.
Sheraton Hotel	John works at a **hotel** in Hollywood, Florida.
Dunns River Falls	I must cross a **river** to get to my house.
Mother Theresa	Susan's **mother** works 12 hours per day.
Senator Edwards	My brother is a **senator**.
Congresswoman Meek	In two weeks, **congress** will meet.
Mayor E. Brown	The new **mayor** of Miami is very friendly.
Judge Colbert	Ebony is a **judge**.
Sandra's dog, Pepe	Sandra's **dog** is her best friend.
United States Army	Jonathan has no interest in the **army**.

Exception: Titles following names are used as substitutes for names that are not usually capitalized.

Examples: John Francis, **mayor** of Macon, Georgia, is very friendly.
                   The **senator** of your constituency is retiring.

Derivatives

Capitalize words such as *Anglomania, Christian, France,* and *Judaism* that are derived from proper nouns and still rely on those nouns for their meaning. This is also true for proper noun derivatives such as *German measles, Kelvin scale, Legionnaires' disease,* and *Mach number* that function as adjectives.

Do *not* capitalize nouns and adjectives such as *baptism, godmother,* and *pasteurize* that no longer rely on their proper noun derivative for their meaning.

Capitalize names of specific academic courses with numerical references, and only capitalize course names if they are derivatives of languages (*French, Spanish, German, Italian,* etc.).

Specific Course:	Manny is taking **Psychology 2000**.
Subjects:	His plans are to take **mathematics** and **Spanish** next semester.
Specific Course:	Amber is teaching a course titled the **Benefits of Good Nutrition**.
Subjects:	My best subjects this semester are **English** and **humanities**.

Directions

Capitalize specific locations (*north, south, east, west*) when they are used as substitutes to refer to designated areas of a country.

However, do not capitalize them when they are used as compass or to give direction to someone:

Location:	I once lived in the **North**.
Direction:	My bedroom faces **west**.
Location:	Iraq is in the **Middle East**.
Direction:	To get to Palmetto Senior High School, go **east** on Kendall drive.

Months, Days, Holidays

Capitalize the months of the year, days of the week, and holidays.

Months:	January, February, March, April, May, June, July, August
Days:	Sunday, Monday, Tuesday, Wednesday, Thursday, Friday, Saturday
Holidays:	Thanksgiving, Halloween, Christmas, Memorial Day, Washington's Birthday

Seasons

Do *not* capitalize the seasons: spring, summer fall, autumn.

- The spring term starts in January.

Exception: Capitalize the seasons when they are used in formal titles.

- The **Summer** Olympics will be held in Barcelona.

Titles of Works

Capitalize the principal words in the titles of compositions, books, magazines, newspapers, articles, films, record albums, songs, poems, television series, and plays:

Book: I am using the textbook *Writing for Skill*.
Magazine: I subscribe to *Time* magazine.
Television: *America the Beautiful* airs Tuesday night at 8 p.m.
Newspaper: The *Sun Sentinel* is delivered to my house every weekend.
Album: Fantasia's first album, *Free Yourself*, has made it to the top of the charts

However, do *not* capitalize words like **short prepositions** that have less than **five** letters (*with, from, at, in, of*), **short conjunctions** like *and, but*, or, *nor,* and the **articles** *a, an, the*. No matter what the first letter of the first and last words are, though, always capitalize them.

- Every Christmas I look forward to watching my favorite movie, *Gone with the Wind*.
- Jennifer Hudson, former *American Idol* contestant, has the lead role in *Dream Girls*.

Quotation Marks

Use **quotation marks** to enclose short works such as chapter headings from books, magazines, newspaper articles short stories, essays, poems, songs from record albums, and scenes from plays. However, do not use quotation marks to enclose the titles of your *own* essays.

- I enjoy the song "Hypothetically" from the album *My Life Story*.
- The poem "Little Bee" was written by Isaac Watts.
- The title of the essay that won the contest is "Someone I Admire."

Underline/Italics

Underline or use **italics** for the titles of longer works such as textbooks, novels, magazines, newspapers, movies, television programs, and record albums.

Examples: The title of Annette Johnson's book is <u>What's Your Motivation</u>.
                  The revised version of *What's Your Motivation* will be out in May 2010.
                  The <u>New York Times</u> is an award-winning newspaper.
                  Most law professors require that their students read the *New York Times*.

However, do *not* underline, italicize, or use quotations marks with names of religious books like the Bible, the Talmud, or the Koran.

Trademarks

Capitalize trademarks or brand names:

Popsicle	Coca Cola
Dumpster	Irish Spring soap
Blue Mountain coffee	Michelin tires
Microsoft Word	Sheetrock

Government and Business Organizations

<u>Government</u>	<u>Business</u>
the White House	Sears and Roebuck
the House of Representatives	the Miami Heat
the Library of Congress	the New York Yankees
the Senate	Humane Society
U.S. Supreme Court	Delta

Note: When the word "the" is not part of a name, it is *not* capitalized unless it is the first word in a sentence.

Historical Periods, Documents, and Events

Capitalize the names of important historical periods, documents, and events:

<u>Periods</u>	<u>Documents</u>	<u>Events</u>
Victorian era	Declaration of Independence	World War I and II
Great Depression	Bill of Rights	the Bay of Pigs
Renaissance period	Emancipation Proclamation	the Spanish Inquisition

Exception: Do not capitalize numbers that refer to centuries (eighteenth century).

Nationalities, Races, Religions

Capitalize the names of nationalities and religions:

- Oprah Winfrey is a generous **African-American** talk show host.
- This semester most of my students are **Hispanics** and **Brazilians**.
- I like **Italian** food.
- When I was younger, I attended a **Pentecostal** church.
- Most of my family members are **Baptist**.
- Most of my **Hispanic** friends are **Catholic**.

Names that Indicate Family Relationships

Capitalize family relationship words when they are used in front of a person's name or when they are used alone as substitutes for the person's name:

- Last summer I visited **Aunt Sally** and **Uncle Charley** who live in Brazil.
- When **Mom** and **Dad** went on vacation, I was left in charge of my brothers.
- I wish my **grandpa** and **grandma** would visit me for summer.
- Most **moms** and **dads** want the best for their children.

Note: In sentence 4, *moms* and *dads* are not capitalized because they are used as common nouns.

Additional Uses of Capitalization

Capitalize the salutation of a letter:

- **Dear** Ms. Manna:

Capitalize the complimentary close of a letter:

- **Sincerely yours**,
- **Best wishes**,
- **Yours truly**,

Capitalize the names of God:

- **God** the **Father**
- **He, Him, His** when referencing God

Capitalize the names of holy books:

- the **Bible**
- the **Talmud**
- the **Koran**

However, *do not* capitalize the name of the bible when it is not associated with Scripture:

- The **Bible** says that God is love.
- A journalist **bible** is his or her reference book.

Capitalize the names of the planets:

- **Mars, Venus, Mercury, Jupiter**
- **Milky Way**
- **Earth**

Do not capitalize *earth, sun,* and *moon* when they are used as common nouns.

- My mother lived on **earth** for 81 years.
- We used to watch the rising of the **sun** at 6 a.m.
- We also watched the eclipse of the **moon**.
- Some cultures worship more than one **god**.

Note: In sentence 4, the word *god* is not capitalized because it is used as a common noun.

Capitalize geographic areas defined by a collection of states or provinces:

- the **Sun Belt**
- the **Bible Belt**
- the **New England** states
- the **Middle Atlantic** states

PRACTICE 1

In the following sentences, underline and fix all necessary and unnecessary capital letters.

1. Sammy Sosa beat Mark McGwire for the national league mvp in 1998.

2. The miami heat's Point Guard Dwayne Wade earned a new title, mvp.

3. I have never had korean food, so in the summer when I am on leave, I will visit a korean and mexican Restaurant.

4. Joshua graduated from killian senior high school in june.

5. In fall 2011, when Josue starts college, he will take Mathematics, Psychology 2112, and Criminal Justice classes.

6. When I go on vacation in Summer, I will visit aunt Rosa and uncle Gilbert, who live in the dominican republic.

7. The name of Sandra's dog is nola; she is a playful Dog.

8. My children's favorite holidays are thanksgiving, christmas and easter.

9. In my family, no one drinks pepsi, coco-cola or sprite.

10. Fannie always says, "mother, don't worry about people who do you wrong; god will repay them."

11. I know several Veterans who survived world war I and II.

12. Keith attends carver senior high school in Atlanta, Georgia.

13. Next Summer, I will take an exercise class, and the instructor wants me to purchase jane fonda's, album, fun and fitness.

14. Did you read the article in the phoenix herald about the number of soldiers who died in iraq in the month of june?

15. When I first came to the United States, I lived in the north for ten years.

B. TITLES

A title indicates a position of authority, profession or status. Here is a list of titles:

Academic (principal, chairman)
Courtesy (Mr., Mrs., Miss, Ms.)
Legislative (senator, representative)
Military (major, sergeant, colonel)
Nobility (duke, marques, earl)
Religious (reverend, rabbi, monsignor)

Note: Only use courtesy titles when quoting someone who used them or when male or female relatives with the same last name appear in your writing.

Capitalize formal titles that precede names; however, do not capitalize formal titles that follow names:

- **Professor** Julian Anderson
- Julian Anderson, **professor**
- **Mayor** Marlon Reid
- Marlon Reid, **mayor**

Note: Someone's job description is not a formal title.

- **quarterback** Brent Moss, not **Quarterback** Brent Moss
- **actress** Nia Strong, not **Actress** Nia Strong

Capitalize formal titles of high-ranking individuals when used alone:

- **Secretary** of State Condoleeza Rice
- **secretary** of state
- **Supreme Court Justice** John Roberts
- **supreme court justice**

Capitalize abbreviated formal titles that precede names; however, lowercase and spell out when used alone:

- **Sen**. Phillip Thomas
- the **senator**
- **Gov**. Sheila Ferguson
- the **governor**

Lowercase modifiers that help simplify describe or identify an exact title:

- **department** Chairperson Linda Watts
- **production manager** Colin Harris

PRACTICE 2

Underline and then correct the titles that should be capitalized.

1. Is general manager Brooke Nelson available?

2. The president will visit our campus next week.

3. The bailiff will bring Warren to appear before judge Bill Randall.

4. He went to the academy before entering the Navy.

5. An aide said the petty officers will arrive soon.

6. Our minister of music, Jeff Stewart, wrote the new song.

7. Did you meet Author Irwin Myers at the book signing?

8. Perhaps, chancellor Owens will change the rule about freshman.

9. The county approved area superintendent Jon Weems' promotion.

10. Who knows Newt Gingrich, former speaker of the house?

C. ABBREVIATIONS

Acronyms

An acronym is a word combination formed from the first letters of the principal words in a title or series of words as a means to reference that title or series:

FBI	**F**ederal **B**ureau of **I**nvestigations
LASER	**l**ight **a**mplification by **s**timulated **e**mission of **r**adiation
MADD	**M**others **A**gainst **D**runk **D**riving
NATO	**N**orth **A**tlantic **T**reaty **O**rganization

When some acronyms are mentioned for the first time, it is always better to spell out the acronym on the first reference, and then put it in parentheses. Then on the second reference, remove the parentheses.

- **Acquired Immune Deficiency Syndrome (AIDS)** continues to be a phantom killer. Last year alone, more than 20 thousand people died from **AIDS**.

However, some acronyms have become so popular that using the complete name may confuse readers (*CIA, NATO, FBI*). These acronyms can be used on first reference.

Addresses

As a matter of choice or per style guide, you may abbreviate the names of streets, avenues, and boulevards when they are included in addresses:

- Mrs. Monica Brown of 151 Pearson **St.** will be the new director of purchasing.
- Mrs. Monica Brown of 151 Pearson **Street** will be the new director of purchasing
- Mr. Bowers once lived at 665 Stout **Ave.**
- Mr. Bowers once lived at 665 Stout **Avenue**.

States

Spell out the names of U.S. states when they stand alone. However, when they appear with a city name, the state name should be abbreviated with periods.

- Marlon's sister has lived in **Florida** for 36 years
- Marlon's sister has lived in **Miami, Fla.,** for 36 years.

The names of states with six letters or fewer (*Alaska, Hawaii, Idaho, Iowa, Maine, Ohio*) should never be abbreviated in your writing.

Ala.	Md.	N.D.
Ariz.	Mass.	Okla.
Ark.	Mich.	Ore.
Calif.	Minn.	Pa.
Colo.	Miss.	R.I.
Conn.	Mo.	S.C.
Del.	Mont.	S.D.
Fla.	Neb.	Tenn.
Ga.	Nev.	Vt.
Ill.	N.H.	Va.
Ind.	N.J.	Wash.
Kan.	N.M.	W. Va.
Ky.	N.Y.	Wis.
La.	N.C.	Wyo.

Note: The U.S. Postal Service uses only *two* letters without periods (*FL, GA, NY*) to indicate state abbreviations. This style should *not* be adopted in writing.

Dates

The names of months with five letters or fewer (*March, April, May, June, July*) should never be abbreviated in your writing. Abbreviate all the other months only when used with a specific day.

<u>Correct</u>	<u>Incorrect</u>
Jan. 14, 1927	January 14, 1927
January 1927	Jan. 1927
Tuesday, June 26	Tuesday, Jun. 26

Titles

You may only abbreviate an individual's title if it is followed by his or her first and last names:

<u>Correct</u>	<u>Incorrect</u>
Rev. John B. Alexander	Rev. Alexander
Reverand Alexander	
Prof. Frank Downing	Prof. Downing
Professor Downing	
Sen. Daryl Jones	Sen. Jones
Senator Jones	

Note: Abbreviate junior (Jr.) and senior (Sr.) when indicated as part of someone's name:

Examples: Manuel R. Jones, Jr.
Karl George Brown, Sr.

Proper Names

Abbreviate the type of entity (Co., Corp., Inc.) only when using the full formal name of a company.

- Atlanta Bond Co.   (OR)   the bond company
- Parody Printing Inc.   (OR)   the printing company

PRACTICE 3

Cross out all errors in abbreviation; then write the correct version above it.

1.   The members at Southland Bapt. Church love to hear Rev. Brown speak.

2.   Sen. Jones would be an excellent running mate for Sen. Hilary Clinton.

3.   Prof. Brown is on a six-week leave this semester. He will return to work in Aug.

4.   Last Thurs. I saw several accidents on Hwy. 27 when I was returning home from Dis. World on Sun. night.

5.   Col. Anderson moved to Cal. to be closer to his parents.

D. NUMBERS

Numbers Used as Words

Spell out numbers from one to ten:

- My grandson has **ten** birds.

Spell out ordinal numbers (*first, second, third, fourth, fifth*, etc.).

- Marjorie lives on **Seventh** Avenue in Brooklyn.

Spell out numbers that begin a sentence:

- **Twenty** of the students will be exempt from the exam.

Spell out fractions that are used alone:

- Maria encouraged **two-thirds** of the students to leave because the teacher was late.

Spell out the shorter of two consecutive numbers:

- For Melissa's birthday, I bought her 25 **ten-cent** party hats.

Numbers Used as Figures

Use figures to indicate numbers above ten.

- Martin will be in town for **11** days.
- Bill sold **2,000** copies of his book.

Note: In special situations, however, discretion must be used in expressing a series of numbers. For example, if a series of numbers is written as figures but *one* number is spelled out, express all in figures to achieve consistency.

- I went shopping and bought **ten** scarves, **11** hats, **15** pairs of socks, and **20** towels. (**Inconsistent** - "ten" is spelled out, and the other numbers are figures.)
- I went shopping and bought **10** scarves, **11** hats, **15** pairs of socks, and **20** towels. (**Consistent** - all numbers are written as figures.)

Use figures in dates:

- On **July 8, 2007**, I am going to Israel for 14 days.
- On **August 14**, Debra will go to Africa.

Note: If the month is written first, it is not necessary to add *st, nd, rd,* or *th* to the day.

Always use figures to indicate money.

- I have only **5 cents**.
- Congress needs **$3 million**.

Note: Combine the dollar sign ($) along with word for amounts above $100,000.

Use numerals to indicate time.

- It is **6 a.m.**
- He left at **10:30 p.m.**

Note: Use *midnight* and *noon* to avoid confusion.

Use numerals for people's ages from 1 month to 100 years.

- The child is **10 days** old.
- We will celebrate his **50th** birthday next week.

PRACTICE 4

In the following sentences, cross out any error you find in number, and then make the correction above it.

1.   6 of my students missed 3 of the 10 exams although they were told they could only miss one.

2.   I have already completed 2/3 of the manuscript, which is due on January 10th.

3.   On August twenty third, I will go to Chicago for fourteen days.

4.   At Macy's, winter coats are on sale for fifty-nine ninety-nine.

5.   Glenna has lived on 1st Street for thirty-two years.

6.   100 guests are all I can invite to my retirement party.

7.   My neighbor has ten birds, 14 cats and six dogs in his small apartment.

8.   October 22nd will be 15 years since Lola has not worked.

9.   It is said that only twenty-five percent of welfare recipients voted in the last general election.

10.   For my children's back-to-school supplies, I bought 12 notebooks, ten pencils, three dictionaries, and five dividers.

REVIEW

In the following exercise, cross out any errors you find in capitalization, punctuation, abbreviations, and numbers and then make the corrections above it.

Last week i received a letter from aunt Sally who lives in new york. It was the happiest day of my life because i had not heard from her for 3 years. She said that she was in the Hospital for 3 Weeks, and no one called or visited her. With all the Aunts, Uncles and Cousins she has, one would think that her Hospital Room would be running over with visitors.

When Baseball Player Sammy Sosa from the Dominican republic beat Mark McGwire in 1998 for the national league mvp award, president Clinton called both players to congratulate them. Can you imagine getting a call from the pres. of the united states?

For the past 7 years, I have been watching American idol, the only tv program I enjoy. Every Tues. night, I rush home from work just to watch this prog. Every time I say I am not going to watch it, i end up watching it. Next yr. I am going to try hard not to watch it because 2/3 of my reading time is spent watching it.

T